Abigail Clark House, Josiah Atkins

Memoirs of the religious experience and life of Abigail House

Abigail Clark House, Josiah Atkins

Memoirs of the religious experience and life of Abigail House

ISBN/EAN: 9783337132200

Printed in Europe, USA, Canada, Australia, Japan

Cover: Foto ©Lupo / pixelio.de

More available books at **www.hansebooks.com**

MEMOIRS

OF THE

RELIGIOUS EXPERIENCE AND LIFE

OF

ABIGAIL HOUSE,

LATE OF LENOX, OHIO, AND RELICT OF THE LATE

COL. E. N. HOUSE.

PUBLISHED ACCORDING TO THE LAST WILL OF

THE AUTHOR

JEFFERSON, OHIO:

ASHTABULA SENTINEL STEAM PRESS.

· 1861.

ADVERTISEMENT.

———

THE manuscript sheets of the following work, collected and arranged agreeably to their present order, were, by their Author and Compiler, entrusted to the care and keeping of the Subscriber, on the seventh day of November, in the year 1860; accompanied by a request that in the event of her decease,— which was then expected to be near—I would at some convenient, or practical time, thereafter, look them over and make such grammatical and verbal changes as should be thought desirable; when having in view their publication at some future time.

A few days before her decease, which event occurred on the 10th day of February, A. D. 1861, in a conversation held with her, a portion of which related specially to the subject of her manuscript in my hands, above mentioned; she urged it upon me as a matter not to be lightly disregarded, that there should be no such alterations, or additions, made to that production, either in needless changes or alteration of the forms of expression, or in a close adherence to nice grammatical rules, as would so affect it, as to make it appear in any important or considerable sense, to be other than the veritable production of the Original Author and Compiler:—and it is confidently believed that the course taken, with the intention of fully carrying out her expressed wishes in the case, has left the work in a condition, that she, if living, would approve; so far as regards any false light in which she would be placed thereby, or any obloquy that will attach to her name or memory, in consequence of any alterations or changes that have been made in her original manuscripts entrusted to me so as above represented. And the reader of the Volume, may take the fullest assurance, that, aside from such verbal (a few) and grammatical (many) corrections as it is believed, the instructions of the writer and compiler fully contemplated, it is the unvitiated and veritable production of the late Mrs. ABIGAIL HOUSE, of Lenox, Ashtabula County, Ohio, deceased.

JOSIAH ATKINS.

MEMOIRS.

I WAS born the 8th, of November 1790, in the town of Bloomfield, Hartford County Connecticut. My father's name was IRA
CLARK. I was the youngest of the family, and at the early age
of ten, was deprived of my Mother by death. At the expiration
of one year, my father married again. I soon discovered my loss,
and the dying counsel of my mother was often brought to my
mind. I remembered many of her religious conversations with
her pious mother. My trials at home were very severe and
unfortunate, as regarded temporal things, but perhaps nothing
else could have had so happy an effect upon me in other respects
as did the privation of my home. For me a young girl, at an age
so tender, to be deprived of the best earthly friend, whose counsels was so much needed, was a sore trial indeed. I often mourned
over my condition, and although I had the sympathy of many, I
would frequently say I did not wish to live, but the thought of
death would fill me with horror, and produce serious impression,
knowing I was not prepared to die and meet God in peace. I
knew I was a sinner—and perfectly ignorant of the course I
should take, to obtain a knowledge of the way of Life and Salvation. Such thoughts, however were soon over, as I was young
and death, as I thought, at a great distance.

Storms of wind and thunder would always alarm me, and at
such times I thought that I would sin no more, but as soon as the
storm was over I would return to my former cheerfulness. At
length I became more thoughtful, and some took me to be under
concern of mind. At such times I would try to appear as though
nothing were the matter, for I did not like to be called serious—
neither did I know that it was conviction. Often passages of
Scripture would come to my mind, such as, "Come unto me all

ye that labor, and are heavy laden, and I will give you Rest." I did not think it alluded to me, for I was not coming to Christ. The first I remember that did mean me, was, one night as I lay in my bed in a sound sleep, I was suddenly awakened as if called by name, with these words: "Turn ye, turn ye, for why will ye die?" I had no more desire for sleep that night, for I was alarmed, and I was sure that was for me, and that it was high time to turn from my sins. These words ran through my mind day after day, but I did not know for certain that they were Scripture. I thought, however, that they were, because they came with such power, though I had never read them. At length I broke the subject to the woman with whom I was then living. She told me it was a loud call from God, and I ought not to slight it. After that I felt more disposed to read the Bible, and other good books, such as the Pilgrims Progress. I knew there was something in it I did not understand, and would often weep while reading it from pity and sympathy for the poor man whom it represented.

Again those impressions wore off, and I returned to my follies, but as yet could take but little pleasure in them, knowing I was mortal and must die.

About this time an alarming disease broke out in the neighborhood, and swept off a number of my schoolmates and others: my mind was greatly agitated in consequence of sudden deaths.

"Oh that I were prepared to die, what would I give if I were a Christian?" One thing I was resolved to do, and that was to forsake my young associates, especially in the ball-room. That resolution I always kept. I took courage, thinking I was gaining ground, and perhaps I might overcome some of my follies.

When I heard the gospel preached (and as I trust I did) it would make me shudder, and the blood would run cold in my veins. Then I would resolve again to break off my sins. But alas! as soon as I was out of the sound of the preacher's voice, something would turn my mind from it, and not having deepness of root, it vanished away, and I was as light as before—being rather of a cheerful turn of mind naturally, I would often run into folly, and soon found it a most difficult habit to overcome.

There being a number of young people in the place, I saw it to be impossible for me to make much progress by way of reform; so I made a promise if my life might be spared about ten days, I wou take my fill of pleasure with my youthful companions, and then would seek my soul's Salvation. I thought such a delay was dangerous, but thought my comfort almost to an end. To be a christian was a gloomy thought. While at this place, I listened one day to the experience of a Godly woman, which made some serious impressions on my mind, but I shook it off as soon as possible, for my time was short for enjoyment; my promise was before me constantly, so much so, it destroyed my anticipated pleasure. My probation had expired, and I left for a mor retired place, but was still the same. I was disappointed to find in myself no desire to turn and live. At length I concluded to give it up, as it was too great an undertaking for me. I felt very easy and composed, more so than for months, yet I still thought it strange to feel such an indifference on this subject, but went on in this way a few days. O! what reason I have to praise my God that he did not leave me to myself. In a few days from this time being alone in the house, and busy at my work, suddenly, in my imagination, I saw the yawning pit open before me. I was struck with horror, and dare not move for fear of falling into that dreadful place. While thus gazing it was made plain that I had rejected the offer of mercy. O, what shall I do! was my cry. I moved my work, and in an instant the terrific scene disappeared. Again I said what shall I do? I had no sooner made the enquiry than I was directed to read the Bible. I made no delay, but took it from the shelf, opened its pages, and the first words my eyes rested on; were these: "Hell and Destruction are never full, so the eyes of man are never satisfied." I then realized my dangerous condition, and strove hard to shut my eyes from every enjoyment. I had never tried to pray, only to say the Lord's Prayer, taught me by my mother in my childhood. I was in constant fear for the vision had made a deep impression on my mind. If any one came in, it was with the greatest difficulty I could hold social converse with them.

In the lapse of a few weeks those solemn feelings wore off in some measure, so I ventured to leave my childish prayers. One day as I was about to leave on business, in the act of getting on the horse, I felt heavily laden in consequence of sin, and said, I feared the horse could not carry me. On being asked why? I replied I cannot tell why, only because I am so wicked. After the lapse of a few years, this woman became pious, and in her relation to the Church made mention of this same circumstance, and thought if I was so wicked, what would become of her? One day I was accosted by a young man with whom I was acquainted, calling me Miss Christian; as he had heard that I had become pious. I told him it was not so, but sincerely wished it was the case; he did not expect such an answer and passed on. It appeared, as though I had accomplished much with my reply. Though vain and rude, yet I never saw the time I could sport or trifle with serious things.

I had less desire to associate with my young companions and that gave me courage. And the desire for holiness became more frequent and that I should yet be a Christian, I was led to hope, for these desires came more frequently, and continued longer, which led me to think that God did take notice of me, and to his praise led me in the way I knew not.

"Not of ourselves, but the gift of God."

I met with a book entitled, "Grace abounding to the Chief of Sinners, Or come in welcome to Jesus Christ," written by John Bunyan. It was a treasure indeed to me, as it pointed out my condition as nothing else had done. I carried it with me and read it over and over, for nothing gave to me so much instruction. I had some reason to think I was coming to Christ or at least trying to come, and felt some animation of heart, but my greatest fears were that I should not come aright. I was now about sixteen years of age, and the world was losing its pleasant look. I had no comfort in the world, nor in religion.

I attended a funeral one day, and the text on the occasion was, "I heard a voice from heaven saying unto me, write, blessed are the dead who die in the Lord from hence forth." The text arrested my attention and needed no improvement for me, for if the labors of the righteous followed them, where would my end be? After returning home I felt still more solemn. In the evening I sat reading my Bible, when a young man (a neighbor) came in. I would have been glad had the bible been laid aside before he came, but was obliged to make the best of it, and laying it upon the stand, commenced conversation, when he rather jocosely, asked if I could find the text? I turned to it and read it, but while doing so I burst into a flood of tears. This betrayed me and I knew not what to do, but I left the room to hide the emotion of my heart and give vent to my feelings; for I perceived that weeping relieved me. I felt some mortification to think that I could not command my feelings any better. The next day I had occasion to go to the house of this neighbor, and some of the inmates commenced laughing, for what had occurred on last evening. The report was, that I was under concer.. of mind, but they thought it was feigned. I was perfectly speechless for some time, and then replied that I was sorry any one should form such an opinion of me, as it was untrue, that if it were so, that if I were under concern of mind I should be glad; I went home with a heavy heart: oh thought I—I am undone, what shall I do? To trifle with such serious thoughts I dare not. No hope nor enjoyment in anything. Soon after this I thought I would go to a school exhibition. I could not see much harm in that, and should meet with my young friends, and then, what if they had heard the report of my being serious? that would destroy my happiness. However, I was resolved to go; but had not proceeded far, when I suddenly stopped, and thought to proceed no farther. I retraced my steps a little. There the tempter took the advantage of me—my proud heart too came in contact with the teachings of the good spirit, the struggle between the flesh and spirit became weaker, and the flesh prevailed, and on I went. I did not enjoy myself as I expected.

As Spring advanced, instead of feeling gay and cheerful as formerly at that season of the year, I became more dejected. This passage of Scripture came to mind and gave me some encouragement: "Come unto me all ye that are weary and heavy laden, and I will give you rest."

I still read my little book, and pressed it to my bosom, and said there was no comfort in anything but religion. I read the Bible, its threatenings were against me, and the promises were none of mine, because I knew not how to come to Christ.

My heart burns within me as I record the dealings of God with me, while in a state of ignorance, and far from Him. How kindly, how gently, does he lead us on! And alas, how little one can know, unless he touches us by his holy spirit! It matters not how much of merely human knowledge we possess, we must work out our own Salvation with fear and trembling, knowing that "God worketh in us both to will and to do, of his own good pleasure." May gratitude flow from our hearts for his long sparing mercies, and that he has not cut us off in our sins.

In the month of May the same year, two men from abroad sent

in an appointment to hold a meeting: they were exhorters, accordingly our Minister (Elder Gillett) gave the notice, and my heart leaped for joy, and from that moment I could scarcely think of anything else.   After the lapse of four days the evening of the meeting came, although the precious time had passed so slowly, and I was on my way thither.   Sometimes I would find myself on the run and then slackening my pace, however, I found it extremely difficult for my body to keep up with my mind.

Elder G. preached a short discourse, and gave liberty for improvement; when one after another of those before alluded to, arose and spoke with power in the Holy Ghost.   Every word went to my heart like an arrow.   They sung praises to God in the spirit as he directs, and as they sung these Lines, it seemed as though my very heart would burst:

" Come and taste along with me,
Consolation running free,
From my Father's wealthy throne,
Sweeter than the honey comb."

" Goodness running like a stream,
Through the New Jerusalem,
By its constant breaking forth,
Sweetens Earth and Heaven both."

" Heaven here and Heaven there,
Comforts flowing everywhere.
This I boldly can attest
That my soul has got a taste.

They appeared to be happy in their Master's service.   Were I in possession of all the world I would freely exchange it for the enjoyment they appeared to possess.   I then came to a much stronger resolution than ever before; so thoroughly convinced was I that there was a reality in religion, that I intended to seek for it as long as I lived.   In this condition I began to weep, and wept so loud that some of the old ladies came to me to know the cause of my grief.   I could not utter one word nor suppress my feelings; tears were my only relief, for my heart was too hard to break as I then supposed.

Thanks be to God, for the strong resolution I was enabled to make that night.   I trusted that my conviction would never leave me.   On retiring to rest, I fell upon my knees to implore mercy

of Him, whom I had slighted, and asked that my life might be
spared until I had sought and found mercy at his hands.
A night long to be remembered, I imagined I saw the finger of
scorn pointed at me, as if I had began a great work, and should
not be able to perform, strove hard to overcome such temptations,
then would think what I had read in my little book.
" Come in welcome, &c." I began to feel more alarm that I
should miss my way and not come aright, for I was still ignorant
of the way. The next morning I felt more strengthened and
my tears still flowed freely, I strove hard to prevent discovery,
for though I had resolved to seek religion, yet I was ashamed to
be found weeping. I would often wash to prevent any notice
being taken of me, I sought an opportunity to be alone that I
might give vent to my tears. I retired a little from the house
when I thought my head was water, and my eyes a fountain of
tears; the excitement was so high I feared that I should alarm
the family. I strove so hard to suppress my tears that the blood
ran freely from my nose. I became more calm and relieved.
This was the first time I had any realizing sense of Christ having
shed his precious blood for sinners like myself. I viewed him
on the cross in the agonies of death for me. My heart went out
in love towards Him in return for what he had done, and
thought I could let all the blood flow from my veins if that would
make amends. I returned into the house but sought to keep out
of sight as much as possible.

The next Sabbath I went to meeting, and thought minister and
people all felt solemn as myself, and learned that two men were
struck under conviction at the previous evening meeting. If a
natural heart could rejoice at the appearance of good, mine did.
Meetings were given out for the week and I returned home, glad
to hear that others were going from the City of Destruction.
Now thought I the way will be made easy, and I shall soon be a
Christian; but I soon found lions in the way.

Soon after this, the Minister came to see me, and made sundry
inquiries. I told him that I thought myself a great sinner. He
asked if I thought my sins were so great that Christ would, or
could not have mercy on me? I replied I had no doubt that He
could and would, if I really came aright. I knew not the way;
and this was my greatest trouble. He gave good advice, but
could not show me the way and left. I set myself to keeping

the Sabbath, but that was not very hard, as I was accustomed to, from my early childhood; and was willing to do anything whereby I could make myself better. I was also strict to attend meetings. but cannot remember that I received much benefit except the one before mentioned. Thus I lived for some weeks, yea months, while the reformation was in progress, and heard of many conversions, that brought my sincerity into question, and led me to doubt whether I was in the right way. I concluded, however, that I was the greatest sinner of them all, of course more difficult to find pardon. I also tried to be more fervent in prayer, that I might feel more my need of a Savior's blood. I had great respect for Christians, and thought I loved them. I conversed with some of those, styled young converts, but no one complained of so hard and wicked a heart as mine. I tried to examine my past life, to find wherein I was worse than others of my age. I was never disobedient to my parents, nor unkind; and had been kept from outbreaking sins, and what was the matter? My burden appeared to be in my breast, not on my back as represented to be the case with Christian's in the Pilgrim's Progress.

One day an old Lady came to me and said, there was a man also expecting to join the church, and inquired if it was not my duty? I told her no; for I had never felt such a change as some others had. From that time I was fearful of being left to stop short of a sound conversion. What have I neglected that should have been done? It occurred to my mind I had some trifling ornaments that must be given up, that lead me to believe pride was lurking in my heart, of which I had not seriously thought. It was not long before they were disposed of; for I thought they were not compatible with a Christian character. I continued so for some time.

Another circumstance lay with weight on my mind, and that was singing, for it appeared to me I could not sing rightly or acceptably, with such a heart. I therefore left the gallery. It was not long before a woman belonging to the church asked me why I left my seat? My reply was hasty, but just as I felt: "That the Devils in hell could sing as well as I could!" I was growing worse, and sinking in discouragement. The reformation so much anticipated, was about over; ELDER G. visited me again I could not converse much with him;—he saw my condition and said he was concerned about me, or to that effect. After he left, I felt very bad, and was sorry I did not give him a more full description of my real condition, still fearing he would say something that would make me think I was a Christian. This conversation however had a very different effect, he had not gone far when I burst into tears, and thought where shall I go for counsel? I shall certainly ruin my soul by such a course. I felt sad, thinking I had grieved the Holy Spirit. I resolved to call on our Presbyterian Minister, living some eighty or one hundred rods from us. Wishing to know the worst of my case I proceeded to his house, after a considerable conflict; he asked me how I got along? I told him not much, if any. He said no more, and left the room. I returned home with a heavy heart. No one cared for me, and I thought myself an outcast, and knew not what to do; I tried to pray and that was all. Soon I was encouraged, by these words: "Though your sins be as scarlet, they shall be as white as snow — though they be red like crimson, they shall be as wool." I was enabled to resolve again to keep a double watch over my besetting sins, hoping I was not entirely forsaken of Him who hath called me.

Meetings became less frequent, and nothing had done me any good, the circumstance of the woman that had spent all her substance on Physicians, and was no better but rather grew worse, was truly my case. I had attended many of the meetings and denied myself every enjoyment, had done everything that I could for the most of two long years, had been mourning over my sins, and what more can I do? If it were a journey to be performed by traveling, I would go until my limbs were worn off. I was conscious that was not the way to obtain religion. There was a secret involved in it, that was yet unknown to me. Despair was coming upon me, as I had long desired a revival and it was granted, and where was I? a sinner still! I thought that if I was sick, nigh unto death, then should I be more fervent at the throne of grace, and God would hear and perhaps answer. Everything on earth wore a gloomy aspect. I thought my time upon earth was short,—distress and horror filled my mind,—I wished that I were some beast or reptile, not accountable; it would be far better than my present condition. It was now September and I was almost eighteen years of age.

No hope, nor anything in prospect, upon which I could rely.

I went to Meeting on the Sabbath as usual, have no recollection
what transpired through the day. At evening sat down to read,
and found the threatenings pronounced against the wicked to
suit my case. Retired to rest, but did not find much, for I
thought of Him whom my sins had pierced, as looking with
wrathful countenance upon me would say :—" Behold, O Lord,
for I am in distress!" The next morning I arose being Monday,
with a heavy heart; it being a stormy day, my fears were
increased. Nothing appeared to be written on my mind, but
"Lost!" "Lost! forever Lost!" "My daily bread like ashes
grew, unpleasant to my taste." Towards evening walked into
the garden, and then met with a temptation; and that was to
walk a certain number of times across the garden, and if I did
not feel better give it up, for I could not live so.—I commenced
walking, stopped suddenly, said: what am I about? Discovered
my fault, in making an effort to bring God to terms; in this critical moment our neighboring Minister passed by, I could hardly
refrain from taking hold of him, anxious to catch at everything
that could possibly save me.

A little previous to my going into the garden, these words fell
with power on my mind: "The harvest is past, the Summer is
ended, and my soul not saved." This so exactly suited my
case, that it was difficult to keep from utter despair, for all my
works were as filthy rags, and I knew not what to do, only,
"Lord if thou wilt, thou canst." Why is it that I must so long
be bound in Satan's chains? Lord what wilt thou have me to do,
was all that I could say. I went into the house as evening drew
on—took my Bible and sat down to read; it was in vain for I
could not read, my distress was so great, I walked the room and
wrung my hands—never can I forget that agonizing pain of
heart. "Oh, blessed God who leadeth the blind by a way they
know not." I went into my chamber not knowing whether I
should see another day, for the pains of hell had got hold on me
—fell upon my knees and tried to pray once more—sought God
with all my heart. I saw if I was ever saved, it would be by
grace, and free grace too. I never saw my perfect helplessness
before, and entire dependence on the mercy of God, could say,
"Lord save, or I perish. I never knew what it was to lay my
soul at Jesus' feet before. then thought I had done the very last.

"Here Lord I give myself away,
'Tis all that I can do."

I went to bed, and strange as it may appear, went also to sleep, whether from exhaustion, or how, I know not or did not then. Early in the morning before it was light, I was awakened by the tears streaming from my eyes; at the same instant found myself happy, and free from that load of sin which had borne me down for so long a time. I was almost ready to think that I was not awake; but the first sense of consciousness found me in a flood of tears, and my soul filled with love. I questioned in a moment what this should mean, and what had become of my burden. I asked what? is this a change of heart? Is this being born again? Are my sins forgiven? Then I exclaimed, no! it cannot be, that God has taken any notice of me—such a worthless, hell deserving creature, wondered why my tears flowed so freely if this was conversion—surely it cannot be. Something seemed to whisper so sweetly, will anything else answer? No! no! I replied nothing was ever like this before. I praised God till morning light. Now the secret was revealed, now I had found "The way, the truth and the life." I saw that none can come to God only through Christ the door. O why could I not have found the way before. I felt as though my whole life had been lost until the present moment. Oh how thankful to think that I had not been left to myself, and perished in my sins,—how near I came to grieving the Holy Spirit, from time to time for the last time. Oh it was too good and great for me. I never expected to be troubled with my own heart any more—all the enemies were slain. I arose in the morning and found all nature changed as well as myself. I felt like singing, but feared to, on account of my silence so long, I suppressed my feelings for a little while, but soon gave vent to my full soul. And thus I sang:

"When God revealed his gracious name,
  And changed my mournful state,
My rapture seemed a pleasing dream,
  The grace appeared so great."

"The world beheld the glorious change,
  And did thy hand confess,
My tongue broke out in unknown strains
  And sang surprising grace."

"Great is the work my neighbors cry'd,
  And own'd thy power divine,

Great is the work my heart reply'd
And be the glory thine."

"The Lord can clear the darkest skies,
Can give us day for night,
Make drops of sacred sorrow rise
To rivers of delight, delight—delight."

In the course of the day I fell upon my knees as often as I could find a secret place, to give thanks, for I had nothing to ask for, as I was in possession of everything. It was the first time I ever felt conscious, it was enough, yea, more than enough; it was too good for me. I thanked God that I was ever made to hear His voice, and entered while there was room. I thought it strange why I could not have found the way before, and yielded sooner to the calls of Mercy, instead of losing so much of my life. Thus I went on praising and wondering at the goodness of God through the day, never suspected that another trouble would arise.

However, as night came on, I began to question the nature of my exercises which so delighted my soul; at this I was much alarmed, thinking it possible I had been deceived. Oh dreadful thought! If this is not religion, what is it? I was jealous of my heart, thinking that it might be a delusion and that I could not know it. I walked out a little from the house, for I dared not rest in sleep until this point was settled; the thought of being deceived was distressing. I seated myself beside a stream of water; the moment I heard the sound of the rill and saw the stream gliding gently down its course; mercy appeared to flow to sinners just as free, but Oh Lord decide this doubtful case with me; although I felt something of the glowings of peace in my bosom, gazed upon the water, saw the moon and stars all in their appointed order. All nature looked pleasant and I should be happy if those doubts were removed. Oh how little did I realize that when one temptation was overcome, another was prepared to try me.

I went to the house and repaired to my chamber, feeling as though I could not be deceived; fell upon my knees and prayed that I might know the worst of my case, when suddenly these words came with force to my mind: "Daughter be of good comfort, thy faith hath made thee whole." I arose, embraced the promises and enjoyed the sweet comforts of religion for some days. I had succeeded in keeping all my joys and fears from any one until Thursday evening, on going to meeting I fell in company with a young lady, with whom I was conversant, and asked her how she got along in her mind? (she had been somewhat serious,) she replied she was about the same. I told her I had never been so happy before, as I had been for a few days past; she burst into tears. I was almost sorry I had told her on account of the grief it had produced; but felt as though I could not keep it to myself much longer. To make it more easy I said, perhaps it was not anything, but felt as though I had done wrong—went into meeting and thought everybody was happy, they looked different from what I had ever seen them before. The house was full and I had no seat, thought nothing of being weary whilst listening to the preached word. The text was, "And looking unto Jesus"—how sweet the Gospel sounded, when he described what it was to look and live—and gave instruction for future life. I gained strength that evening; it being the first I had heard with an understanding heart—it was truly refreshing. On our way home, I spoke again of the blessed effect of the Gospel, did not try to hide my feelings from her any more, and every time my lips were opened to speak of the goodness of God, my faith grew stronger; and thus went on my way rejoicing and sang:

"Oh tell me no more of this world's vain store
The time for such trifles with me now is o'er,
A country I found where true joys abound
To dwell I determined, on that happy ground."

"The souls that believe, in Paradise live
And me in that number will Jesus receive.
My soul don't delay, He calls thee away;
Rise, follow the Saviour, and bless the glad day."

"No mortal doth know, what He can bestow,
What light, peace and comfort, go after Him go.
So onward I move, to a country above,
None guesses how wondrous my journey will prove."

"Great spoils I shall win, from death, hell and sin,
Midst outward afflictions shall feel Christ within,

B

And when I'm to die, receive me, I'll cry,
For Jesus hath loved me, I cannot tell why."

"But this I do find, we two are so joined,
He'll not live in Glory, and leave me behind.
So this is the race, I'm running through grace,
Henceforth till admitted, to see my Lord's face."

"And now I'm in care, my neighbors may share
The blessings, to seek them will none of you dare?"
In bondage Oh why, and death will you lie?
When one here assures you free grace is so nigh!"

Every word suited my case and I felt as though my sins were separated from me, as far as the East is from the West; was reconciled with God, and at peace with Him. It was now my greatest pleasure to converse with my Heavenly Father, neither would I do anything without asking counsel of Him. I felt and spoke like a child, yea I thought like a child; my cup ran over, and I felt a drawing and reaching after sinners, often wept in secret, my exercises were so strong, I was filled with distress before unknown. I saw such a fullness in Christ, I could hardly hold my peace. The words of the Poet were on my mind continually:

"On what a slippery step,
The thoughtless wretches go!
And Oh the dreadful fiery deep,
That waits their fall below."

While in this frame of mind I went to a meeting in the neighborhood, where I had formerly associated in my early days, had not been in the house long before I felt a yearning over my young friends and others, to such a degree that I could hardly keep my seat. It was the first time I was called to speak in a meeting. My anxious mind was filled with perplexity the thought of allowing those who were blind, and dead in trespass and sins, to go on without warning them to flee from the wrath to come, made my spirit faint, I loved sinners, and christians were loved almost to excess. On my way home I was overtaken by the Minister. He inquired into the state of my mind: I told him how anxious I felt for sinners; he asked if I found any crosses by the way? I told him no, for I did not know I had been suffering under the cross. Before reaching home my mind became clouded. I thought it was in consequence of not warning my friends.

I felt as though I could not retire to rest until I had made known my feelings to a neighboring woman, and while relating it, the same sensation came over me as at the meeting. I told her it was my duty to pray with her if she had no objections. She expressed a willingness; and I fell upon my knees, with my full soul raised to Him who hears prayers, and was carried beyond this world as it appeared to me, giving myself away as it was all that I could do. In a moment I lost sight of the object, and my mind returned to earth, and I was perfectly speechless. I arose from the attitude of prayer, it being the first time I had ever attempted it in the presence of any person. I returned home in peace, although performed in so blundering a way. I was resolved to do my duty whenever it was made known to me as well as I could. For some days that heavenly peace before experienced flowed like a river. My Heavenly Father did not give me a stone, when I asked for bread, nor a serpent instead of a fish. He gave "the sincere milk of the word that I might grow thereby." I was still more and more convinced that God looked at the heart and its motives. I was "Led into the Garden of nuts to see the fruits of the Valley, where the Vine flourished, and the Pomegranate budded." Already I had enjoyed more than a compensation for all my trouble and sorrow. Soon after this I became desirous to unite with the church. A covenant meeting was approaching at which time I had concluded to make the application; the time came, and the cross also, and as the subject had not been divulged to any one, it being late in the fall I thought it best to wait till Spring—fearing I might not live like a Christian, I had better remain as I was, than wound the cause of God. Thus my conflict abated for a time,—yet to my great astonishment, found I could not live happily at all, and now my hope was called in question, and my fears were increased; lest after all I might be deceived, and fall short of eternal life. I called to remembrance the joys and fears that had been so recently experienced, and why this sudden change? Notwithstanding all, I felt a drawing to the church, my doubts and fears were increasing, love growing cold and that too gave me anxiety. I would call to mind the kind dealings of God, but my strength is perfect weakness. "Oh thought I, that I had the wings of a dove, then would I fly away and be at rest."

One day I went out alone to pray that I might know whether I did really love God or not, for if not a Christian, I had no wish to do those duties that belonged to them. I went from place to place to pray, but found no access. Continually while seeking, these words came to mind: "If ye love me, keep my commandments." I tried to prove my love in various ways. One night I dreamed I was baptized, and was very happy. As soon as I awoke these words came to my mind very forcibly: "And now why tarriest thou? Arise and be baptised and wash away thy sins, calling on the name of the Lord." I did not recollect ever reading this passage, but thought it to be scripture. I regretted that I did not go forward when the season would admit of it. This scripture dwelt on my mind day after day. I knew it was a dream, but its condition led me to think it was in consequence of my omission of my duty, and promised if spared till spring nothing should hinder. Next Sabbath evening a neighbor came in and told me, that a number had presented themselves for baptism at the meeting from which I was absent that day. What to do now I knew not, and to let such an opportunity pass I dare not, although it was winter and the earth was bound in snow and frost, and I never had heard of the baptism of any person by immersion under such circumstances. I retired to rest but sleep departed from me. Spent most of the night in prayer that I might be directed; I had no desire to return to my former ways of living, my fear was that I should bring a reproach upon the cause of Christ. I was tossed to and fro like a drunken man, and took no rest day or night. Oh thought I, if some one would direct me, and concluded to visit the Minister. Before I went, these words came to my mind: "If the Lord be God serve him,"—told the Minister I did not know what to do; instead of giving me any encouragement, as I expected, he said I must be fully persuaded in my own mind. Then the enemy took advantage of my weakness and my fears. Suspected the Minister thought I was not a fit subject; told him I did not know whether I should go or not. While there it appeared to me I must go and consult with my father, not expecting to meet with any objections. He readily gave consent and said he would come after me. Now my difficulties were all removed, and had become more calm; being resolved once more to take up my cross and follow Christ.

The day appointed for the meeting drew on, being Thursday, Jan. 5th, and we repaired to the place of meeting, which was a private house, for convenience, and many came from afar to witness the scene. Just on our arrival Elder GILLET came to me and enquired, if I had changed my mind? I replied no! He soon commenced the meeting, and on naming his text, was somewhat surprised to find it was the very same words that came to my mind on awakening from my dream. Had never told any one of it. After the services were through, I related the dealings of God with me, and gained admission to the church. As we approached the water of baptism it was a delightful place to me, as I arose from the water, I could realize the words of the text, 'And wash away thy sins.' Again I felt relieved of my burden, found peace, and went on my way rejoicing with the answering of a good conscience, not in the abundance of water. For many days no clouds appeared, all sunshine and peace. I feasted on the blessed promises, read the scriptures with more delight; and could say with the Poet:

> "Give me the Bible in my hand,
> A heart to read and understand
>   And I desire no more."

Whenever I passed that blessed book as it lay on the stand I would open and read a few words. I loved the saints of God and delighted to commune with them,—waited with intense anxiety for the time of our covenant meeting. I was present, and after hearing others express their feelings, I arose, being the youngest in the church. I had now arrived at the age of eighteen years, my feelings could not be expressed more suitably, than with the words of the Poet:

> "Had I ten thousand hearts dear Lord,
>   I'd give them all to thee.
> Had I ten thousand tongues, they all
>   Should join the harmony."

One day after returning from meeting I took my bible and read the fourth chapter of John, first epistle, and when I read these words:—"Beloved, let us love one another, for love is of

God; and every one that loveth is born of God, and knoweth
God. He that loveth not, knoweth not God, for God is love."
I thought "Oh Lord ever give me this love!" It was the first
time I understood the scriptures, speaking of being dissolved in
love—then thought I, who can love any object with all their
hearts and not know it?

All was well for some time, and I hoped peace and joy would
be my lot, I had no trials. It was not long, however, before
these words fell with remarkable force: "Behold I will refine
thee, but not with silver; I have chosen thee in the furnace of
affliction." I shuddered at the very expressions, especially the
last sentence. I said, Oh my Father, what shall I learn by this?
I always expected difficulties through life, yet the impression
these words produced did not leave me for a long time. I beheld
a promise in them that I should be refined, but not with silver;
that showeth me as I thought that I could not have much earthly possesions. Well thought I, they are not what I mostly
desire—give me food and raiment suitable for me, and I can be
content. But Oh! the furnace was what I mostly dreaded. "In
the world ye shall have tribulation, but in me peace. Be of
good cheer, for I have overcome the world."

In the year of 1811, a difficulty arose in the Baptist connection
which resulted in the expulsion of one of its most worthy members; on account of some difference of opinion in regard to
worship, and the support of the Ministry. He was a Preacher of
the Gospel, in the City of Hartford, Connecticut, by the name of
HENRY GREW. He had previously left the church and a large
salary, and many false reports were in circulation. It was
thought best by himself and others, for him to have an opportunity of declaring his true sentiments; accordingly an appointment was given in the neighborhood where I then resided.

Previous to the meeting ELDER GILLETT visited the church,
recommending its members not to attend the meeting, as it came
in contact with the proceedings of the Association, as they had
adopted measures to silence him, he had however, succeeded in
his visits but being young, he had overlooked me. The time
arrived and thinking it best to hear for myself and—"Prove all
things, and hold fast that which is good," I went and found a
large assembly, though but one member of the church present
beside myself. I gave attention to what was said, which brought

to mind some exercises while under conviction, in regard to the singing of such, as were enemies of, and far from God. At the close I was asked, how I liked what had been said? I replied: "Never man, spake like this man" of all I had ever heard before I resolved from that time to search the scriptures, and see if these things were so.

The more I read, the more I saw the need of separating from every unholy alliance with the world. I was convinced that the sacrifices of the wicked, were not acceptable to God; that he was a spirit, and whoever worshiped him Him, must do it in spirit and in truth. Myself and a few others, met with much opposition which led me often to frequent a throne of grace. Those I had loved with such vehemence, ceased to inquire after my welfare as usual, sometimes my affection would twine around those with whom I had taken sweet council. As often as I had an opportunity to converse with them I did so. I began to feel more for the church than for the people of the world; the church was getting rather low. In the Spring of 1812, I went to live with a person who employed a number of young females, this I feared would operate against my spiritual interest, as they were gay and frivolous, and being myself of the same tempermament my danger was apparent. Often would I ask the Lord to keep me, I would tarry in my room resolving to be careful when going to the shop, fearing I should wound the good cause, and my own soul, I as often found my resolutions to fail, a continual warfare in my breast, "The flesh lusting against the spirit," etc. Oh thought I, when will the combat cease!

Soon after this ELDER GILLETT gave an appointment for preaching in the district were I then resided,' and I attended. At the close of the discourse I was so pressed in spirit, that I could scarcely breathe, feeling it my duty to bear testimony to the truths of the Gospel to which I had been listening. In my mind objections were soon raised such as these: if I do say it is the truth, the Minister will be proud and lifted up, and again, my life stared me in the face, my time was short in making the decision. I cried to God to let this cup pass for this time, and if I ever felt so again I surely would do my duty. I had no sooner made the promise, than the impression left me and I was perfectly calm. While this conflict was going on in my breast, the meeting closed by giving out another appointment one week from that evening—I sincerely wished something might occur to prevent me from being present at the contemplated meeting—I felt assured that the Lord heard and answered my request, and knew the secret workings of my heart, for no one knew what was passing in my mind. I tried to live day by day so that I might have strength if I were called on again, still had a secret hope that something would interpose. Sure enough, it so happened that I had occasion to leave town the day previous, and did not expect to return till the day after. My business being accomplished, 1 returned home just in time for the evening meeting, made no delay but repaired to the place of worship, being filled with many fears, and having promised was bound to obey—being much excited did not enjoy the preached word, and have no recollection of what was said. At the close liberty was again given for any remarks. It is impossible to describe the power and weight that rested upon me for a moment or two, when my heart arose in rebellion; that moment my breath stopped, and I dare not disobey, and sprung upon my feet, and burst into a flood of tears. What I said I cannot tell; it was only to be a witness for Christ, and to yield that moment was needful. And now, I believe as I did then, if I had refused I should have been made amonument of God's wrath. From that time it appeared to me that something different, from what is of most females, was and would be required of me. I felt somewhat cast down fearing the consequences, for I did not enjoy such peace as formerly, after such a struggle with my corrupt heart. It occurred to my mind that it was "The willing and obedient that eat the good of the land." I saw plainly that I was not willing; and that obedience was forced. On my way home my young companions forsook me, I felt very lonely, fearing God had forsaken me too. The man with whom I was living was very pious, and as soon as I returned home he arose from his bed and inquired what had taken place that evening, for his exercises were such, that he could not rest. He saw that I felt so bad, he did not insist upon an answer. From that time I found more strength to overcome my vain passion. The church was in a low condition, therefore I could not receive much benefit from them.

Previously I had become acquainted with a pious young man whose name was SIMEON FISH; his character was such as to insure to me help on my pilgrimage, and we entered into arrangements to join our fortunes together. Accordingly we were married in the fall of 1812. We went on prosperously for some time having meetings in our locality now and then. It was thought proper to appoint a church meeting at which time I was led to speak my views on the order and discipline of a Gospel Church. This brought fresh trials, and began to understand the former passage of scripture, "Behold I will refine, etc." One of the Deacons who attributed wrong motives, spoke harshly to me. I was grieved. His wife sympathized with me and told me to stand firm for the truth—however I was much hindered from that sweet fellowship I had formerly enjoyed. One circumstance occurs to my mind which happened about this time: An elderly man and his wife belonging to the church, being poor and not calculated to obtain a living, were cast upon the town for support, thus placing them outside of the limits of the church, and of course depriving them of all its privileges. My mind was so exercised about them, that I could not rest. Feeling that my work was not done in the church, I went to one of the leading members and told him my feelings, and views, on the subject, inquiring if something could not be done whereby they might live near the brethren, I told him of the duties which belonged to the church in regard to the poor saints, and how to administer to their needs, and thought we had reason to call our love in question. If we love God we will love his children. Well, he said I do not know who wants them. I told him we must deny ourselves in regard to such things. He asked me to set the example if my judgment was right. I expressed my willingness to share with the rest in the burden; but my suggestion prevailed nothing, and I returned home somewhat disappointed still more weaned from them than before.

Not far from this time the church was deprived of their Minister by death. A man greatly beloved who under God, had done much good, though I was obliged to dissent from him; yet I loved him as a Spiritual Father. The church felt her loss and became less spiritual—Church meeting accasionally—seeking for a new Minister, I was surrounded with many cares and was flung off my guard, overcome by temptations, mixed with a worldly spirit, causing my doubts to arise higher than ever. I saw that I needed the rod more than ever—plainly saw myself in the furnace, and as plainly felt my unreconciled condition. I tried to pray that I might be carried safely through. One day while at work in my chamber I thought, if I were in such or such a place I could pray. But I found no place of repentance, and weep, I could not, my heart was so hard. I could not dis. tinguish between the spirits; I thought it was all evil, surely I never was in so deplorable a condition before. I could not break my mind to any one; no, not even to my dear husband. As night drew on, I walked out to find some place where I could pray, and went from place to place, but found none. I do not know how long I had been absent, but all had retired to their rest. O! thought I, if a christian why is it thus? I called to mind some of my former exercises; but they were not so vivid as formerly. I began to sink and give up all for lost, I knew no more how to free myself from this wretched dilemma than in my first outset. I cared but little what become of me, for I was fully persuaded that if I were not a christian, I never should be; and how can a christian possibly feel as I do? A temptation too horrid to relate was presented to me—Judas like. Oh blessed God! to save and bring me in a way I knew not. I was alarmed at the temptation, and made my way toward the house; my husband had arisen from his bed, lighted his light and was in pursuit of me—he wished to know why I was so long absent. I told him I did not think it was so late.

The next day being by myself, I thought if I only knew what to do I would do it. To be guided by the spirit I could not; for I did not know the difference. It, notwithstanding seemed to be the point that I must walk in the spirit. After struggling for some time I felt to consent; if I could know the Good Spirit, I would follow it, let it lead me where it pleased—It was but a short time before something seemed to say, go and pray. I began to listen, and reason on the subject; that it could not be a bad spirit, for that would not teach me to pray, unless it was to be seen of men, and no one knew the commotion of my heart. I thought I would go, and try, and see where it would lead me- I retired to my chamber, I do not know that I found any access, but felt no worse. I watched every motion of my heart, for it was a thing, a time of choice, between life and death with me. It was but a few moments when the same whisper came again: go and pray, I went without any hesitation, and fell upon my knees. I do not know what I asked for, but felt encouraged— found some little access,—felt assured I was on the right track.

A few moments elapsed, when again it was said: go and pray; with a proviso, that I should go down stairs and into the garden. I did not hesitate, went immediately out, and fell upon my knees, and asked God to forgive me, and that was all. I had no sooner done that than my soul was made like the Chariot of Aminadab. Now I could weep, and say, thanks be to God for all his goodness shown to me, instead of the chastening rod, which I so justly deserved.

Something seemed to say, now will you doubt again? I said no,—no, I never will; if I thought transgression got low in my mind I will always remember this days beliverance. If I do not feel this Heavenly joy and peace always, I will search after the cause and not say "I do not know anything about religion." And from that time until the present has my mind been steadfast, when my life does not correspond with the word, my duty is, to confess and forsake; then receive the promise, and find mercy. This trial being over, went on for some time until a new one was presented:—and that was a worldly spirit with somewhat of a discontented nature. I did not then understand that it was not compatible with the christian character.

One day while in secret asking for guidance in all the affairs of life, these things were presented to my mind, in which I was called to choose one of them: 1st. Live where I was and have all I desired in regard to temporal things, or 2d. Go away and be poor; and 3d. Lose my husband. It did not take long for me to choose, although proud spirited and having a desire to gain a competency. Yet I could say: "Put forth thine hand and touch anything, in preference to my husband." O how little I knew, that an inordinate desire for wealth brings our minds into a certain species of idolatry which is forbidden. Our circumstances were changed and arrangements were made for our removal to the town of Sheffield, in 1815. We had been there but a few weeks when a former neighbor from the place we had just left come rushing in and inquired for my husband, I told him where he was, and asked what was the matter? He did not wait to give an me answer, soon they come in, and said what we possessed of a temporal nature, was at stake, and it was needful to go immediately and secure it, if possible; but in all probability all was lost. We had gathered a few hundred dollars for the purpose of obtaining a small place, as we had then relinquished the idea of going West. They made all possible speed and went off—I immediately sank in discouragement and began to weep; was soon reminded of the choice I had made a little previously, and perhaps should never have known how closely my affections were united to it, if it were not for this circumstance. I felt the loss most keenly, but to mourn over it was not profitable—felt more calm and opened my Bible and read these words: "Though he slay me yet will I trust in Him." I felt peaceful and thankful that my Heavenly Father laid his chastening rod on me so gently, and spared my best friend. I saw I was in the furnace and felt its purifying fire; and desired to be purged from every kind of dross. "Behold I will refine thee; but not with silver" was verified in every deed.

Not long after this a revival of religion commenced and many were turned from darkness to God's marvellous light. The church in the place was like a City set on a hill. Their worship was carried on by the church, and the church only. If any were sick, they were visited and prayed with, and poor, their necessities were relieved, without the need of appointing a committee, each one felt their own responsibility and all were careful that each should do his duty. Thus I went on having food and raiment was therewith content, not fearing but that I should have a supply, while my Heavenly Father was so rich.

One cold night in the winter of the year 1816, I was much distressed on account of a poor man living about a mile from us. My rest was poor, but I fell into a sleep and dreamed. As I awoke these words came to mind: " For unto you it is given to know the mystery of the kingdom of God." I had known him for some time but never had any particular concern about him, until that night. I woke my husband, and told him my exercises, notwithstanding all our misfortunes I felt it to be my duty to go and administer something to them. Having gained his approbation we went into the cellar, I could not refrain from tears. My heart flowed with gratitude, we were supplied with the necessaries of life, while many others were quite destitute; I was sensible from whose hand we received them. It came to mind that " God loveth a cheerful giver." After gathering from our little substance what I supposed needful, my horse and cutter were made ready, and I set out. I never shall forget the emotions of my mind—being ashamed of myself when considering over circumstances, while so many others in the neighborhood, worth thousands, whose dwellings I passed, were living in pride and affluence;—but I must do my own humble duties: On reaching the house I made known my errand and delivered what I had brought, which was received with gratitude. I went in with a bottle of milk I had brought with me and gave it to the woman—she burst into tears and sobbed aloud for some time. I knew she had a babe that did not nurse; as soon as she could speak she made this reply: I verily thought my babe would have died last night, as I could get no milk in the neighborhood to nurse it. When I saw that broken-hearted mother I could easily account for the exercises of my mind on the previous night. I returned home and can truly say that day was a day of great peace and comfort. I praised God for his loving kindness towards me. O I thought it was my meat and drink to do His will. Let my sowing be as it may, I am reaping bountifully. I found it a blessing to give and also to receive. Thus I sang:

Jesus all the day long, was my joy and my song,
    O that all, his salvation might see.
He hath loved me I cried, He hath suffered and died
    To redeem such a rebel as me.

On the wings of his love, I was carried above
    All my sins and temptations and pain;
And I could not believe, that I ever should grieve:
    That I ever should suffer again.

Had I possessed the Indies, I would have disposed of them all not feeling desirous to call anything my own. Oh! I could have wished that my summer would last all the year. But I have found the day of Adversity set over against the day of Prosperity.

One other circumstance I will relate:—In the Spring of the same year I became acquainted with a young woman that was truly pious, and she was taken sick—I went to see her and found her in a blessed state of mind, she continued in this feeble state for some time. Visiting her occasionally; after some lapse of time, other members of the family were taken sick also. My mind became considerably exercised as to her condition, many sleepless hours passed away to know what my duty was in in regard to her, I thought it my duty to bring her home; but having so recently lost our little substance, the duty appeared closed. I contented myself for a short time, when one day I saw her Physician and he said she needed more care than they could possibly bestow while the others were sick. That tended to stir up my mind still more. I made mention of it to my husband; he told me to do as I chose; he had no objections. Nothing appeared to quiet my mind, I consented to go and make her the offer. She thanked me kindly, and said she would most gladly accept of the offer, but was too feeble to ride that day, a day was set, and according to appointment, I went and brought her home; it was too much for her; and she was taken worse, and for ten weeks she was only moved by a sheet, and at the expiration of sixteen weeks was just able to sit up a little. She was a poor girl and an orphan. My mind was calm and serene all the time, I waited upon her, and these words would often occur to me: "As much as ye do it unto the least of these my little ones, ye do it unto Me." With what pleasure and delight did I enjoy, when I could realize I was doing it to my Saviour—it appeared there was nothing too hard for me to do.

It was proposed we should make application to the Overseers of the poor for her support and our benefit. Then came the trial of my faith and principles. My mind was referred back when I went to a certain brother to see if something could not be done with a certain case, before mentioned, when he told me to set the example. What thought I,—shall my faith be shaken, or principles be sacrificed for such a trifle as this? No, it is the fire that tries every man's work, what sort it is? I saw the need of of crucifying the carnal mind that is at enmity with God, it was evident to me that every step in religion, was crossing to our natures.

In the Spring of 1817, a christian brother was preparing to move to the West, I called on him just before he left, and it aroused in me every desire I had formerly possessed for a new country. On my return home, I proposed to my husband that we had better go where we could have a home of our own; the difficulty was the want of funds. We had received encouragement that a certain per cent. could be drawn from our little stock, but did not know precisely when. However, we concluded to venture, and preparations were being made for our removal. In

tho month of June, I made my last visit to Bloomfield. The
brethren and friends drew near my heart, while we were about
taking the parting hand. The Sabbath came on and I felt a
heavy load resting upon me, I thought of retiring from the after-
noon service, for I feared what would be the consequences.
Tho Minister was a stranger to me and the house full, my proud
heart shrank at the cross ; the conflict was so severe that I was
drenched in perspiration. I dare not refuse nor delay, I arose
to bear testimony to the truth of God's word ; just before the
commencement of the sermon, I felt as I would like to express
it a strong solemnity ;—at the close of the meeting one of the
brethren spoke to me, and asked me whether I could tarry
another day: if so, he would appoint a church meeting. I not
only consented but was glad of the opportunity. The next day
we assembled and after some preliminaries, the question was
asked me, if my views were the same as when I left, I told them
they were. After telling me the consequences of such a course
I was permitted to answer for myself. I made as brief a statement as I could, and said, I did not believe a Church of Christ
needed any assistance from the world, for they were opposed to
each other; neither could the people of the world offer spiritual
sacrifices. Unto the wicked God saith : "What hast thou to do
to declare my statutes, or that thou shouldst take my covenant
in thy mouth ;" again, "The sacrifice of the wicked is abomination unto the Lord." I also said, that it was the duty of the
church to come out from such things, and not to be unequally
yoked with unbelievers. After sundry other remarks they inquired if I intended to abide by such views? I told them I did, as
long as I lived. On returning home I reflected on the abundance of comfort I had enjoyed with the people of Bloomfield,
and that I was now about to remove from the home of my
nativity, to spend the remainder of my days in a far distant
land and to form new acquaintances. After a few days I
received a letter of dismission. The next trial of separation was
at hand, for we were about read y to bid farewell to almost every
thing that was dear to us. The numerous friends and brethren
began to entwine more closely around our hearts. And after
many salutations and prayers with the exchanges of many little
keepsakes we set out on our contemplated journey. Never
shall I forget the scene of parting. Some accompanied us a part

of the way and as we passed along, frequently looking back
upon everything that was dear, while changing those beautiful
towns on the Connecticut river, for a wilderness unknown to us.
Soon those painful sensations subsided and we found ourselves
well on our way, with brightened hopes of being in a better
condition to be more useful.

In a few weeks of heavy travelling, with much difficulty on
the beach and in the mud, we were feeling the fresh breeze of
Lake Erie, and our feet were at last planted on the long anticipated soil of Ohio. How pleasing the prospect! land beautiful
and just at our adopted home! I was so elated that I could not
ride—woman's heart was never raised higher in anticipation,
than was mine. But oh, how soon were my prospects changed,
and my hopes cut off? A canker worm lay at the root unseen.
My husband complained of being unwell. I thought we should
soon arrive at our place of destination, and give him rest, when
with good attention, he would get better. But, before we reached our journeys end, he failed and sat down beside a tree. I ran
to him and administered some medicine, when he revived a
little. We were within two miles of the place where we intended to tarry awhile, which was Chardon, Geauga County, Ohio.
It was with much difficulty we reached this short distance as our
team had gone on. I began to be strongly impressed that it
would be his last sickness, still hoping that after rest, the fever
would leave him. With much of my strength he walked a piece
and came to a spring of water; being thirsty he sat down having
nothing to drink with, I called to a lady some distance off—she
came with her cup and he drank. After our arrival at the house
he was taken from the wagon and carried in, and never went out
again! Medical aid was sought after, and procured. Yet he
constantly grew worse. Gloom and despondency filled my
mind, for I often moved to say: O, Lord spare the rod or 1
shall perish by the stsoke—I had had my choice; now God
would have his. I had no spirit of prayer, only that I might be
reconciled to have my only, and dearest friend separated from
me in this wilderness, among strangers, and in a distant land—I
saw God's dealings just; but how should I submit! What a
struggle my poor soul was in from day to day! Some would say
he was better, perhaps to cheer my disconsolate heart; but
nothing encouraged me. The trying time was at hand my

anxiety and great want of rest overcame my strength. As he drew nearer his end, reason and speech failed him in some measure. One day I was left alone with him under peculiar circumstances. I thought my burden of grief was more than I could bear, and that I must sink under it. I walked the room in keen anguish, for I thought my very heart would burst. My loud weeping awoke him out of his death-like slumber. He called me to him and said: "Weep not, I am happy;" and exclaimed:—"O the beauty and excellency there is in Christ! My soul is ravished with his love! I leave you in God's hands. He *will* take care of you, and supply your needs. He will comfort you under all your afflictions.' He embraced me in his dying arms, and then swooned away, and from that time he spent his remaining breath in prayer for me :—that I might be supported, though his ideas were broken. How evident that I was chosen in the furnace of affliction. The greatest struggle with me was over. I felt calm and more resigned; my strength was evidently failing me, having fainted two or three times during the night. On the morning of November 10th, 1817, his happy spirit departed to rest till the morning of the Resurrection. My pained heart was at ease; my tears were all shed as I supposed, and I became like a little child. All was silent. On the day following, his lifeless remains were borne to the grave. ELDER HANKS preached from these words:—"Many are the afflictions of the righteous, but the Lord God delivereth him out of them all."

Before service was ended I was assisted out from the place of the services into a public house, where I remained some ten days not able to return or even sit up. One evening while there, I was much distressed in view of my situation, sick and having no real friends in this, a strange land; I knew not how to bear it. I felt the same resting against the kind hand of Providence. The person tending on me that night became alarmed, and called up the inmates of the house; my Physician was sent for unknown to me. I tried to yield my all into the hands of Him, who so often had brought me to trust in his name. At length I become more submissive. The inquiry Elijah made to the Shurnamite came to mind :—"Is it well with thee? Is it well with thy husband?" I could say, "It *is well!*" The Doctor came and made inquiry in regard to my

C

distress. I told him *all* was *well*; an uncommon sweetness of mind came over me. After a few weeks of tender nursing, I was able to write to my Christian friends, making known my condition. Some weeks after, all of a sudden, a sweet peace of mind rested on me that was unaccountable, as I had not experienced any peculiar trial just then. While meditating to find out the cause—something seemed to say: Did not you request your Christian friends to remember you in their prayers? On recollection I found it even so; and that it was just about the time my letter would have reached them. I praised the Lord that distance nor time could prevent a sweet flow of Spiritual affection in the fellowship of the Saints: and also thanked Him that they could bear one another's burdens. I had been cast down; but not destroyed or forsaken. I found a God at hand and not afar off.

In the fall of 1818, I took a short journey, to visit an old acquaintance. who had recently removed to the State of Ohio, and on my way back a gentleman inquired my name, and place of residence. I replied to his inquiries and in the course of a few weeks received from him, a letter by the hand of one who afterwards became my husband. His bosom companion had been separated from him by death and left him with three little daughters. The prospect of such a change of circumstances as marriage would involve, did not give me much joy; as we were strangers to each other. I was not entirely ignorant of the great responsibility that would naturally rest on me. My mind was like the troubled ocean that could not rest. I often questioned the propriety of placing myself in such a relationship. After some length of time, on returning from church, I felt as though perfectly free from every desire of my own, in the matter of so much importance, and entirely given up to the will of my Heavenly Father. While in this frame of mind the anxious question was again asked,—shall I go? The answer was returned with the promise. "I will be with thee;" from that time my mind became more calm. I thought of the prayers of my dying husband. Nothing appeared too hard, if the Lord would be with me. His presence would clear the darkest sky and give me day for night. I had formed pleasant acquaintances in that place, and found it difficult to bring my mind to leave those that had been so very kind in my sickness. Our nuptials were to be celebrated on the 28th of January, 1819.

After the union, preparations were made for moving to the town of Lenox, Ashtabula County. I again took the parting hand of kind friends, to form new acquaintances with him, who was up to this time a stranger. While on my way I found myself often in tears, and would as often suppress them; fearing it would be painful to my husband. When within two miles of our residence, the badness of the roads,—or rather the want of any, obliged us to put up with his brother for the night. The next day we arrived at our log dwelling, in good spirits and willing to bear with the inconveniences of a new country—with few inhabitants in the town, and consequently no meetings on the Sabbath.

The first Sabbath, I read the Bible the most of the day; felt much inclined to weep, and as I read these words in Isaiah, "Thy Maker is thy husband." I did believe He would be with me, as He had promised. On the following day our two eldest daughters were brought home, aged six, and three, the babe still at her nurse. Their little prattles prevented many a gloomy thought, and as they advanced in years they were kind and affectionate. I took delight in reading the scriptures to them, having put myself in a condition to bear the responsibility of a mother. One day we went out of town to meeting. When we returned, the children said there had been a meeting at our house.

A Methodist preacher had sent an appointment but it had not reached us before we left. From that time he preached occasionally, for more than a year. My soul was often blessed. It was with difficulty I could wait from time to time. I often felt the Macedonian cry to come over and help us; being sensible we needed help, as there were but very few christians in the place. One day as I sat weeping, my eldest daughter came to me to know the cause, with her little arms around my neck. I told her I was thinking about poor sinners, desiring that they might be saved. She turned from me as though she did not understand. These words came to mind: "Thy children shall rise up, and call thee blessed." From that time I had a stronger desire than ever, that God would bless this people, and some of our children would be sharers in the work, especially our eldest. One day while in company with two pious woman, we mutually agreed that at such an hour, we would try to pour out our souls in prayer, and do every duty that was made plain to us. Thus we continued to do for a short time. Soon after this we had a nephew come to live with us; a boy aged 13 years. After awhile we employed a pious young lady to teach our school. One day they all came home, and I discovered something to be the matter, for they had been weeping. I feared at once that some of them had broken the rules of the school. After inquiring what had taken place, they said Miss L. had been talking to them, and praying with them. This impression lasted some time; I felt the need of living more carefully. A Congregational brother moved into the place and set up meetings; there were few believers, and they were divided, (or scattered) as to local residence. I desired a reformation, but was between hope and fear. One day while at our little meeting, realizing our condition, our little nephew, being under serious impressions, and not strength enough in this portion of Zion, I was impressed to go to an adjoining town, and say to a preacher who was laboring there: "Come down, ere my child die." He came and preached once, and gave encouragement for some future time. I was moved with compassion for sinners, knowing that unless they were born again, they must perish.

Not far from this time a Missionary from the State of New York, came along and held one meeting. His exercises were so powerful, he dare not leave, and preached the next evening. As soon as the people were convened an awful solemnity rested on a number present. I felt as though the Holy Ghost had breathed upon us; a cry was begotten in my heart for sinners, that never left me until the desire was granted. To hear the Gospel but now and then was not sufficient. I viewed poor sinners standing on the brink of ruin; yet by what means the work could be brought about, I had yet to learn—but felt assured if he could tarry with us, his labors would be blest. In the morning my burden was increased; such a responsibility resting on me, as pen cannot describe. The time of his departure had arrived. After prayers I left the room. I could not bear any more. After a little space of time my daughter came in and told me he was waiting, wishing to see me. I came out and took his hand and told him I must die; he said he would come again in two years. I remarked that I could not live that length of time. He left, commending me to God. My head was waters that day—we still kept up our little meeting : but the next Saturday I desired to go out of town to meeting and spend the Sabbath. As night drew on I began to feel lonely and distressed: I retired to rest but sleep I did not. These words were constantly running through my mind: "By whom shall Jacob arise, for he is small." In my cogitations I found it was wrong for me to leave home; our meetings were small, but by whom shall we arise? As soon as I arose, I said to my friends, I must return home; they were surprised after making so much exertion to hear preaching, and then leave. Without delay my horse was made ready, and I was on my way; arrived just in time, as our family were going to church. They too were surprised at my return. I met with our little cluster of friends and was much encouraged that God would yet hear and bless. My strength was increased and I felt to draw near and claim the promises, believing I should see better days. Soon after this, I saw a young preacher from Pennsylvania, whom I invited to come and preach with us. He gave an appointment. At the time appointed the people assembled, and just as I was entering the house, he commenced reading this hymn:

"When pity prompts me to look around,
    Upon my fellow clay ;
See men reject the Gospel sound,
    O God, what shall I say!"

"My bowels yearn for dying men,
    Doom'd to eternal woe,
Fain would I speak, but 'tis in vain,
    If God does not speak too."

"O! sinner, sinner, wont you hear
    When in God's name I come,
Upon your peril don't forbear,
    Lest hell should be your doom."

"Now is the time, the accepted hour,
    O, sinners come away.
The Saviour's knocking at your door,
    Arise without delay."

"O don't refuse to give him room,
Lest mercy should withdraw,
He'll then in robes of vengeance come,
To execute his law."

Every word of this spoke the feeling of my heart, and it leaped for joy, for it touched the tender chord of love; so long felt for poor sinners. We had a solemn time and one was struck under conviction; he put up at our house. When about to leave, before doing so, he fell upon his knees and prayed. Our eldest daughter left the room in tears. This gave me courage, for it was the first time I had seen the penitential tear. It gave me reason to hope the time was not far distant when I should hear the cries of the wounded, and God would heal them. I closely watched every tear and every sigh. One day one of our children came to me and said, they found their cousin behind the door reading the Bible; he separated himself from our laboring men, that they should not discover that he was serious. After that, one night he arose from his bed and came into my room weeping bitterly, and I inquiring after the matter: he said he wished me to pray for him. I got up and gave him the best instruction that I could, but thought I could not pray with him. I would pray for them, but not with him. I thought I had no gift, I had lost all through disobedience in my early out-set.

Soon after this, one night as I lay weeping, my husband awoke wishing to know the cause of my grief. I told him I had been anxious for poor sinners for a long time, and now I feared that they would all perish; it was my duty to pray with them. I saw plainly I was in the way, or did not help forward that work as was my duty, for a heavy burden lay on me almost continually.

Not long after, I resolved to call in the children and converse with, and pray with and for them. I found it needful to take up my cross at all hazards; to delay was only keeping back the work so much desired. The meeting on account of the children was misunderstood and our house was full of all ages and classes of people. The next Sabbath Elder CHENEY sent an appoiniment at the hour of four, but his mind was so wraught upon, that he come at one and preached to a large

congregation for a new country. He remained with us for a
few days visiting from house to house. I was much engaged
in prayer during this time; a solemn and weightly spirit was
manifest. The first evening but very few attended and these
words were on my mind: "And great grace was on them all."
The next evening two young females testified publicly that
they had found mercy. Soon after this a number of the youths
and children accidentally met at our house. A prayer meeting
was proposed; Elder C. opened the meeting, all was silent for
some moments, when it occurred to my mind that there was a
lad here who had a few small fishes. I had scarcely spoken
it before they were all upon their knees, crying for mercy in
deep distress. While these precious little ones were in this
condition, I commenced laughing. O thought I what does
this mean, when so much of my time had been spent in solemn
prayer. I strove hard to suppress my emotions for fear they
would be misunderstood; for I had never been exercised so
before, neither have I since; but I remembered this passage:
"There are divers operations, but the same spirit." I should
have been alarmed had it not been for this. O blessed ones!
how they strove to enter into the straight and narrow way—
I was convinced some were not far from the Kingdom of
Heaven. I was soon seized with a sort of trembling, which
produced almost agonizing prayer. Our exercises were mostly
over when this hymn came to mind, with force:

"With hands uplifted to the skies,
Stop, Gabriel stop, the Herald cries!
All-conquering power, forbids thy wing,
Till Heaven born souls, begin to sing."

"Ye listening crowds aloud rejoice!
Angels shall mingle with your joys;
Ye bands of death and bars of hell,
All bursting, let the chorus swell."

Lord where's the soul within these walls,
That unto Isaac's arms now falls?
Shall Angels round the throne appear,
And say not one's converted here?"

"Stop, Gabriel stop, one moment stay
Nor bear such dismal news away;
Some trembling sinner may believe,
And Heaven and Jesus now receive."

"Then wing thy way to worlds of love,
Fly, Gabriel fly, and tell above,
One sinner more begins to praise,
Unbounded, free, and sovereign grace."

Our eldest daughter dated her experience from that evening.
A young man came in carelessly, was struck under conviction
and brought out within a short time. Our nephew felt differ-
ently, but did not receive the evidence until the next evening.

The work went on slowly and surely for some weeks, when
some fearing that heresy had or would get among us; went to
a neighboring town and invited the Minister to come over
and teach us—he came but the result was not profitable—his
feed was doctrine which produced stagnation. Milk for babes
and meat for those of strong minds. Thus the work was hindered. A second came soon after, which put an end to conversions, which distressed me much. I thought of the words of
the Prophet when he spake of being pressed as a cart with
sheaves. [Amos 2.] Just previous to this, a church was
formed of seven members, and soon after three were baptised.
There were additions of such as we hoped would be saved
and great care shown for each other; were any afflicted, or in
trials, we sought to bear their burdens; if any reports came
out against any, personal inquiry was made; if in fault, prayers
were made for the occasion if not comforted. They spoke
to themselves in Psalms and hymns; all gifts were used and
improved, in accordance with the scriptures as we thought;
and all things were done decently and in order. Thus we
went on for some years, and never met in prayer or conference
without the Great head of the Church meeting with us. And
blessed be his name.

Soon after the church was formed I dreamed seeing a few
men trying to raise a small building not far from our house.
Whilst gazing with much anxiety and fearing they could not
accomplish it without more help I ran, thinking woman's help
might be necessary, when arriving, I looked up and it was

finished without the sound of ax or hammers, with the King's crown framed into the top of it. I thought I never saw such a beautiful sight. I awoke with a pleasant sensation that God would take care of his own church, while they walked in the light of His countenance; it was my greatest desire that we should walk in the truth, and grow in grace, and knowledge of our Lord and Saviour.

We had connected with the Quarterly meeting; and it was proposed that one should be held in our place. My mind was was very much burdened with the cares of this life, with some peculiar trials, and add to this, the care of the church, and burden for precious souls were all more than my nature could bear. I was seized with ague and unable to sit up. I thought I could not live; my prayers were that my life might be spared to see the dear brethren once more. A preacher from Massachusetts came a week previous to the meeting, and visited our house and held meetings at intervals, and intimated that a reformation was at hand.

I thought otherwise, although so cast down and distressed, still thought my time short. The day having arrived the brethren began to assemble; Elder ROLLIN rode up and inquired are you prepared for a revival? I told him something was about to take place, but what I could not determine. He told me that he had the witness, and then I told him what the other preacher had said, (they not having as yet seen each other. The meeting commenced, I never saw them look so lovely before—they rejoiced and sang praises, but still I could not be cheerful under such a heavy pressure. The next day the people gathered into a barn to hear the word, and it was preached with power,—poor sinners were pricked to the heart. At the close of the meeting some arose and requested prayers My second daughter was one of them—from that moment I understood the cause of my distress.

In the evening had a powerful meeting, and many cried for mercy. Afterwards our beloved brethren left, except Elder ROLLIN, who tarried for a few weeks, and the work went on. I felt the case of the poor sinner, and desired their salvation, let what would become of me.

During this time a neighboring woman whose mind was powerfully wrought upon, feeling it to be her duty to pray, became greatly agitated and requested me to go out with her. I did so; she could not for some time disclose her situation on account of her flow of tears, but on doing so she became calm and expressed surprise to find herself relieved so suddenly. I told her she would very probably feel the same cross again, and warned her to do her duty, as it was a time of life or death, and not trifle with the offers of mercy, but to confess her Saviour; upon the peril of your life do not refuse. We returned to our seats, the impression came again, she fell upon her knees for the first time. The Lord appeared for her deliverance soon after—and made her happy in believing and in becoming a member of the church. In 1841 she removed into another State, but such was the oneness of spirit that she was always remembered in our prayers when we met in our meetings of fellowship. In her absence I received a letter of which the following is a copy:

"You do not know the extreme anguish I passed through in parting with my *dear dear* Lenox friends. Time in a measure has softened my grief, but time nor distance can ever cause me to love my dear sisters or brothers less than when I parted with them—oh no, dear sister, my more than sister; my mother, how many times would it have relieved my own burdened heart if I could have fallen on your neck and wept. I find here and there a poor starved soul like myself—oh! that they and myself might be restored to our former estate. I do sincerely desire your prayers, that I might be revived. I still desire to keep my standing in the church with that little chosen band—happy hours have I seen there, when we were striking with one accord to serve the Lord."   Yours,

                                                J. H.

In the winter of 1834, Elder WISE came with his family to reside with us, and preached a year; being somewhat discouraged he began to labor in other places; he was the Missionary before referred to. We went on from strength to strength with a good degree of union and good order—with now and then an occasion of church discipline. There was one man which had caused grief, and the church was under obligations to to take notice of it; he agreed to make resttitution before the next Lords day, being the day set apart for communion, but he failed in doing what was required; and while seated around the table, I was very solemnly impressed all was not right—it appeared to me the cause of Christ was about to suffer. I felt to tremble with fear, when these words came with force to my mind: "Ye are clean but not all." I dare not make any delay as the bread was raised in the hand of the administrator to pass, when I arose and repeated those words of our Saviour. The ceremony was deferred a few moments, and remarks being made, when the offending brother left, and I have never seen him since.

In the fall of 1835, our nephew left for the South, in consequence of ill health. At our monthly meeting previous to his leaving, he arose to speak, when it appeared to me my heart would break, as though something was about to happen to him as he was low in his mind, but at this time he had never thought of leaving [the church.] I wish here to make mention of a circumstance which took place in his early out-set in religion: Although young, he possessed the mind of a man of years—his experience was such, that no one could be depri ved of his sympathy, while in his early love and walking in the ways of God. On returning from meeting one evening, I made a misstep and dislocated my ankle; my pain was severe: the night was mostly spent in obtaining the Doctor and replacing the joint, after which I found no rest. The next day he was very sad; in the evening all our family had retired except our eldest daughter who was to wait upon me through the night, and himself. After being seated he took the Bible and commenced reading; he closed his book and said, he could not retire until he had prayed with me. They both fell upon their knees in a childlike manner and offered the prayer of faith, for he had no sooner commenced than my pain left me, to my great surprise. I was *perfectly* at ease—after rising from prayer, I told him to take courage, for I believed that God not only heard, but answered prayer, for it was the first moment of relief since the accident—a hymn came to mind and I requested him to read it:

> " Blessed be God for all,
>   For all things here below,
> For pain, for grief, and joy and thrall,
>   To my advantage grow."

"Blessed be God for pain,
   Which tears my flesh like thorns,
It crucifies my carnal mind,
   To God my soul returns, etc."

After this blessed family interview, I fell asleep and rested some thirty minutes; found my nature refreshed, when my pain returned again, but my mind was calm and serene. When I reflect on past scenes of joy and pleasure in our family circle, I can say, hitherto the Lord hath helped us.

In after years when we took the parting hand I was pained; his mind was somewhat clouded and I feared the consequences. No one to watch over him with care, we could only recommend him to the grace of God.

In the Spring of 1835, our eldest daughter was married, and in in April '36, a little less than one year we were called to part with her by death; leaving an infant to suffer in her stead. A few days before her death, she inquired why it was that everything looked so gloomy? I raised the curtain; she smiled, but her heart was sad. She asked for her hymn book, and read a short time, turned down a leaf and laid it the head of her bed. The symptoms of alarm were visible; her mind was calm. She expressed great love for her friends, and O! what consolation to surviving friends that she did listen to the Saviour's voice in her youth, and never brought a wound upon his precious cause. Her extreme pain of body caused our fond and cherished hopes to disappear, she became deranged; and death was at hand to mow down its victim. In the bloom of life, she resigned her spirit into the hands of Him, who gave it. Thus she died as she lived, a christian. All that I could say was, "Oh Lord thou hast touched me." The wound was deep, and He only that wounds can heal. After her death, her Hymn Book was taken up and we read these lines, by the leaf which was turned down:

"O could I soar to worlds above,
That blessed state of peace and love
How gladly would I mount and fly,
On angel's wings of joy on high."

"But ah! still longer I must stay,
Ere darksome night is turned to day;
More crosses, sorrows, conflicts bear
Exposed to trials, pain and care."

"Well, let these troubles still abound,
Let thorns and briers fill the ground,
Let storms and tempests dreadful come,
Till I arrive at Heaven my home."

My father knows what road is best,
And how to lead to peace and rest.
To Him, I cheerful give my all,
Go where He leads, and wait His call."

"When He commands my soul away
Not kingdoms then shall tempt my stay
What raptures! I shall wake and rise,
To join my friends above the skies."

In the Spring of 1835, a young man came into town to follow the mercantile business, and boarded with us. In July we were called to part with a neighboring woman, who died happy, trusting in God. While on my way home from funeral I was thinking how pleasant it made our lifeless remains appear, that it had been a fit temple for the Holy Ghost to dwell in. My mind was cited to the poor sinner, dying without hope in Christ. My mind was settled on him, I felt an uncommon desire for his eternal welfare. When in secret his case was always before me; I had a desire to converse with him, but no suitable opportunity offered. At times I could not refrain from tears, but believing when he was prepared to receive instruction, there would be an opportunity; I had some fears that it would offend, which it took some time to rise above, my heart being slow to yield. This anxious frame of mind continued some two or three months, when one day in our little monthly interviews, some manifested a desire to be revived; and others for a general revival. Soon after, a young preacher came to spend a few weeks by request; the first day being the Sabbath the people gathered to hear the word. After service was over he called for an expression of their mind, if any would seek religion, make it manifest. No one arose. He, fearing it was not understood, made the second attempt, the people not being prepared for the decision, still kept their seats, he closed the meeting, and sank in discouragement, with a determination to leave the next morning. On his way home, I told him upon his peril, not to leave, for the people were gathering unto him; beside there was a cry in Zion for help. But he left and he has never been here since. The desire for a reformation was increasing slowly.

The case of the young man before alluded to, was continually presented before me, with the addition of two or three more of our neighbors. Just about this time a new circuit preacher, (Methodist,) came on to this circuit. He soon manifested a desire for precious souls:—we entered into one mind, and one judgment; he appointed a two days' meeting. But few attended. The next day being Sabbath, the house was full, and a solemn spirit was visible. The appearance was such, as to encourage him to protract the meeting from day to day. We soon heard the cries of the wounded—What shall I do to be saved? My distress was so great, I feared my nature would sink under it. I prayed the Lord to give me an opportunity to converse with the young man; my heart had become reconciled to do my duty in the fear of God, and risk the consequences. I thought he would believe I was sincere, and compelled to speak in love and tenderness.

Blessed be the name of Him who ruleth the hearts of his people! As soon as my heart yielded, the way was made ready, but not till Saturday evening when my burden left me, so that I could converse with him. Our family retired early, being fatigued—the young man left the store, and came in to retire also. Now was the time. I sat down and said, I had a desire to converse with him on the subject of religion, if he was willing. He, very gentlemanlike, said he was willing; and frankly opened his mind to me and said:—he believed there was a reality in religion, but it was not for him; he had tried to obtain it, but could not. I gave him the best instruction I was able. After conversing till one o'clock he retired. The moment he left the room an agony of spirit rested upon me—I fell upon my knees and implored the God of mercy to have mercy on his precious soul. I cried to high Heaven that He would give me strength. All my true desires were answered, and I felt confident that God did hear, and faith that he would answer; I felt the promise sure: "When Zion trusts its,"—etc.

I went to bed but could not sleep, on account of the deep distress which lay upon me. The night being far spent and the day following being big with events—I prayed to my Heavenly Father that he would permit me to have a little rest. I had no sooner made the request, than I was easy and calm. I fell into a sweet sleep about an hour, when I awoke still feeling easy, and as quiet as usual. Fearing I had been too careful for the body in such a critical moment. I said, Oh Lord if I have done wrong forgive, and grant me thy Spirit again, till his soul shall be set at Libarty, and basking in the ocean of God's love. I had no sooner made the request than it was granted.

I arose in the morning with a pained heart, being much exhausted, but felt as though I must attend church. We all went. An individual asked me on reaching the church.: " Do you think the Lord will be here to-day?" I replied yes, for his spirit is with me. The house was filled to over-flowing and a deep feeling pervaded the whole assembly; many from adjoining towns were present. The preacher could not preach but a few moments, when he called for mourners; and the first one that arose was that young man. Neither my pen nor tongue can describe the anguish of my soul, having no doubt but that he was near the Kingdom of Heaven. I fell upon my knees, child like, and prayed. I still felt the struggle; I prayed again, and was relieved a very little, when meeting was dismiss. ed. At intermission I felt as though I must go to him, and encourage him to seek with *all* his heart. As I turned from him to take my seat, I found I was not able to walk alone. Two of the brethren took hold and assisted me. Some said I was a dying; one old brother knowing the effect of a soul in travail, said, No: she cannot die now! "No," I replied. Some thought that I was not in my right mind. I said I was clothed and in my right mind: and God's strength was sufficient to remove mountains! Before evening meeting, our own family with some others had a special time of prayer; the young man for the first time fell upon his knees and asked for pardon.

The next morning before day I awoke and my heart was filled with perfect peace; and felt assured he was born again;

but I thought he did not know it, or had not the evidence. I felt the witness in my own breast.

> "My heart it was humble, and fell to the ground;
> What a wonder of mercy at length I have found."

On awaking my husband I told him Mr. W. was born again, he wept in silence. Oh! how my heart did leap for joy, at such a transporting thought—to think one more precious soul had escaped the power of the enemy, and was plucked as a brand from the fire; how thankful that God had a way whereby He could be just, and justify those that come unto Him.

The next day he was very sad. In the evening I told him whatever he found duty to do it. After the people had assembled, he arose and declared publicly, that his sins were forgiven—"there was joy on earth," as well as in Heaven. He went on his way rejoicing; and admiring the wonders of redeeming love. I will just relate one other circumstance:

Not long after this, he did not return after church as usual; I felt the same care and burden for him as before. I could not account for it. There was a prayer meeting not far distant, our family thought I had better go, as I was in such distress: perhaps the cause of my distress could be ascertained. I consented and my horse was made ready. Just as I was about to start, my distress left me. I then concluded that it was not in consequence of that meeting, however, I went on, but nothing occurred that evening. On returning home, just at the very place where I left my burden, there found it; then I thought something was about to happen to the family. I continued in this situation until the middle of the next day, when I left my work and took my bible, and prayed that God would instruct me; if he had anything for me to do, or learn, I wished to know it. I opened to the first chapter in Luke, and read until I came where Christ was circumcised, when the neighbors and cousins wished to know what he should be called, etc.; when I read the sixty-sixth verse, "And all they that heard them laid them up in their hearts saying:—What manner of child shall be be? And the hand of the Lord was with him." As soon as I read these words all my distress left me, and I gave him into the hands of God. I thought he would be a useful man in the cause of religion, which has been the case, as I am informed.

Why the Lord made use of such feeble clay, is not for me to know, only what He has revealed in His word, "He takes the weak things of this world to confound the wise and mighty."

Notwithstanding all the kind dealings of God to me, I would still wander from Him, and grope in darkness which would cause deep sorrow of heart. I well recollect on one occasion, my mind became engrossed in the cares and perplexities of life. I had become cold and indifferent as to my spiritual exercises, my heart was growing harder and harder, neither could I have access in prayer; concern was awakened in me, and I dare not live in this condition. I tried to enumerate the Lord's mercies, but my heart was still hard:—I found that creature's love shared too great a portion of my affections, and must be removed.

One night as I lay in bed my exercises were so great that I could not sleep; some part of a hymn came to mind which met my case exactly. I arose and searched my books and at length found it. Hymns and Psalms express my situation better than I can myself. These are the words:

"With tears of anguish I lament,
    Here at thy feet, my God,
My passion, pride and discontent
    And vile ingratitude.

"Sure there was ne'er a heart so base,
    So false as mine has been,
So fruitless to its promises,
    So prone to every sin—

"My reason tells me thy commands,
    Are holy, just and true—
Tells me whate'er my God demands,
    Is his most holy due.

"How long dear Saviour shall I feel,
    These struggles in my breast.
When wilt thou bow my stubborn will
    And give my conscience rest.

D

"Break sovereign grace, O break the charm,
    And set the captive free,
Reveal Almighty God thine arm,
    And haste to rescue me."

"Reason I hear, her counsels weigh,
    And all her words approve,
But still I find 'tis hard to obey,
    And harder yet to love."

At an other time there was a large meeting in the town of Austinburg, and having enjoyed some precious seasons about this time, I felt a desire to go. When I arrived my heart was inflamed with love towards the whole people, saint and sinner. Oh how I loved them! Something appeared to whisper,—are you willing to tell them how you love them? At that moment I felt a trembling for fear that the impression would come, that I could not, or dare not resist. I felt my heart revived at the thought. There appeared to be the company of two armies in my breast, one battling against the other. I said, O Lord I pray thee have me excused, it is more than I can do. In a moment my request was granted, and all was silence in my tumultuous breast, but it was a deathlike feeling as though I had grieved the Holy Spirit. Oh what a sudden change, just before full of love and now like our first parents cast out of Eden. On my way home I could not refrain from tears; but my tears were of no avail, for the spirit had fled. My spirit was like a bone out of joint—I felt to mourn and grieve, that I had offended my Lord and Master. I was afraid of offending the people, but now I had offended God; and how could I be restored? I was ashamed to call for mercy.

The next day being the Sabbath, I could not go to church as usual; I felt like having a day of prayer and fasting. My husband inquired the cause of my sadness and tears. My reply was, I had grieved the Holy Spirit and I feared it had fled forever. I told him how I had prayed to have it depart, the cross was so great. I would not be comforted. In the morning of the next day I went out by myself, lamenting the pride of my heart; promised if placed in such a condition again that I would be faithful. My soul was humble, and that sweet heavenly peace

returned. I felt to praise God, for his Fatherly care over such
a disobedient creature. The lines of the poet were sung in
spirit and in truth.

> "Seizing my soul with sweet surprise,
>   He draws with loving bands
> Divine compassion in his eyes,
>   And pardon in his hands."

> " Wretch that I am to wander thus,
>   In chase of false delight.
> Let me be fasten'd to thy cross,
>   Rather than lose thy sight."

Within a few months after, my love to God and former
promise of obedience was tried: Subsequently another meeting was held in the town of Jefferson; the inquiry arose, shall
I go? Again my proud heart trembled under a sense of duty
but my eyes were up unto God. One day while singing, the
impression came upon me that I must go. It was brought to
mind how Abraham offered up his son Isaac, and perhaps all
that was desired of me was a willing mind. Those keen sensations were not forgotten which were experienced a few months
previous. I attended, but I had not been in long before my
impressions to speak were so strong that my emotions were
manifest, and some came to me and inquired if I was sick. I
made signs that I was not, feeling determined to take my life in
my hands; come life or come death, I would yield all into the
hands of Him who had preserved me thus far. I arose and
opened my mouth in behalf of the cause. Some took offence,
but I believed it to be right to obey God rather than man.

Another trying circumstance which took place in the same
town. The minister preached all day on the doctrine of
Election. I was so distressed that I made an effort to return
home, but not having the opportunity at intermission, I went in
again; but had not sat long before I discovered the cause of my
distress. A sense of duty came over me: sometimes I regretted
that I was there, and the thought of giving offence to some, as
before produced an unpleasant sensation. I had long held the
doctrine myself, but now it appeared to wear a different aspect

from what I had realized before, as the grace of God, to the poor sinner, was not freely proclaimed. I thought there was no need of preaching at all, for the effect upon sinners was injurious. I knew we were helpless creatures but the claims of God ought to be pressed upon the minds of all. The inquiry ran through my mind whether I should ask liberty; but that did not appear right, but wait until the close of service; the word for me to speak was to invite sinners to come to Christ. I saw such a fullness in him I dare not refrain. At the proper time I arose in much weakness and was relieved by giving utterance to my feeling, for it was like a fire shut up in my bones.

I think in 1836 Brother DUNN came into the country a young man, and preached with us some time; he was but eighteen years of age; we did what we could in our feeble state to sustain him. When I first saw him it was at a Yearly Meeting, a young man leaving his parents and native country to promulgate the gospel. I felt to sympathize with him, when these words fell upon my mind,—"Woman, behold thy Son." I felt from that time to seek an opportunity to invite him home with me.

In the Spring of 1837 a young man in the practice of medicine came into town, intending to make a permanent residence, and board with us. After remaining a few weeks, as I was alone in my room meditating on the goodness of God, for my mind had been calm and serene for some time, I felt a drawing out in love towards the human family, especially the unconverted. My eye was turned upon our own household, and this young stranger in a special manner. I saw the blessed plan of the gospel, that whosoever believeth might find pardon of sin, free salvation was my song, while my heart was uplifted to God, who made the sinners way of access possible. Very suddenly I saw as it were a light which reached from earth to heaven, beyond the brightness of the Sun, and this young friend was encircled in it. From that moment a cry was begat in my soul, and my vision disappeared. I had already learned that he was somewhat skeptical. My anxiety was increasing and in the silent watches of the night the tears would flow for my relief, so that in the morning I would appear cheerful, I did not hesitate to speak of the realities of religion before him, but was not prepared to talk with him. My experience had tanght me that it was of but little use to speak to any one without a proper time and place, and—"Thus saith the Lord." I always found it important to watch God's time, not being too fast, nor too slow, but ready at his bidding.

He began to be somewhat cast down and thought of leaving. That would distress me much, for it appeared to me if he went away he would not be as apt to think of his situation, for that reason it was my duty to make him happy and contented.

One day while sitting after church, with the family, I took my hymn book and while reading a certain hymn, I felt it my duty to read it aloud to him, or in his presence. While my mind pondered upon it, my emotions were such as to cause my daughter to observe it, when she inquired the matter: I told her nothing: only I was thinking of reading a hymn, it was so applicable I read it, it was so expressive of the uncertainty of life:

"Ye lovely bands of blooming youth,
Warned by the voice of heavenly truth
Now yield to Christ, your youthful prime,
With all your talents and your time."

"Think on your end—nor thoughtless say,
I'll put far off the evil day;
Ah! not a moment's in your power
And death stands ready at the door."

"Eternity!—how near it rolls,
Count the vast value of your soul;
Beware! and count the awful cost,
What they have gained whose souls are lost."

"Pride, sinful pleasure, lusts and snares,
Beset your hearts, your eyes, your cares,
Take the alarm—the danger fly,
Lord save me, be your earnest cry."

He began to feel more uneasy as his practice was not sufficient. I did all I could to retain him, but did not manifest my greatest desire to have him tarry, I could not suffer him to leave without giving him to understand how anxious I felt concerning him. He received it very kindly, saying that he was not aware that any one had anxiety about him, and expressed friendship and increased confidence. The time of separation came, and I was not sufficiently on my guard, and found myself completely overcome, being obliged to leave the room, yet feeling somewhat mortified on account of my weakness and the thought that I could not suppress emotions in a moment, but the current of feeling was so strong that I was forced to yield. We took the parting hand with many tears, our family wondered why I felt so bad. Oh thought I, how can I be denied my request.

After the lapse of a few days we received a letter from him, of which I give a copy :

CLEVELAND, Oct. 19, 1837.

DEAR FRIENDS :

        As I write, the remembrance of the past, presents a thousand tokens of friendship to my mind, and I am happy in cherishing the thought that I have been so fortunate, as to acquire the friendship of a family so kind, so generous and amiable as yours. It is with feelings of pleasure that I recall in my meditations, the tranquility and harmony, that always exists under that roof, and the happy hours I have enjoyed when blessed with your society. It was with feelings of the deepest regret, that I gave the parting hand ; I have several times bid adieu to my relatives and a large circle of near friends, but never with so much reluctance as I left your house. You may possibly think that I am exaggerating, but you must believe me when I say, that no parting to me was so bitter. I shall always feel a deep interest in your welfare, and always wish that you may long enjoy your state of retired and tranquil happiness. I flatter myself that I have in some degree gained your esteem and confidence, and hope that my remembrance may not soon pass entirely from your thoughts, for it is with a sensation of pride and satisfaction that I look on the acquaintance, and the degree of interest that I flatter myself I have found with you as one of your friends.

Yours,   H. H.

He pursued his journey until he was impeded by a break in the canal, in consequence of which he returned to his father's house in the State of New York. My mind still pursued after

him, and his case was always presented before me in secret
luty. The church observed something unusual in my appearance, and wished to know the cause. I gave them to understand that it was an individual out of my reach; and what to
do I knew not, to pray was all that I could do. I feared my
faith nor strength was sufficient. I found no relief from them;
for the burden rested on me, and me only. After the elapse
of months I felt it my duty to write to him, and let him know
my fears in regard to his situation. As I commenced writing,
passages of scripture applicable to his condition, flowed into
my mind. I was almost confident if they were presented to
him he would embrace the truth and believe in the christian
religion. My faith increased and my impression grew
stronger, and my constant cry was, Lord bring him to the
knowledge of thy truth. Thou canst turn his heart as the
rivers of water are turned. Do not let this long and painful
struggle be in vain—but do thou grant my desires. One night
when deep sleep was upon me, I thought I beheld him in
deep agony, and no one to take care of him but myself,
everything I could think of was administered to him. He
arose from his bed and said: In all his practice and all his
books he never heard nor saw such a case before, neither did
he know what to do, and declared he had felt those symptoms
ever since he was at our house.

I awoke and behold it was a dream. However, I could not
refrain from having some hopes that his mind was troubled on the
subject and perhaps there is a meeting in progress, which I very
much hoped was the case. I felt anxious to know what his
condition was; my mind was more at ease than it had been for
some time. An opportunity was presented that I could make
him a visit. It was sudden and unexpected, nevertheless I
embraced it, and in a few hours I was on my way, feeling
perfectly at ease. After traveling by stage a little short of one
hundred miles, I arrived at his father's dwelling, and was received courteously, being somewhat surprised. [I soon learned of
a protracted effort commencing the evening before. On the next
evening I went with the family. I had not been in long, before
I felt those same impressions as before, but they did not tarry
only a few moments at a time. I could think of nothing but
a bird lighting from bough to bough. At the close of service

the Minister spoke to this effect:—If any desired a revival of religion, to meet at the house of brother W's in the morning of the next day. I had a desire to attend, and precisely at nine o'clock I was at the house. Being the first one, and a stranger, they had some curiosity to know who it could be. I made myself known, and as soon as they heard my name, they asked if I was not the woman that wrote to their friend and neighbor, Dr. H., I told them I had written to him, and desired they should tell me how this had been learned. I was told that he had disclosed it himself, some remarks were made and people began to come in. I learned by this time that I was at the house of their congregational minister. He soon opened the meeting and made mention of the case to this young man, when suddenly I was so pressed in spirit I could scarcely breathe. I fell on my knees and prayed,—O Lord give strength this once, unto Zion ; I felt greatly agonized in spirit. There was no one present who ever saw the like before. At the close I bid them farewell, and entreated them to remember that dear young man; I expecting to return home on the next morning. I did not feel as though I could leave without conversing with him, (the Doctor.) They had company and he was full of business. I tarried until the next morning. Some time in the night I awoke in great distress; could scarcely keep my breath, found my strength relaxed; and thought I had come here to die, and perhaps it was the only way to bring him to the knowledge of the truth. I desired that my life might be spared until I could have an interview with him. With difficulty I arose from my bed, and when breakfast was announced I sat at the table for fear that my excited condition would be discovered. But to eat was impossible, I drank a very little coffee. After arising from the table we sat down a moment, when the Doctor earnestly said to his mother, that I was sick. She soon made preprations to administer something, when I arose and went into my room, fearing I should fall.

It caused considerable excitement. His mother desired me to let her son come in and administer to my relief. I then saw God had prepared the way for conversation, I readily gave my consent. He came in full of anxiety and inquired where my distress was. I took him by the hand, and told him I did not need any medicine, it was the desire I had for his future welfare; he sat down and said he believed there was a reality in religion.

I then told him more fully than I ever had done, and how it caused distress of soul to see those I so much esteemed putting far away the voice of mercy. He promised me he would seek religion but could not attend to it now. He had so much business that he could not, it was impossible, I could not bear that he should settle down with such an excuse. Oh, those words,—"I cannot now," pierced my very heart. I strove hard to make him think that now was the best time, and the only time. I told him of the case of Felix, when, trembling under a sense of what Paul was saying, he said : "Go thy way for the present when I have a more convenient season I will call for thee."

He treated me with the utmost tenderness, but seemed to wish that I would be satisfied with his answer—I cannot now ; I feared the consequences. Oh what a view I had of the free agency of man. It was then in his power to choose or refuse. I saw him standing as it were on a pivot, it was,—"Choose ye this day whom ye shall serve." He thought he could seek God at any time ; but when the creature has been shown what is required of him, and an opportunity given to decide, he then has taken his choice. Then his free agency is at an end in the case ; I saw him hanging on the brittle thread of life and my heart was sick within me, instead of pain my heart was faint. I found his unbelief was changed into a belief of the truths of religion ; and now my cry was :—"Take not thy Holy Spirit from him, and lead him into the truth."

Early the next morning the minister came in and wished me to tarry one day more, and they would have a special meeting on the occasion. I was at a loss to know what was duty, I feared it would give offence ; however I consented, hoping it might turn in his favor. Again I met with the brethren ; his case was the subject of prayer. My heart sank deeper and deeper in sorrow on account of these words,—"I cannot now."

The next morning I left for home, said nothing more ; felt quiet, as if all was done that a poor creature could do ; rode twelve or thirteen miles where I was to take another line of stages in the morning. As night drew, on the burden of soul returned, which caused many fears to arise with such questions as these : Have I left too soon ? Or not soon enough ? Or is he engaged in the protracted effort ? Many such inquiries rushed into my mind. The cry of my heart was: "O Lord take not thy holy spirit from him." At evening I was conducted to my room, when I fell upon my knees to implore God's mercy in his behalf. I felt such a wrestling in prayer that I never closed my eyes in sleep. I think that I never experienced such a night as this before; how many times I arose from my bed to give vent to my sighs and tears I am not able to say. My Heavenly Father knows, and his grace was sufficient, but "Oh Lord take not thy holy Spirit from him." Just at daylight I left this place (Fredonia, N. Y.) Oh what a heavy heart. When I seated myself in the coach I could scarcely speak through the day to any one. At night I put up in Erie, Pa., still pressed in spirit as a cart with sheaves; rested poorly but slept a little. Let not thy Spirit take its everlasting flight, was the cry of my soul. Oh! what a precarious situation he was presented to me as being in. One decision of thought would place him where hope could never come, for God hath said, "My Spirit shall not always strive with man."

In the morning I proceeded on my journey, and as I advanced towards Ashtabula, and found persons of my acquaintance, I was able to converse a little and my burden was some lighter. For ten days it was all that I could bear. After that more moderate until the month of December, when it appeared to me I could not endure it alone. At this time there was a protracted meeting held in Wayne, O., by Mr. DAY. The way being opened I went, and as I drew near the place I felt a sort of strange trembling emotion for I had thought if circumstances would admit, and duty presented, I would bring his case before the meeting. As they were mostly strangers to me, I did not know how to introduce the subject. Where I stopped the good lady said I could stay with her, as she had no company but Mr. DAY. I thanked her, and accepted the favor.

After dinner we repaired to the place of worship, when Elder DUNN spoke from these words: "Grieve not the spirit." That being the burden of my mind it created in me a more lively sense of duty. In the morning I told the kind lady I would assist her if she would direct me. She said she would like to have me set in order Mr. DAY's room, she went in with me and made an introduction. I thought this a favorable opportunity to introduce the subject, I told him my mind had long been burdened and if there was strength and union in prayers, it was an urgent case, and I desired help. He said wait till evening and I should have an opportunity to bring in my request. It was a long day indeed and I was much cast down. Evening came and with it a solemn spirit. After the ceremonies and order of the meeting for one hour, I thought my strength was not sufficient and I delayed. Mr. D. left his seat and came to me and said he wished me to bring forward my request. Fear and doubts were in my bosom. I arose heavily and made as short a statement as I consistently could. There were certain ones selected to pray, but that did not answer for me, it being my duty to pray; and I therefore broke in upon the order of the meeting. The cross was so heavy, I found myself in a high state of perspiration. Come life or death, I must submit. Being almost exhausted I felt as though my strength was perfect weakness, and it was in vain to rely on man. The next morning we repaired with a little circle for prayers. As soon as I entered I felt constrained to bow myself again, and thought,—Oh that I could feel for the two middle pillars, and die to everything, that should hinder the work of grace in the heart.

There was but one man that appeared to know or understand anything about such exercises, when he prayed, he bore the burden in some measure. I was convinced there was nothing more for me to do, and resolved to leave in the morning. While at the family altar I was again constrained to breathe out my desires to God, in behalf of him in whose case I had taken so deep an interest While thus engaged, these words rushed into my mind: " Be it unto thee even as thou wilt." My distress left me, I thought I had obtained the promise and nothing now remained to be done, but wait in patience for any change that God by His spirit might produce upon his heart. I returned home again and in a few days after this my soul was blessed abundantly and I was left to praise God for all his kind dealings with me. But the enemy was near at hand though I was unconscious of it. Not many days after, ere I was aware my heart began to sink and distress followed. It was distrust, and it increased upon me so, as to amount to almost complete horror. I could do nothing but fall on my face and cry unclean, unclean. It appeared to be in consequence of my faith, as I never could "pray nothing doubting," for in this case I always

saw the will of the creature, and could say,—"Lord thou canst
turn the heart of man as the rivers of water are turned." I
was so near dispair on my own account I trembled at the consequence; my reason was in danger and I cryed mightily to God
that He would in mercy deliver or take it from me.

My prayer was speedily answered. Whether from the weakness of my faith, or unwillingness to bear the burden laid upon
me, or the possibility of Gods' converting his soul at some future
period I know not, or that the spirit of God had taken its everlasting flight, is still shrouded in mystery, but from circumstances, I awfully fear the latter. Many times when reviewing this
heart-rending scene I can say,—"Lord forgive my imperfections
if I have not done all, thou hast required of me to do. Oft-
times my heart is melted within me on account of his goodness
towards me, and lost in wonder and praise. Instead of trembling in the presence of man that is mortal, I ought to realize
the presence of Him who is able to destroy both soul and body.
It is possible for the creature to reject the offer of mercy, and
how alarmingly dangerous it is to grieve the holy, tender, heavenly spirit of God. Oh, these words can never be eradicated
from my mind: "*I cannot now.*"

After a few years his death was announced in public print
and I learned that he died without a christian hope. And here
I would remark—that into whose hands soever, this trying and
solemn narrative may fall, it is the writer's prayer, that they
may shun such temptations as shall make their delay dangerous.
There is a *last* time, and then the desire for holiness fails. May
kind heaven forbid that any should say,—"Go thy way for this
time when I have a more convenient season I will call for thee,"
or "I cannot now."

At an early date I became a member of the Temperance
Society, and felt anxious that those principles should prevail,
and that the church should be active and ready to assist every
good work. My mind was much burdened for a length of time.
One night as I lay in my bed, my mind was so agitated that
sleep departed. The words of the Apostle came to my mind
with much force, and I was impressed that I must speak of
these things to the church: "Add to your faith virtue;
and to virtue knowledge; and to knowledge temperance; and
to temperance patience; and to patience godliness; and to god-

liness brotherly kindliness ; and to brotherly kindliness charity. For if these things be in you, and abound, they make you that ye shall neither be barren, nor unfruitful in the knowledge of our Lord Jesus Christ. But he that lacketh these things is blind, and cannot see afar off, and hath forgotten that he was purged from his old sins." I was resolved to present it to the church as duty directed, and prayed for utterance in such a manner as to free my mind and benefit the cause.

There were differences of judgment and trials with regards to the promotion of the principles. My mind was almost constantly burdened for two years ; and I often said something of importance was about to take place: either a reformation, or the death of the visible church. I very much feared the latter, as they were becoming more and more formal and pride developed itself in various ways. I was compelled to conclude that the desire to be like others would prevail. My faith grew stronger as I saw the temperance reform gaining ground ; and I rejoiced at the defeat of the enemy. I began to despair in regard to the church, for sectarianism began to show its mighty influence and it appeared to me I could see the Good Spirit hovering around and no place upon which to alight. At length the precious, Holy Dove took its flight !

The church introduced worldly worship, and soon forgot to bear one another's burdens, and to pray with and for one another. The result was separation, and in July 1844, I told the church I could walk no longer with them. There were but few who sympathized with me. I wept and mourned to no avail, and forsook the (once) house of God.

I could say : "How is the gold become dim ? How is the most fine gold changed ? How hath the Lord covered th daughters of Zion with a cloud, and the adversary hath spread out his hands upon all her pleasant things, for she hath seen that the heathen entered into her Sanctuary." I saw the vanity of putting confidence in man, for every brother will utterly supplant—and every neighbor will walk with slander. I saw also that pride was contagious ; and in consequence some had lost both eyes and strength. Satan takes dominion when the sweet union is broken that binds us together. I could plainly discover that a leprosy was in the camp, and its contagion visible. True religion is the same in all ages, and the heart of man no more in love of holy things than it was anciently. I would ask. When did the church walk hand in hand with the world, and receive the divine blessings of light, life, and love? The Apostles have kept a line of distinction between the church and the world. Our blessed Saviour hath said: "I have chosen you out of the world," Since this is the case, why turn we again to its weak and beggarly elements? They that are of the flesh do mind the things of the flesh. But God is a Spirit and they that worship Him, must do it in spirit and truth; for the carnal mind is at enmity with holy things. The works of the flesh are manifest: Adultery, Fornication, Uncleaness, Idolatry, Hatred, Variance, Wrath, Strife, Envyings, Drunkenness, Revilings and such like. But see the contrast: Love, Joy, Peace, Long-Sufferings, Gentleness, Goodness, Faith, Meekness, Temperance, for such there is no law. How much there is to be learned by searching the Scriptures with an honest heart! May God help.

In the fall of the same year I was taken sick. My life was dispaired of by friends and Physicians, as well as myself. I reviewed my past life and saw many errors, and could see how often my feet had well nigh slipped, and that it was through the grace of God that I was preserved to the present time. I saw the beauty there was in the character of Christ, and felt a longing at times to be free from this tabernacle of clay, and be with Him. I had previously resigned my all into His hands, and had no desire to recall what I had committed. My hope and confidence were stayed on Him, and I could see through a glass darkly, one who had been made a sacrifice for me. I did not wish to make any reserve. I thought my work was done The sinner's case had rested with weight upon my mind, and I could not bring to mind any whom I had neglected while in health.

After I began to amend, the church was still resting on me. I wondered why my life was prolonged and what more there was for me to do. I could not bear the thought of seeing the people of God scattered. As I had often said, it was more than I could bear. But alas! I did see that beautiful crown before mentioned in my dream, now covered with artificials. I saw the danger of being satisfied with the form of religion, without the power. I began to feel a trembling in my heart fearing that my work was not all done. As my health improved I concluded to take a journey to my native State, Connecticut, and visit

my friends once more, and improve my health. While traveling everything wore a gloomy aspect. My father that looked
after me while standing in the door some years previous, was
now buried in the dust, and my brother that called in the
neighbors to rejoice with him, on our arrival, he and wife too,
were in the silent grave.

I visited his orphan children with much delight and satisfaction, and when the time came that we must part, I felt it my
duty to commend them to Him who careth for the fatherless.

After returning home I found myself quite well, and felt a
strong impression to write some of my exercises, in regard to
what God had done for me. I had often thought of it but as
often banished it from my mind. This impression somewhat
alarmed me. I made more apologies and excuses than Moses
did. I thought it could not be, as my acquired abilities were so
limited. Frequently would passages of scripture rest so heavily
my mind that I could find no rest until I had written it down on
some scrap of paper my understanding concerning their import.
The impressions grew stronger and stronger, and more frequent.
The cross appeared great, and I felt more and more convinced
I must submit to it. The thought was forcibly impressed upon
me what trials those had, who were called to preach the gospel,
feeling that "woe is me if I preach not the gospel." They left
all and followed Christ. And why should such delicacies and
pride arise in my heart, when God had done so much for me?

According I sat down to write, and was often prevented by a
flow of tears. My desire was that He that had called me would
assist and be with me; and while writing down His dealings to
me I was strengthened, and made to rejoice, that I was a monu-
ment of his grace and mercy. The more I thought upon these
things, the more inclined I was to separate from those things
which the church generally delighted in ; such as conformity to
the world in their worship. We are commanded to come out
from the world. Christ saith,—"I have chosen you out of the
world."

One night while in my wakeful hours of meditation the 18th
chapter of Revelation came with force to my mind, which
produced these lines :

" Come out of her my people,
    And partake not of her sins,

Her crimes have reached Heaven,
    And thus the Judge begins.

" Come out of her my people,
    And receive not of her plagues,
All nations have drank of her wine,
    For which, my wrath assuage.

" Come out of her my people,
    The cup which she hath fill'd,
Reward unto her double,
    For this is now my will.

" Come out of her my people,
    Before you hear their cry,
Alas, alas! for in one hour—
    Thy judgment they must try.

" Come out of her my people,
    For the Lord thy God is strong—
Although she setteth as a queen,
    Surely her heart is wrong.

" Come out of her my people,
    From false idolatry,
There is but one true God to serve
    To serve Him, let us try.

" Come out of her my people,
    From the doctrines of men,
And ever keep before your mind,
    His holy precepts, ten.

" Come out of her people,
    Be governed by the plan,
Then you shall surely be a guest
    At the supper of the Lamb.

" Come out of her my people,
    And touch no unclean thing,
Ye shall be Sons and Daughters,
    Saith Jesus Christ our king.

'Come out of her my people,
    And I will dwell in you,
You must be separate from the world,
    Like the nation of the Jews.

"Come out of her my people,
    And let the work begin,
You must not be unequal yoked,
    With the wicked ones that sin.

"Come out of her my people,
    From alcoholic drinks,
Or many devils you will see,
    And in degradation sink.

"Come out of her my people,
    For Slavery presses sore—
This nation can't be free from guilt.
    Unless she yields its power.

"Come out of her my people,
    And use your liberty,
All they that walk within the light
    Shall happy, happy, be.

"Come out of her my people,
    Come out once more I say,
Come out, though you may think it hard,
    Come out, come out, I pray."

Christ's teachings were, that His kingdom was not of this
world. A new commandment was given, "To love one
another." And is it abolished? The covenant now in force,
and the relation it bears to our divine Master, is entirely spiritual. The distinction is already drawn between him that serveth
God and him that serveth him not. "For they that are after
the flesh, do mind the things of the flesh." For the carnal
mind is at enmity with God, for it is not subject to the law of
God, neither indeed can be, so they that are in the flesh cannot
please God. Would to God that we might tremble at his word
and separate from those things with which we are to hold no
fellowship.

After the Jews had fallen into idolatry, they married those of another nation, which was forbidden. Not only the common people, but the Priests also were in the same fault, in taking to themselves strange wives, and after many prayers, and tears, they made a covenant to separate from their wives and children, that were born unto them. Now, after they had made their confessions they could go on to rebuild the walls of Jerusalem. I am sure the church must mourn over lost privileges. Isreal hath cast off that which is good and may we yet hear her say :— " My God we know thee." May heaven favour and set a guard of angels about us that we sin not. Therefore stand fast and hold the traditions which ye have been taught whether by word or our epistle. The Apostle has said,—" Ye have therefore received Christ Jesus, the Lord, so walk ye in him, rooted and built up in the truth."

The sinner receives pardon when in a low condition, separate from the love of the world and its alluring charms.

How soon we break the first command : " Thou shalt have no other God before me," So given to idolatry, that the Apostle saith : " My little children keep yourself from idols."

It is needless for me to say that we are " Prone to evil as the sparks to fly upwards," for every Christian feels the warfare in his breast, as the company of two armies, one lusting against the other ; the evil trying to keep the ascendency over the good. But love to God and to one another is the character of the true church. " If any man have not the spirit of Christ, he is none of his." " As many as are led by the spirit of God they are Sons of God." Then we are builded together for an habitation of God, through the spirit. Thus we see, that the spirit of which we were born should dwell in us, as we are the temples for the Holy Ghost to dwell in, being knit together in love. That church where the Spirit of God dwells not, is no church of Christ's, yet it must be said that the spirit is grieved, and hindred in its perfect work, as there are divers operations of gifts by the same spirit. For while we say, I am of Paul, or Apollos, are we not carnal ? May we study the scripture more diligently and walk in its rules for where else can we go for knowledge ?

The burden of my mind still is, that Zion may arise and trim her lamps, and no longer sleep with the foolish, or as do others, until the Bridegroom cometh. " For then he that is filthy shall be filthy still, and he that is holy, shall be holy still." How can we expect to feel settled peace, while our hearts are lusting after conformity to the world? May the dear saints come up out of the wilderness, and lean on the breast of their beloved. How gladly would he fold them in His arms and carry them in His bosom, for they are dead and their lives are hid with Christ in God. How safely can we venture our all on His promises, for He doth care for us. How barren and lean we go from day to day, when there is such a fullness of joy and peace appointed for us, if we but willingly consent to be transformed into the likeness of God's dear Son. It becomes the Saints of God "to be dilligent and make their calling and election sure, that they may be built up into their living head, and grow to the perfect stature of a man in Christ Jesus ; and be fitly framed together, and be not unequally yoked with unbelievers, for what fellowship hath righteousness with unrighteousness, and what communion hath light with darkness, and what concord hath Christ with Belial? Or what part hath he that believeth with an infidel? If the fountain is corrupt, the waters that flow therefrom will be corrupt also;" for that reason we are to keep the heart with all diligence. Where the Spirit's influence urges us on to obedience, we should obey and not grieve the tender Spirit, that was sent into the world to reprove it of sin, I do not know what greater sin can be committed than to grieve the Spirit of God. For this reason the church, as well as the indivi dual, first relapses into vice. When the Holy Spirit is not owned and received as the whole power and life of the Gospel, no marvel that Christians have no more the Gospel virtues, which were intended by our union with God.

"Eye hath not seen nor ears heard what joys there is laid up for those that love God." There is a crown laid up that the righteous Judge will give all those that love His appearing. Then turn not away from the holy warnings of that blessed comforter, and be resolved that nothing shall separate us from the love of Christ Jesus, our Lord. "To him that overcometh will I give to eat of the tree of life which is in the midst of the Paradise of God, and be clothed in white raiment; because they keep my word, they shall be heirs and joint heirs with Jesus Christ." What honor! What nearness! Oh free grace! Free mercy! Who will not rejoice in contemplation of such a prospect? Let me say to such as think their mountain strong. "Let him that thinketh he standeth, take heed lest he fall." "Keep thy heart with all dilligence for out of it are the issues of life." "The heart of man is deceitful about all things and desperately wicked, who can know it." Let it be proved by love to God and one another, not merely because we belong to the same sect, but because we behold our Saviour's likeness and drink into the same Spirit, and then will our fellowship be with the Father, and His Son Jesus Christ.

A thousand delightful thoughts spring up in our hearts, and; which cause us to adore Him for whose salvation we wait, therefore " fear not little flock for it is your Father's good pleasure to give you the kingdom." Oh what a gift,—a kingdom!

Not merely because you belong to the nominal church, but because your name is written in the Lamb's Book of Life—Yes a kingdom too that is not of this world. The unregenerate know not the mysteries of the kingdom of God—neither can the unsanctified work the work of God. "What hast thou to do to declare My statute or My covenant in thy mouth, seeing thou hatest instruction and casteth My words behind thee."

How often has my mind been led to meditate on the means by which the Gospel should be made beneficial to us! It was committed to earthen vessels, to go and preach. "My Gospel to all Nations, and lo! I am with you always." The Apostles went as they were commanded, and what did they receive? Stripes and imprisonment hunger and nakedness, and perils by sea and land, and some like their Master, of no certain dwelling place. They strove hard to show that they were no longer under the law; and when many signs and wonders were wrought, many believed on them, and they were gathered together and the Holy Ghost descended upon them and spake to be understood. They soon began to make merchandise of the Gospel. A certain sorcerer, a false Prophet, tried to turn them from the faith; but nothing could "turn their steady feet aside." And to their tempter was said, "O full of all subtility and all mischief, thou child of the devil, thou enemy of all righteousness, wilt thou not cease to pervert the right ways of the Lord?"

It is to be feared now, as well as in the Apostles' days, that many preach for doctrine, the commandments of men, not laying aside their own tradition. What a contrast between the true and false shephards. One will jeopard his life and all ease and comfort, for those under his care, and those are all the Saints, he comes in connection with, or even those of whom he but hears. Like their Master lay down their lives for their sake, or for the flock of God. This is the way with them to manifest their love to God and one another. And when they feel the woe resting upon them, they forget to inquire what shall we eat, or what shall I drink. Godliness is all their gain.

"They despise all earthly treasures,
  Having one above the skies,
Worldly honors, pomp and pleasures,
  Are but trifles in their eyes."

How great the contrast! While we behold one craving for nothing but the fleece, who appear to think that gain is Godliness, and like Eli's sons, thrust the hook into the seething pan or cauldron, and draw from thence the sodden flesh, saying:— "We will have it." Seemeth it a small thing unto you. Oh ye shepherds! to have eaten up the good pasture, and trodden down the residue with your feet? As for my flock, they drink the water they have fouled with their feet. A wonderful thing is committed in the land saith the Lord: "The Prophets prophesy falsely, and the Priests bear rule by their means, and my people love to have it so." How easy it is for the children of God to be led astray by false teachers! Our Great Head and Shepherd has declared that many had gone out into the world in that day; and is there any less now? He said.—"My sheep hear my voice and they follow me; but a stranger they will not follow." How careful we should be in proving them to see what manner of Spirit they possess? For if the blind, lead the blind, how true it is—what shall befall them.

Can we not easily see, that the church is in a fallen state, and cannot discern between truth and error; in consequence of the thick mist of darkness, which is spread out over them:—for "If the light in us be darkness, how great is the darkness?" Therefore, the true Gospel is not owned, and received in its whole power and life, which were intended by our union with our head.

My heart is pained, many times, when I see those so desirous to feed *on* those *they* feed.

Oh Lord look down with pity upon such as are so unfortuate as to be under the care of such instructors!

I have thus given a short account of what God in his mercy has done for me, sincerely hoping, that such of my views and principles as are according to the scriptures of truth, may find a place in the hearts of God's people; though sown in much weakness. May we ever strive to bring every proud and selfish desire into sweet conformity to the will of our Heavenly Father! I conclude by making the following inquiry:

"Is the worship of any person or persons acceptable to God, but that of the saints, and are they justifiable, who by their doctrine, or by their conduct, contribute to, or encourage the worship of any, that are not manifestly saints?"

NOTE BY THE EDITOR.

The Authoress of the foregoing Autobiography, when she intrusted to me her manuscript, expressed a wish, that a concise notice of her life, from the time she ceased to write upon that subject up to the time of her decease, should be added, and signified, that, should I be in a condition, to do so much in remembrance of her, she hoped that I would do it. As she, in her own work now prepared for friends, and all such as take an interest in the cause she advocated, has made so full developments of her native characteristics, her "Ruling Passion," but little remains to be done, to close up the record of her somewhat extensively useful, and always exemplary life. Beneficent, conciliatory, and forbearing, almost all with whom she formed an acquaintance were her friends. Industrious by habit, and economical from choice, her house was well kept, and her pantry abounded in the necessaries, and moderate luxuries, of a rational subsistence; to the unstinted use of which, all her household were freely, and cordially invited; and her satisfaction was only complete, when the members of her household, all, and her neighbors as well, partook of, and enjoyed them also. Children worshipped at her altar, and luxuriated in her approving smiles; she was ever active in doing good. From the first, to the close of her residence in Lenox, she was an undeviating, and consistent advocate, and supporter, of every social and moral movement, having for its object, the civilizing, and christianizing, or the ameliorating of the condition of the entire human family; at all times and at all places. And thus she has "gone to her rest," her "fine gold undimmed," to the last. She might truly say "Our Father," for she truly seemed to feel, that, in moral, and social privileges, and responsibilities, she belonged to the whole human family.

On the 21st day of June, in the year 1854 her second husband, Col. E. N. HOUSE, died, at the age of about sixty-nine years, (a little less,) after a long, and very harrassing, and at times, very painful, chronic visceral derangement, of some two years continuance,—more or less—during almost the whole of which time, but more especially the closing months, the subject of this sketch was being almost constantly annoyed by, and deeply suffering from the malign influence, of broken rest—constant watchings, and attendance, deferred hopes, and abiding fears; the unceasing restlesness of her sick, suffering, and dying husband, and then the catastrophe, which all combined, left her in a condition of physical and mental depsession, little more to be desired, than that of him, her late husband, whose remains had been so recently interred. But the restorative properties of a constitution generally healthy, soon enabled Mrs. HOUSE to take note of, and prepare herself for that portion of the pilgrimage of life, yet remaining, for her to accomplish; and she removed within a few days after, the interment of the body of her late husband, from the dwelling lately occupied by the family, to one which had been in the process of construction, during the sickness of Col: HOUSE, on premises owned by Mrs. HOUSE, in her own right and to the occupancy of which, it was expected that the family would remove, when the necessary work on the same was accomplished, to make a comfortable habitation for such a household; the premises where her late husband died, having been previously sold, and in the occupancy of the family of J. M. RAY, a son-in-law of her late husband, E. N. HOUSE, aforesaid. To this new building she removed, as before stated; and here she gathered around her the objects of fancy, desire, and affection; here she passed the last six and a half years of her useful life, in rural pursuits; in the cultivation of her flower and kitchen gardens—in the humanizing of her pet animals, (no cat or dog among them,) in the society of such friends as she chose to select in her accustomed acts of benificence, in the daily searching of the scriptures and contemplation of scripture truths, in the

perusal of many religious, ethical, and political works, (mostly
religious) and in wishing and doing good to all mankind as she
had opportunity. Up to the time of her sickness she spent these
last years of her life, as she many times said, more to her satisfaction, more happily, than any other portion of her life of equal
extent—and up to the said time of her last sickness, made
frequent allusions to the many blessings clustering around her
earthly home. But the adversary was at hand. The worm in
the fruit was gorging itself at the core. The pall of fell disease
was about to be laid over and to remove under its direful folds,
this not oft recurring instance, of a rational and satisfactory
enjoyment of the secular bounties of the Almighty Being; and
in the latter part of September, A. D. 1859, she was again almost
helplessly prostrated on a bed of sickness, by an attack of the
same disease, of which she came near dying, in the fall and
winter of the years 1844—1845, but of which she had been in
good degree free, from that time to this. She was now seriously
and severely affected by the attack, yet after several weeks of
quite harrassing, and at times painful indisposition, she appeared
to be in part restored; and gradually resumed some portion of
the less laborious parts of her previous occupations, and seemed
in some sensible degree, again to appreciate and enjoy her home
comforts, and neighborhood society; but she never again
attained any satisfactory measure of health or strength, and at
about one year after the time of the commencement of the
above mentioned indisposition, the imperious destroyer,
placed his iron hand upon her much debilitated body.
The same disease was again developed in its most virulent, and
fatal form, and after long protracted, and most excruciating
sufferings, all borne with the patience and heroism of one
believing in the advent of a bright and glorious future, at five
(5) minutes past three o'clock, P. M., on the tenth (10) day of
February, in the year 1861, her organs of life ceased to act; her
blood was stayed in its course, and her breath passed into the
keeping of Him who gave it. No groan or struggle distinguished her expiring moment; but she passed away with the
quietness of sleeping innocence; noiselessly as the rays of the
morning sun, remove the early dew. From its commencement,
her disease was characterized by paroxysms, extremely distressing and unbearable—and some fifteen or sixteen hours before
she ceased breathing one of these paroxysms came upon her,

F

of more than usual vehemence, greatly exceeding all the ones preceding it, in its intensity of pain, and distress; as was most clearly indicated by the almost unearthly groans, and screams of the pitiable sufferer. As this aggravation of symtoms subsided and passed away. She apparently fell into a condition of unconscious existence, manifesting no more pain, or suffering of any kind; and entirely unobserving of all surrounding objects or circumstances, and in this condition she left us, and passed away from among men, into the rest of the grave, at the time above mentioned, aged seventy years, three months, and two days.

From the last of her intelligent communications, on the subject of her views of a future state, or the condition of the dead, we undoubtingly infer that she believed in the vicarious atonement of the Son of the Highest, and that at the last day, He would take *her* up, with the full myriads of the Redeemed from among men, to meet Him in the air, and so to be forever with the Lord. An after death examination of her body, disclosed the existence of very great derangement of the organs of nutrition. The billiary and pancreatic organs with no apparent healthy function remaining; and of the abdominal viscera, the stomach alone perhaps showing any indications of being in a healthy condition, and the left mamillary organ in a most virulent state of induration throughout its entire structure—a scirrhous tumor of the most obstinate class.

On Tuesday, the 12th day of February, two days after her death, her remains were interred in the burying ground at Lenox Center, at the right side, south, and near to the grave of her last deceased husband, Col. E. N. HOUSE, whose body was laid there, June 22d, A. D. 1844, the day succeeding his death, (June 21st, 1844.) The funeral services for Mrs. HOUSE were commenced at her late residence by the meeting there of mourners, friends, and others, at eleven o'clock, A. M., and after suitable preparations, the body was moved by the assembled in procession, to the Free Will Baptist and Methodist meeting house, where at twelve meridian, Elder WILKINSON of the Methodist persuasion, preached a sermon on the occasion, taking for a text, the last clause, of the first verse, of the twentieth chapter of the second book of Kings. Thus saith the Lord:—"Set thine house in order, for thou shalt die, and not live." After the sermon, her remains were taken to the grave, prepared for them, at the Center Cemetery, accompanied by a respectable concourse of mourners, friends, and acquaintances, and the true regrets of all those who knew her best; where (as she supposed,) they will rest until "Christ, The Life shall appear."

In the Ashtabula SENTINEL, dated February 20th, A. D. 1861, was inserted the following Obituary notice:

"Died, at her residence in Lenox, on Sunday, Feb. 10th, A. D. 1861, ABIGAIL HOUSE, relict of the late Col. E. N. HOUSE, of Lenox, aforesaid, from the time of his decease, June 21st, 1854. She became his wife on the 8th day of February, in the year 1818, since which time she has constantly been a much distinguished resident of this township. Known among us from the very first, as eminently endowed with many, (almost all) of the christian's moral and social virtues and graces, she soon became distinguished here as one 'of the most strenuous advocates, and consistent supporters, of religious, moral, and social rights, and rational liberty of conscience; and by her active, and generally effective benevolence, she readily came to be distinguished by the necessitous, as their always prompt and ready helper, and well deserving the proud appellation of the "Good Mother House," accorded to her with universal consent, in the pleasant savour of which title she has moved for many past years; surrounded and enwrapped in which she has now descended to the grave, her final earthly rest: aged a little more than seventy years. Her mortal disease a complication of many ailments."

Thus, as far as practicable, in view of other business, necessarily occupying a considerable portion of attention, and subjecting to interruptions innumerable and inimitable, and my fitness for the work, have the wishes of the subject of the foregoing brief memorial sketches, as expressed by her during her last sickness, been cheerfully complied with. "Nothing has been extenuated," nor "aught set down in malice." The offering is of gratitude. The altar friendship. From an acquaintance, extending over more than forty years, the sterling qualities, of her who is no longer among us, are known, and declared: And having received, during all that time, from her, and every member of the family with which she was connected by her last marriage, favors great, and innumerable, untiringly and ungrudgingly bestowed, I should be intolerably mean and contemptible, and worse than altogether brutish, were I not grateful. I have done.

JOSIAH ATKINS.

Lenox, May 27th. 1861.

REFLECTIONS CORRESPONDENCE, ETC.

ON ST. JOHN XVII, 20.

"Neither pray I for these alone, but for them also which shall believe on me through their word."

"That they all also may be one, as thou Father art in me, and I in thee, that they may be one in us; that the world may believe that thou hast sent me."

This chapter shows us a oneness with the Father and his Son Jesus Christ; and the Holy Ghost has been given to us, that we may have fellowship with the Father and the Son, and all those that are born of the Spirit. By this same spirit we have access to the Father through the Son, by the Holy Ghost; whereby we, cry, "Abba Father." Is it not our duty, made so by His revealed will, and declared in his word? When the word and Spirit agree, we may rest assured that we have a right knowledge of the Scripture of truth, and may rely upon our faith. Christ speaks largely of his love to his disciples, and to be such, we must manifest our love one to another.

He saith again, "As thou hast sent me into the world, even so have I sent them into the world." "I have given them thy

Word." Blessed be God for his word, which makes us wise unto salvation. Is there no joy in the hearts of the children of God for such blessings? The promises are not to one individual Christian, but to all that believe on his precious name. Fait' questions none of the promises. If Christ has received any, w must receive the same, to the glory of God. This principle of love led our blessed Saviour to sufier; he whose blood was the shed, is still the Lamb that was slain, and to him is the worshi; of heaven directed. Worthy is the Lamb that was slain t receive glory and honor, and power, and blessing forever and forever. We know that the sheep of Christ are widely scattered now; but by and by they will sing one song, and be united in heart. But why should we not strive more to be united in the one spirit, and to be of the same mind and of the same judgment; glorifying God with our spirits, which are God's. Ye were without God in the world, but now are made nigh by the blood of Christ.

ON ROMANS VIII, 32.

"He that spared not his own Son, but delivered him up for i all, how shall he not, with him also, freely give us all things?

In the first place let us look at the cross, look at Gethsemane see him hanging on the tree, and hear him crying to his Father, *Eloi! Lama! Sabacthania!* his soul was exceeding sorrowful, even unto death; but he changed not from his purpose, for tha was his errand into the world, and how was he straightened until it was accomplished.

He prayed, O my Father, if this cup may not pass away from me except I drink it, thy will be done!

This is love beyond degree! God's purposes and grace could be exhibited in no other way. He was alone, and in consequence no one could bear any part. There was an Angel sent to minister unto him, an inferior spirit, yet he was commissioned to strengthen him. He was bruised for our iniquities; Satan triumphed for a short time, and man joined with him; but the sacrifice was made in spite of death and hell.

What sorrows when we look with nature's eye, but when we discover that our eternal all depended upon his atoning blood, our hearts rejoice; for there is no other name given under heaven, whereby fallen man could be saved. Thus we see that God first loved us. It was disobedience that caused such a moral distance from God then, and it is disobedience and unbelief that is now our ruin; the sinner does not believe that the blood of Christ is absolutely necessary to save; and many are ready to think they have good works enough to save them: but the Apostle tells us our works are as filthy rags, while we trust in them, for "By grace are ye saved through faith, not of works least any man should boast. Let our boasting be in the Lord, for he is our rock and our high tower, and in Him let us trust."

LINES.

Jerusalem hath greviously sin'd,
   And the Lord hath afflicted her sore,
She mourns and she weeps in the night
   Saying, I will not trangress any more!

The ways of Zion do mourn,
   Because none come to her feasts;
She called for her lovers and friends,
   And also, for some of her priests.

Her bowels are troubled within,
   While Zion spreadeth her hands,
Lord accept of the offering she brings,
   That sin may depart from our land.

The enemy hath spread out his hand.
   The Priests and the Elders gave way,
All you that are now in the land,
   Must hearken and also obey.

The Lord is more righteous than I,
   Zion's enemies prosper and thrive,

For this reason we sigh and we cry,—
O Father, do save us alive.

O Lord consider our grief,
    For we have become very vile,
Believe us, when we are so brief,
    And pardon us, as a dear child,

Did I not suffer for thee?
    And can you not trust in my grace?
For this cause my pardon you see,
    Nor again be found out of place.

ON MATTHEW, XV, 14.

"Let them alone they be blind leaders of the blind. And if the blind lead the blind, both shall fall into the ditch."

Now if preachers and writers comfort the formal christian, by telling them that God does not require a heart of sinless obedience, it is a course of teaching or leading of the character spoken of in the above quotation, and is blind indeed! and *all* our *sincerity* is not of the right kind, for all the outward works of religion, may be performed by the natural man, without grace in the heart, he can adhere closely to the doctrines of the church and observe its creeds, and still be a stranger to the new birth. Notwithstanding all this will show, that the man is still defiled and blind. Away then with volumes written upon church union, nor ask council of those that styles themselves divines.

In vain they do worship me, teaching for doctrines the commandments of men. Can we realize that he says it is in vain to do such things. "Are ye also yet without understanding?" For out of the heart proceed evil thoughts, murders, adulteries, fornications, thefts, false witness, blasphemies; these are the things which defile a man."

The Pharisees thought that to wash their hands, that would make them sufficiently clean; but their blindness prevented them from seeing themselves naked and filthy. Let them alone; they are blind leaders of the blind. These are they that

·make the commandment of God without effect. This people draweth nigh unto me with their mouths, and honoreth me with their lips, but their heart is far from me.

We have Scribes and Pharisees now, which say—why do thy disciples transgress the traditions of the Elders? How many there are in these our days that abide in the sayings of their Elders and teachers, instead of examining the scriptures for themselves.

Study the scriptures, for in them ye think ye have eternal life and they are they that testify of me. Let not the power of the beast have dominion over us; but trust in the power of his word.

ON HAGGAI, II, 3.

' Who is left among you that saw this house in her first glory? and how do ye see it now? is it not in your eyes in comparison of it, as nothing?"

Thus we see how sin defaces the works of good men, and causes deep sorrow of heart to those that have seen the glory of God in his temple, or his sanctuary, where he has formerly dwelt, and where he has met with his Saints! And how humiliating to see Satan sitting in the place from which he has formerly been thrust out. Whose heart is sufficiently strong to bear the sight of our nominal churches? Once the place where God delighted to dwell, and where his children met with the previous promise. "Where two or three are met together in my name, there am I in the midst." The promise remaineth the the same, but the fault is on our part. We meet it, it is true, but as our text says: "And how do ye see it now?" Why the glory is departed from Israel. O my soul put on strength. So shall my strength be like an armed man, for God will surely punish for this! He says in verse 17: "I smote you with blasting and with mildew!" We are now as then commanded to touch no unclean thing: even a dead body should not be touched, nor a dead church. So is this people, and so is this Nation before me, saith the Lord; and so is every work of their

Hands; and that which they offer there, is unclean. How often we are reminded of our frailty by the word and also by our own experience, There are two classes clearly pointed out in the sacred scriptures—one who whet their tongues like swords, and bend their bows to shoot their arrows, even bitter words. They encourage themselves in an evil matter, but God shall shoot at them with an arrow that they fall suddenly.

But the righteous shall be glad in the Lord and shall trust in him, and all the upright in heart shall glory in him. Who then is safe but such as trust in the merits of him, who died to redeem us from the penalty of his righteous law? Who shall answer?

LINES.

Now come to Christ whoever will,
While Jesus sits on Zion's hill,
And taste free pardon at the rill,
O come to him and drink your fill,
      And love the Lord your God.

If you should say I dare not go,
For I have disobeyed thee so,
Death will come, and down thee mow,
Before to him you'll willing bow,
      And feel the wrath of God.

Oh why should you, longer delay,
And choose to walk the crooked way,
Now look to Christ and to him say,
From thy blessed word no more I'll stray.
      And Heaven shall shout for joy.

Then sing to him, who is divine,
And say be all the glory thine,
So I'm resolved to spend my time,
That I may rest in yonder clime.
      The place prepared for me.

Now pardon Lord my many sins,
May I to thee my tribute bring,
My soul be ever on the wing,
Then I will hallelujahs sing:
      Christ Jesus died for me.

Come christians all, come hear the call,
Before you in transgression fall,
Be more like the Apostle Paul,
And shun the worm-wood and the gaul;
     Which Christ did drink for you.

And when we pass this vale of tears,
And Christ shall take away our fears,
May not our souls be in the rear;
But ever prove ourselves sincere.
     In following Christ the Lamb.

Then shall we sing without a sigh,
As Christ the Lord is drawing nigh,
Angels are shouting from the sky,
Hosannahs to our God on high.
     Salvation through him came.

ON PSALM, IV, 6.

"There be many that say, who will show us any good? Lord lift thou up the light of thy countenance upon us."

The Psalmist had great confidence in God—when every refuge fails, God's love sustains us, and we like David can say:—"Thou hast put gladness in my heart more than in the time that their corn and their wine increased." Notwithstanding he complained of his enemies and said—"Destroy thou them O God! let them fall by their own counsels—for they have rebelled against thee."

ON ISAIAH, LXIV, 9, 10.

"Be not wroth very sore, O Lord, neither remember iniquity forever; behold, see, we beseech thee, we are all thy people."

"Thy holy cities are a wilderness, Zion is a wilderness, Jerusalem a desolation.

The Jews were a peculiar people, as a Nation, highly favored of the Lord, through which the Saviour was to make his appearance upon the earth; and the same that should betray him; he was wounded in the house of his friends. But the believing Jews, the Church, prayed in the language of the text—"Be not wroth very sore;" and acknowledged Zion to be a wilderness and desolate. For these things they were rejected and God would not spare their natural branches, but broke them off and engrafted in the Gentiles—wild by nature—and we are to stand by faith: for if God spared not the natural branches, we must be careful and not perish through unbelief, as they also perished. "As the new wine is found in the cluster, destroy it not for a blessing is in it." God saith if you will put away your abomniable idolatries out of my sight, then will I receive you; for your sins have reached heaven, and no unclean things can enter there. My sanctuary is holy and nothing can enter. But Zion hath said, the Lord hath forsaken me and my Lord hath forgotten me. Well God will forsake both Jew and Gentile that forsakes him. We may claim we are all his people, but if we do not the things which he commanded us to do to we are none of his, though we say—Lord, Lord, we shall never enter the kingdom of heaven, for their fear towards God, is taught by the precepts of men.

We are careful to obey the precepts of men, for it is much easier than to submit to the ordinances of heaven, for that requireth clean hands and hearts, or our appearings will not be acceptable. Our holy and our beautiful house where our fathers praised thee, is burnt up with fire, and all thy pleasant things are laid waste.

"Be not wroth very sore? O Lord, neither remember iniquity forever."

ON ZACHARIAH, XIV, 8.

"And the Lord shall be king over all the earth; in that day shall there be one Lord, and his name one."

What shall we understand in regard to this day spoken of by the Prophet Zachariah, if it is not of the down-fall of the spiritual Babylon, and the Jew's infidelity and superstition brought to nought, and Christ's kingdom set up. The prophet Daniel makes mention of a day when the sanctuary shall be polluted and the daily sacrifice taken away, and abomination that makes desolate, in the place where it ought not to be. But the people that do know their God, shall be strong and do exploits. It appears from sacred writings that we are living near the close of the days of certain prophecies. It is a dark day with the church because Antichrist is in her midst: infidelity is stalking in her streets, but we have every reason to believe that Satan's kingdom shall be destroyed by the brightness of Christ's coming, although it is dark now; Christ is the true light that lighteth every man. But we read of a great battle being fought between the two kingdoms. The princes and the great men shall join hands with Satan. "But in that day shall there be one Lord, and his name one." Christ will be at the head of his church. The church will suffer persecution no more, and will remember the saying of Isaiah, xl, 1,—"Comfort ye, comfort ye my people, saith your God!" The promises will be more full to our minds, but before this blessed day there shall be great falling away in regard to pure principles, and our love will so degenerate that beholders shall doubt whether we believe in the Mesiah. It has been observed before such great events, that darkness prevades the world. So it was before the coming of Christ, and when he came their unbelief was so prominent that they rejected him, and this after seeing the stupendous miracles which he wrought; and learning his teachings, and beholding his life that was without spot or blemish; but still they said, "Away with him; we will not have this man to rule over us;" and so it is now.

Many are they which disbelieve the sayings of Christ and his Apostles in regard to this second coming. For the encouragement of the Saints, he saith, behold I come quickly, as though it were to relieve them of many cares and trials which should befall them on their way, and to cheer them to watchfulness and to sobriety. Not telling precisely the time, but that when we see such and such things, we may know the time is at hand. "Take ye heed, watch and pray, for ye know not when the time is." But in like manner as ye saw me ascend, so shall ye see me descend. Heaven and earth shall pass away, but my word shall not pass away. There is everything in store for the children of God, for he saith: "Ye are they which have continued with me in my temptations; and I appoint unto ye a kingdom, as my Father appointed unto me." Who will not trust his word, and look up when our redemption draweth near. This is called the latter days, pointing to the gospel days. But how is the gospel preached, and by whom? Chiefly by those who are wishing to make merchandise of the same, and have the marks of those that care not for the flock—woe be to such shepherds! Where shall we find those that imitate their Master, by laying down their lives for the sake of those they love? Do we not see a disposition in far too many, only to strive to be the greatest? If we would be humble like a child, (for in that situation we did receive Christ) it would save us the trouble of such bold contentions. But when we see Antichrist sitting in the place where it ought not, and setting itself above all that is called God, then will be a time of lamentation and distress. Then will be the time for the saints to fight against principalities, and against powers, and spiritual wickedness in high places; and ultimately the saints will come off conquerors, although it will be with great tribulation, for many will turn back when trials arise, and go no more with them; but there is no promise to those that do not hold out faithful unto the end.

ON ACTS, I, 10, 11.

"And while they looked steadfastly towards heaven, as he went up, behold two men stood by them in white apparel, which also said, ye men of Galilee why stand ye gazing up into heaven? This same Jesus which is taken up from you into heaven, so shall come in like manner, as ye have seen him go into heaven."

After Christ had chosen his Apostles he also manifested himself unto them by many infallible proofs, was seen of them forty days, speaking of the things pertaining to the kingdom of God. When they had come together they inquired of him, whether he would restore again the kingdom of Israel? But he told them it was not for them to know, what his Father had put into his power, but promised them power after the Holy Ghost had come upon them, and that all should be witnesses throughout the whole earth. And when he had spoken these things, a cloud received him out of their sight. And then comes in our text.

After his ascension the chosen returned to Jerusalem and went into an upper room when the number of names which were together was about one hundred and twenty. These all continued with one accord in prayer and supplication with the women. It appears men and women were all of one heart and of one mind in serving the Lord, as it should be now, for we are all one in Christ Jesus both male and female. How affectionately did women gather around the sepulchre of their dying Lord and Master, and how did they watch his tomb, and who was first at the sepulchre when it was yet dark? Women remained at the sepulchre weeping after the rest had fled into their own houses; by her tarrying she saw two angels, and they said unto her,—"Woman, why weepest thou?" Jesus himself was there to soothe her by saying,—"I ascend unto my Father and your Father, my God and your God."

LINES ON CHRISTMAS.

———

By some it is said, Christ was born in December.
A stable so lowly, but each one remember,
The Shepherds rejoiced at the sight of their Saviour.
In their arms they embraced him as he lay in the manger.

We hear from the lips of those that are vain,
I wish you merry Christmas, (it is almost profane,)
How little they think on our Saviour's birth day,
Who came to redeem us, while in ruin we lay.

Some give of their substance, both silver and gold,
And many fine treasures that cannot be told,
But nothing on earth, will compare with the sum,
That the Lord bestowed on us, like the gift of his Son.

He was here like a stranger, and pilgrim below,
To accomplish his mission, and his love to us show;
Though rejected by many, he ascended on high,
He now lives forever, though once he did die.

We soon shall behold him in yonder bright cloud,
With great power and glory, with trump long and loud,
The wicked will call for the mountain to fall
On them because they, had rejected his call.

The saints will rejoice, at the sight of their king,
All heaven will echo the sweet notes they'll sing,
While the wicked will gnaw their tongues in sharp pain,
With cursing and swearing his name they'll blaspheme.

The eye hath not seen, the ear hath not heard,
What is laid up for those that love him indeed,
Let us still wait for his coming, the time we don't know.
Whether evening or morning, or at the cock crow.

PSALMS, CXXV, 2.

"As the mountains are around about Jerusalem, so the Lord is round about his people, from henceforth even forever."

From this we see God's care over his church as those he loves; his church which represents Jerusalem: which is builded as a city, that is compact together, the only representation of the gospel church, that trusts in their head and leader, for they must be of one heart, and one judgment; and then the rod of the wicked will not rest upon the righteous, nor the rightous put forth their hands unto iniquity; but the Lord is as a mountain, to guard his people from danger, and will do good unto those that be good, and to them that are upright in their hearts.

Our outward walk may be moral so that no sceptic can find aught against us; yet if our hearts are not right in God's sight, the Lord will lead them forth with the workers of iniquity. But peace shall be upon those that are of a clean heart. What a distinction through the whole channel of scripture, between him that serveth God and him that serveth him not. Let Israel hope in the Lord, from henceforth and forever. How wonderfully the Lord manifested his love to his chosen people, the Jews, His love remains the same at the present day towards his church. He changeth not, Thy law is the truth. Therefore I love thy commandments above gold, yea, above fine gold. The idols of the heathen, are silver and gold, and they that make them, are like unto them; so is ev ery one that trusteth in them. Let them all be confounded, and turned back that hate Zion. Blessed is every one that feareth the Lord, that walketh in his ways, for thou shalt eat the labor of thine own hands, and it shall be well with thee. This is my rest forever: here will I dwell, for I have desired it.

Let thy priests be clothed with righteousness, and let thy saints shout for joy, for his mercy endureth forever!

ON ACTS, XX, 28.

————

"Take heed, therefore unto yourselves and to all the flock over which the Holy Ghost hath made you overseers to feed the church of God, which he hath purchased with his own blood."

It appears that Paul called the disciples to him and embraced them, and departed for Macedonia, and there accompanied him certain brethren from divers places. And upon the first day of the week, when the disciples came together to break bread, Paul preached unto them, ready to depart on the morrow and continued his speech until midnight. He then brought to life a young man that had fallen asleep, and fell from the window. And from Miletus he sent to Ephesus and called for the elders of the church, and then declared how he had served the Lord with all humility of mind, and with many tears and temptations which befell him, and how he kept back nothing that was profitable for them, he had taught them publicly from house to house, testifying both to Jews and Greeks repentance and faith towards our Lord Jesus Christ. He was pressed in spirit as he went to Jerusalem, not knowing the things that should befall him there.

But none of those things moved him; neither counted he his life dear unto himself, so that he might finish his course with joy. He was assured that those who had had the opportunity of hearing him preach the kingdom of God, should see his face no more; but he testified that he was pure from the blood of all men, for he had not shunned to declare the whole counsel of God; then he says,—Take heed, etc. He had full knowledge of what should befall the dear people of God on his departure, which was: that grievous wolves should enter in among them not sparing the flock. Also of your own selves shall men arise speaking perverse things, to draw away disciples after them. He tells them to watch, and remember how he had warned them night and day, with tears. He concludes by saying: And now

G

brethren I commend you to God, and the word of his grace,
which is able to build you up, and to give you an inheritance
among all them which are sanctified. He declares he had not
sought their silver, nor gold, nor apparel; for they knew how
he had labored with his own hands and that was not all, he
had supplied those that were with him; for he said it was
more blessed to give than to receive. And when he had thus
spoken he kneeled down and prayed with them all. And all
wept sore, and fell on Paul's neck, and kissed him, sorrowing
most of all for the words which he spoke, that they should see
his face no more.

How much instruction there is to be learned from this chapter,
of the way in which God deals with his faithful children and the
care he had over them. How he appoints those, the pastors, to
have special care and charge over them, and how he teaches
them by his holy spirit what shall befall them under such and
such circumstances, and further how when he calls any to pass
through extreme sufferings he will be with such, and above all
to see their great attachment and love one to another, and in
heart willing to lay down their lives for each others sake. How
little resemblance is there now to the ancients, who made it their
business to serve God in all his holy ordinances:—such were the
ones that God owned and blessed, such will he own and bless in
all ages until he shall come to take home his bride, where there
shall be no more sorrow but where they will partake more and
more of his nature by seeing him as he is. Let the word dwell
in us richly, that we may grow thereby. May our minds be
quickened at the sweet remembrance of Christ's dying love, and
may our fellowship be increased towards one another as the time
draweth nigh that our faith shall be tried so as by fire! May
our lamps be trimmed and burning waiting for the coming of
our Lord.

ON ISAIAH, XXV, 1.

"O Lord, thou art my God, I will exalt thee, I will praise thy name for thou hast done wonderful things, thy counsels of old are faithfulness and truth."

The prophet discovers the goodness and faithfulness of God; he is ready also to acknowledge his strength, for he saith thou hast been a strength to the poor, a strength to the needy in his distress, a refuge from the storm, a shadow from the heat. But the terrible ones are to be brought low. He will destroy the veil that is spread over all nations. He bringeth down them that dwell on high, the lofty city, he layeth it low! What confusion when the judgments of heaven are abroad on the earth; pain and sorrow, wailing and gnashing of teeth, when God frowns! O that we were wise to understand our true condition.

Awake and sing, ye that dwell in dust! for behold the Lord cometh out of his place, to punish the inhabitants of the earth for their iniquity. But there is perfect safety, to those that trust in God. O Lord thou art my God: who is able to call the Lord their God, but such as see his beauty, and can say, who is a God like unto our God, that pardoneth iniquity? One who feels his need of a Saviour and one whose sins are a burden, and one who casteth his cares upon the righteousness of Christ; and entereth into the door, and that door is Christ: blessed and happy are all such as do the commandments and live: for the righteous shall inherit the land and dwell therein forever. But we have seen the wicked in great power, and God rejecteth him, he layeth him low! But mark the perfect man, and behold the upright, for the end of that man is peace. Let us be stimulated to good works that our end may be peace likewise; for what profit is there in gaining the whole world, and yet losing our souls. Make haste to help me, O Lord my salvation!

ON LUKE, XVII, CHAP.

———

This chapter commences by saying: "It is impossible but that offences will come, but woe unto him through whom they come." There is danger of the brethren defrauding one another which in God's sight is reprehensible, which caused our Saviour to say:—Take heed to yourselves. If thy brother trespass against thee, rebuke him, and if he repent, forgive him, and so on until seventy times seven. And when the apostles heard that, they said, Lord increase our faith! and well they might so say when they knew their natural disposition; for our fallen natures are inclined to revenge, or at least let them alone, and not rebuke those which do evil; and let it pass until a hardness is created; then it is harder to gain such a brother than to gain a city. But through faith, we can remove a mountain of iniquities! When we have done all these things which are commanded of us, yet are we unprofitable servants, and have done only that which it was our duty to do.

And as he went to Jerusalem he met ten men that were lepers, which stood afar off, and they cried to him for mercy; and he said, go shew yourselves unto the priests—under the Jewish laws the priests were authorized to make such examination as the law directed and pronounce them clean or unclean as their case should be; for nothing was accounted so filthy as those having the leprosy. They were shut up seven days, and at the end of seven days they were examined again, but not so in this case; for as they went they were healed or cleansed; he obeyed the command and immediately he was healed, and turned back and with a loud voice glorified God—and fell down on his face at his feet, giving him thanks. Then Jesus made the enquiry concerning the rest, but it was ascertained that he was the only one to give glory to him, And he said unto him,—Arise go thy way thy faith hath made thee whole.

Then the pharisees demanded of him when the kingdom of God should come? and his answer was, that the kingdom of God was in them. He was still teaching his disciples things that should befall him, and how he should suffer, and be rejected of hat generation; and told them it should be now as it was in the days of Noah; they were marrying and giving in marriage until the flood came, and destroyed them all. And as it was in the days of Lot: they eat, and drank, bought and sold, they planted and builded, as we are doing daily, and in like manner shall we be destroyed at the coming of our Lord. Even thus shall it be when the son of man is revealed.

Much is said in the scriptures in regard to Christ's coming. That it will be like a thief in the night: but we are too much like those that say, my Lord delayeth his coming, and began to beat his servants, and one another: instead of watching and praying, as we are commanded; for whosoever shall lose his life shall preserve it; for one shall be taken and the other left. Notwithstanding his disciples understood him not, but asked him where? And he said unto them wheresoever the body is, thither will the eagles be gathered together.

How important that we should be ready for such an hour. Although the Holy Spirit is constantly teaching us to deny ourselves of all ungodliness and be prepared to meet Christ in the air, yet how cold and sluggish still! seldom ready to act out own parts; procrastinating from time to time, and crying peace and safety, when there is no peace. But he tells his servants: "*Occupy till I come.*" May we cry unto him like those of old, that were blind,—"Lord that I might receive my sight," for we are blind by nature and we make ourselves much more so by practice: for we shut our eyes against the light:—for ye are blind, and my people love to have it so. May we arise and shine for our light *is come* and that light lighteth every man that cometh into the world, but if the light in us be darkness how great is that darkness.

ON MICAH, IV, 7.

"But in the last days it shall come to pass that the mountain of the house of the Lord shall be established in the top of the mountain and it shall be exalted above the hills, and people shall flow unto it."

The prophet is speaking of the last days, and what shall take place in regard to Christ's kingdom, how firmly it is established in the top of the mountains.

And many nations shall say, come let us go up to the mountains of the Lord, and he will teach us of his ways, and we will walk in his paths. This is the language of the inmates of the mountains, for they wish to be taught by his precepts, for the law is in Zion, and the word in Jerusalem, and they shall sit under the vines and fig trees, and none shall make them afraid. In that day saith the Lord will I assemble her that halteth and will gather her that is driven out, and her that I have afflicted, and the Lord shall reign over them in Mount Zion forever. But the prophets are often speaking of a certain day of destruction that will come upon the wicked. For the day of the Lord is near upon all the heathen, he will send a famine in the land for want of the word, or hearing the word—in that day shall the judgments fall on the fair part of community faint for thirst; the day of the Lord is darkness to all who reject his word—a day of gloominess and thick darkness is spread over them. The day of the Lord is near, put ye in the sickle for the harvest is ripe. Behold the days come that shall burn as an oven! Although God does not punish immediately after the crime is committed; yet his wrath sleepeth not. I will pour out my wrath upon them like water; I will visit their iniquities with judgments, woe unto you that desire the day of the Lord! to what end is it for you? for the day of the Lord is darkness, and not light, to all such as obey not his commandments. Let us retrace the history of God's dealings towards his children in former ages: when they were in danger he sustained them. Amidst all moral desolation the church never became extinct. Noah was saved from the storm.

Israel was conducted through the sea, and had a pillar of fire to lead the way, and in no case has God left his church to pine and die. He tries them, and leaves them for a short moment, but his loving kindness, he will never take from us.

Therefore let us feel safe in relying upon his promises, and let us believe him when he says. "I will never leave nor forsake you." He further adds: "A mother may forget her infant but I will not forget you." Once my fears were great on the subject; but our Father's promises are large enough to quell our fears, and shall we be afraid? Let the subject inspire our hearts, and let us die at our posts, and victory will be ours. A thousand transpiring events secure to us a reliance on his word.

The church then is not in danger, as we oftentimes imagine. Earth and hell united, cannot destroy her; for she trusteth in her head; God is in the midst of his people. So shall ye know that I am the Lord your God—God dwelling in Zion, my holy mountain. Again: For the mountains shall depart and the hills be removed, but my kindness shall not depart from thee. We build upon the same promises that they did anciently. God's love to us is the same to-day and forever.

The Jews are to return to their beloved land. They are *now* expecting the Saviour to come, and be their king and deliver them ; although some of them are giving up their "Traditions" for the Bible; and the Gospel will soon be preached to every Nation, and then will the end be. Instead of looking for Christ as our Redeemer, he will come as Judge: and will destroy the wicked with the brightness of his coming.

Thus we see how carefully Christ, watcheth over those he has purchased with his own precious blood, his children have cost too much to be lost. He says,—" For ye are dead, and your life is hid with Christ in God.

That being the case are we not safe? Were we alone to keep ourselves, then ought we to fear and tremble for our strength is perfect weakness, we ought to be afraid, and if we can save ourselves,then we have no need of a Saviour. But thanks be to God who giveth us a kingdom, it is a gift indeed! When we were dead in trespass and sins, then the Lord brought salvation and it is our duty to accept and walk in his commandments. He has given us a law to keep, and penalties if we disobey. God will not abandon his works, which he has began. His strength remains the same, and his promises will not fail

Let us take down our harps from the willows and praise the Lord, while life shall last. What more can He do? My brethren let us be on the watch. A few more conflicts, and temptations, and our toils will be at an end. Only believe on the Lord Jesus Christ and thou shalt be saved; even so come Lord Jesus, come quickly.

But not so with the sinner, his expectations will be cut off. Confusion of face, when his disappointment is made manifest when the Judge shall pronounce his sentence,—"Depart into everlasting fire."

Methinks I see him weeping, and hear him wailing, and gnashing his teeth, saying, why was I so unwise, as to reject the offers of salvation, when I felt his spirit moving me to accept of mercy? it was once within my reach, but now it is forever hid from my eyes, and I must spend an enternity of despair, where hope can never come. The poor sinner is lost! lost! forever and forever!

ON MATTHEW XIII. 30.

" Let both grow together until the harvest, and in the time of harvest, I will say to the reapers, gather ye together first the tares, and bind them in bundles, to burn them, but gather the wheat into my barn "

After a great multitude had gathered together, he sat down and taught them, and spake many things unto them in parables; he described the sower that went forth to sow, and the differences of soil into which the seed had fallen, and among the various ways there was but one way, that proved beneficial or that yielded fruit after his kind, and that was the seed which fell into good ground. And his disciples came and said unto him Why speakest thou unto them in parables? He answered and said unto them,—Because it is given unto you to know the mysteries of the kingdom of Heaven. There were other reasons too Because seeing they saw not—and hearing they heard not, neither did they understand, for this people, (the Jews,) had waxed gross in their hearts, and he turns to his disciples and saith,—Blessed are your eyes for they see, and your ears for they hear; for many prophets and righteous men have desired to see those things which you see, but were not able. He goes on to describe the parable and tells us we need understanding when we hear the word of the kingdom preached, lest the wicked one come and catch that which was sown in the heart. Again: The kingdom of Heaven is likened unto a man which sowed good seed in his field, and while he slept the enemy sowed tares; the servants enquired what should be done, if they should be gathered out; but he tells them to let them both grow together until harvest, lest when ye gather the tares, ye root up the wheat also.

This world is one vast field, filled with both good and bad. Many apply it to the church, but it cannot so be construed We have no rule laid down in scripture to warrant such an idea, his disciples desired him to explain to them, and he commenced, by saying that he that sowed the good seed was the son of man, the enemy was the Devil, the field is the world, and the good seed is the children of the kingdom, but the tares are the children of the wicked one, the harvest is the end of the world and the reapers are the angels; and as the tares are gathered and burned, so shall it be in the end of the world.

In this declaration we see a clear distinction between him that serveth God, and him that serveth him not. The wicked, the tares shall be bound in bundles, and cast into the fire that shall never be quenched: where shall be wailing and gnashing of teeth. Not so with the righteous; they shall shine forth as the sun in the kingdom of their Father. Who hath ears to hear let him hear.

He spake not unto his disciples but in parables, and yet they understood them not. He oftentimes spake of himself but their minds were darkened although the prophets had prophesied of him, and what should happen to him, how he should be crucified, and the third day he should rise again. They did not know what rising from the dead should mean. He told them that it was necessary that he should go away that the comforter might come, and reprove the world of sin. They understood not his sayings in regard to the Holy Ghost; for as yet he had not fallen upon any. Peter was raised up for the purpose that he should preach to the Gentiles, and after he had seen the vision of the sheet knit at four corners full of all kinds of four-footed beasts, it was to show him that the Gentiles too were to receive the Holy Ghost, and some miraculous vision and singular circumstances must transpire to give him the evidence.

I could enumerate many circumstances and indeed the bible is full of them; if we would read its contents, our knowledge would increase. The righteous ever have been sustained agreeably to the promises, and he never will suffer them to be tempted above what they are able to bear, but will make a way for their escape. Through the whole volume of truth, there are but two general characters designated, that is, saint and sinner; and we can see God's special care over the former, though all hell may rage, and earth join in unison, yet is he able to protect his own, for he governs the world for the sake of his church and they may rest under his protection. It would be as practicable to stop the sun in its course, as to draw his love from those that love him. The Lord will not cease to defend the apple of his eye. The church is as near his heart now, as it was thousands of years ago. "His arm is not shortenened that it cannot save," nor is his ear heavy that he cannot hear.

Therefore let the Lambs of the flock be encouraged and fear not, for it is your Father's good pleasure to give you the kingdom. Wolves may prowl around and threaten to destroy, yet let us bear in mind that his grace is sufficient for such.

But to return to the point,—" Let both grow together till harvest;" one great reason is that we are so closely connected by nature's ties, that many pious persons have unconverted relatives, living without God in the world, and should those be rooted out, it would perhaps awaken less interest for the salvation of souls, the flame of charity draws most towards those we love best, and who are nearest to us. Can we look upon our relatives with composure, and without concern, while we see them walking the downward road? without a heartfelt sense that by and by they must be gathered into bundles to be burned? But let both grow together, and let the angels sever the good from the bad, for we might not know them as well and might take up some of the wheat with the tares, but let both grow together until harvest, and in the time of harvest I will say to the reapers,—"Gather ye togather first the tares and bind hem in bundles to burn them, but put the wheat into barns.

ON ROMANS XII, 2.

"And be not conformed to the ways of this world; but be ye transformed by the renewing of your minds, that ye may prove what is that good, and acceptable, and perfect will of God."

The Apostle begins this chapter by saying,—I beseech you, therefore, brethren, by the mercies of God, that ye preserve your bodies a living sacrifice, holy, acceptable unto God which is your reasonable service. Our bodies as well as our souls are to be in subjection to him who made them, and the Apostles besought the brethren by his mercies, for he knew his mercies were very great, that everything should be done in an acceptable manner for it is our reasonable service. And be ye not conformed to this world, but transformed by the renewing of minds; the mind too is to be sacrificed to the will of God, that it may be good and acceptable; and by doing this we should not think of ourselves more highly than we ought, but think soberly, as he hath dealt to us the measure of faith. For we have many members in one body, and they are not of the same office; and yet composed of one body and many members, having different gifts according to the grace given unto them, and the portion of faith. Faith appears to be very essential to the improving of gifts; they that administer the word should do it in faith, believing in the word, or he that teacheth the same, and must attend to his calling and so on exhortation, and on giving, that he may do it with simplicity, he that ruleth with diligence, he that showeth mercy with cheerfulness; and our love should be pure. "Abhor evil and cleave to that which is good; should be kind and affectioned one to another, with brotherly love preferring one another.

We should prefer our brethren beforeany other one, because they are God's children, and have been born of his spirit and have been made to rejoice in hope. There is a oneness with the saints that cannot exist in those of the world.

We should weep with those that weep, and rejoice with those that rejoice. We should be of the same mind one towards another. We are to remember and conform to those of low estate, neither be wise in our own conceits, we should not render evil for evil, and it is essential to provide things *honest* in the sight of all men, and to live peaceably with all men as much as possible. Such characters should be hospitable towards those that are thus united. He closes this chapter by warning them against revenge, for he saith,—Vengeance is *mine*, and *I will* repay, and if thine enemy thirst, give him drink, and if he be hungry, feed him. Be not overcome of evil, but overcome evil with good.

All mankind are divided in two classes, saint and sinner, friends and enemies of God, and when he speaks of the world in cases of this kind, he means the wicked world, or the inhabitants of such a kingdom; because Christ says my kingdom is not of this world. It is a spiritual kingdom. He then points out the characters of such, and tells them to separate from the opposite, and touch not the unclean things. Wherefore come out from among them and be ye separate, saith the Lord. By faith and good works are we made to overcome by the blood of the Lamb, and he that hath this hope in him, purifieth himself even as he is pure.

Therefore the children of God are called out of this world, or the love of this world, and where shall they go? Why there are but two kingdoms as has just been noted, and of course they must join the one they love, for their inmates are of those they mostly delight in. And by what shall we distinguish them? In many ways they may and ought to be distinguished. In the first their language is different, their conversation is in heaven, and with the mouth confession is made unto salvation, and let your speech be seasoned with grace, that we may know how to answer every man. Ye are the salt of the earth. Let us next consider their dress: they are clothed in white and their garments should not be spotted with the flesh that is the world, they should be clothed with righteousness, they should evince to the world that they have been with Christ. We should not run into the excess of fashion, for that would not be coming out; for this world is a wilderness to the people of God. And here let me say a word in regard to the habitation of the wicked. A wilderness in a dangerous place, the Isrealites would have found it so had not the Lord led them by a pillar of fire by night, and a cloud by day. They were exposed to venomous beasts and serpents. But his presence was with them to make his promise good. God was their sun and shield. How often did they murmur and complain, as it is too often the case with those that travel through the wilderness of this world, homewards. They find many things to allure them and retard them in their progress. It is too unhealthy, and a barren waste, and no water there. And has not the Christian found from time to time, that that was not his abiding place, nor is it supposed that strangers can walk there without a guide. The enemy of the land will make every effort to worry and destroy, but our king is in Zion; the captain of our salvation will feed his flock and gather the lambs in his arms and carry them in his bosom. Let each join this march and arrive at the Heavenly Canaan. Let the enemy flee before your rapid steps, and at the end of your race sing hallelujahs of praise to Him who sitteth upon the throne forever. My dear Christian friends, when we discover the danger of those that are natives of this wilderness, let us plead with them to bestir themselves for their journey, may we live so that we can say: come thou with us, and we will do you good, but if our lives do not evince to the sinner that we are seeking a better country, then with more propriety we could say,—go to Christ for this is not our home; we hear the threatenings of the Almighty every time we look into his word. Turn ye! turn ye! for why will you die, O house of Israel!

ON PSALMS, CI.

I will sing of mercy and judgment, unto thee, O Lord, will I sing. How full of praise and thanksgiving the heart of man will be when his ways please the Lord. The Psalmist saith I will behave myself wisely in a perfect way. O when wilt thou come unto me? I will walk within my house with a perfect heart. He said he would set no wicked thing before his eyes, for he hated the very works of those that turn aside: it shall not cleave to me. The soul that hungers and thirsts after holiness, hates a froward look, and will not take a wicked person for their bosom associate, but you will treat them with kindness, and tenderness.

I will not know a wicked person. The proud in heart and an high look, and him that privily slandereth his neighbor, him will I cut off from his associates. But his eyes were upon the faithful of the land. He that worketh deceit and he that telleth lies shall not tarry in my sight. It seems that it was in his power to destroy the wicked out of the land and from the city of our God. Just in proportion to our uprightness and holy zeal, do we hate sin: for sin and holiness cannot dwell together. The truly pious love such things as their master loves, and their hatred is in conformity with the same rule as far as their knowledge extends. God hath made us partrkers of his spirit, and in that way he reveals himself unto us. It is then we cry out,— bless the Lord! O my soul, and give thanks to his name; so shall our souls rejoice continually; our peace will be like a river. O! the peace that can be enjoyed here upon earth! Great peace have they that love thy law, and nothing shall offend them. But eye hath not seen, nor ear heard the joys that are laid up for those that love Him. What a delightful subject to dwell upon, while here upon earth, and what will it be when we have come off conquerors and passed out of the reach of sin and Satan? It will be what it now is, beyond description.

———

ON MATTHEW, XV, 8.

———

This people draweth nigh unto me with their mouth, and honoreth me with their lips; but their heart is far from me.

The Scribes and Pharisees came to Christ and enquired of him why his disciples transgress the traditions of the elders? To which he replied,—Why do ye also transgress the commandments of God by *your* tradition? He went on to describe wherein they disregarded the commandments of God, and that was they did not honor |their father and mother. He did not hesitate to call them hypocrites, neither did Isaiah when he prophesied of the same people, that would draw nigh with their lips, while their hearts were far from God, which is a crime of no small magnitude. He tells them " In vain do they worship me, teaching for doctrines the commandments of men." Then he called to him the multitude and said, hear and understand: not that which goeth into the mouth defileth the man, but that which goeth out. Then came to him his disciples and told him that the pharisees were offended at his sayings, but he answered and said, every plant that my heavenly Father hath not planted shall be rooted up. Let them alone, they be blind leaders of the blind! and tells them the consequences. Peter requested him to declare the parable; he asked him if he was blind also? or without understanding. Those things that proceed out of the mouth come from the heart, and they defile the man, for evil thoughts of every description flow from the heart, for it is deceitful above all things, and who can know it. But to eat with unwashen hands is not a crime. It was a tradition of the Jews that they should wash their hands at every meal: and also cups and other vessels, which caused Christ to say: Full well ye reject the commandments of God, that ye may keep your own tradition. That was their righteousness, and he told them except their righteousness exceeded the righteousness of the Scribes and Pharisees, they could not enter the kingdom of Heaven.

Our Saviour was constantly warning his disciples of the doctrines of the Scribes and Pharisees, because they were unwholesome doctrines; for they would love those that loved them. They would do their alms to be seen of men, and when they prayed they would stand in the synagogues, and in the corners of the streets. Verily, they have their reward. They fasted not like the disciples of Christ, they would build the tombs of the prophets, and garnish the sepulchres of the righteous, they thought that was a noble act; one step towards Heaven; but could not realize that they were the children of those that killed the prophets. A woe was pronounced against them for making clean the outside of the vessels. A woe too, was pronounced against them for making prosolytes, for when they were made they were twofold more the children of hell than themselves. A very essential charge brought against them was, that they shut up the kingdom of Heaven against men;

neither went in themselves, nor suffered them that were entering to go in. They loved greeting in the markets, and wished to
be called Rabbi! Rabbi! And again they took the advantage of
the widows, and for a pretence made long prayers. Therefore
they should receive the greater damnation. They would set in
Moses' seat, and would bind heavy burdens upon men's shoulders: all their works were to be seen of men. They enlarged the
borders of their garments and chose the uppermost seats, or
rooms, at feasts. They paid tithes of all they possessed, but
omitted the weightier matters of the law, for that was to love
God with all their hearts, and their neighbors as themselves;
judgment, mercy and faith should not be omitted. This people
draweth nigh unto me with their mouth. How careful ought we
to be when we attempt to address Him, who seeth the inmost
recesses of the heart. In vain do they worship me except their
hearts are in their devotion. The sacrifice of a broken heart is
what God delights in. He will not hear the hypocrites. I hate,
I despise your feast days, and I will not smell in your solemn
assemblies, neither will I regard your peace offerings. Take
away from me the noise of your viols, (songs) I will not hear
their melody. But unto the wicked God saith,—What hast thou
to do to declare my statutes, or that thou shouldst take my covenant into thy mouth?

The plowing of the wicked is an abomination; God saith he
hateth the doings of such characters as have been described
above. But this is not all "To what purpose is the multitude of
your sacrifices unto me? when ye come to appear before me?"
Who hath required this at your hands to tread my courts?
Bring no more vain oblation; and again: When ye make many
prayers, I will not hear. The destruction of the transgressors
and the sinners together, and they that forsake the Lord shall
be consumed. But this does not prove that the people of God,
should not call on their God for such things as they want. They
should call on him as true worshippers; but when we lift up our
hearts to be seen of men, then are we resembling the Pharisees,
and God will not hear such. It is the duty and privilege of
Christians to be often at the throne of grace. He suffers us to
converse with him, and come to him through our Lord, and
Saviour, he not only holds out inducements but commands us to
pray always; nothing doubting; for if we ask and receive not,
we ask amiss.

It is the delight of every saint to be humble at the feet of the that mocketh or setteth himself above all that is called God, Holy One, that exalteth him that humbleth himself. It is him or seteth in the place of God; everything that is Antichrist is at war with the true religion of Christ. But when the soul expands and is filled with the love of God, which is like a river, it is then we hate the pharisee and hypocrite that expects to be heard and saved by good works (if their's can be called good.) Let our devotions be fervent and frequent, we cannot be justified by works alone. There are many proofs of the sincerity of our faith and soundness of our repentance. Our faith must rest alone on Christ for salvation. We should have a growing esteem for the sacred scriptures. Our love should increase from a sense of God's goodness, for God first loved us and gave himself for us. It is life eternal, to know the only true God: Let us honor God in our lives that it shall not be said of us: "This people draweth nigh with their mouths while their hearts are from me." But let our lives and lips confess the Holy Gospel, we profess. Let no provocation extinguish the love, which we bear one to another. Our natures are depraved, and we ourselves were sometimes foolish and disobedient, serving divers pleasures.

Lord lay not this sin to our charge. Just help us to realize our condition, if after we have anticipated a crown, we should sink to regions of despair, where hope can never come, because we deviate from the revelation God has given us. What a time! when the hopes of being saved will perish and the Judge will say I never knew you! These are false professors who have trod the courts of Jehovah, paid tithes and spread out their hands, and drew near in words, but their hearts were far from thee. O how does the voice now surprise such when they hear,—"Depart I never knew you! Therefore let us examine closely, that our hope shall not be as the hypocrite; that we may test our love to God and man. If any man have not the spirit of God he is none of his. If you love me saith our Saviour, keep my command-ment, and then shall we draw nigh to God not only with our mouths but our hearts also.

H

ON ISAIAH, LV, 7.

Let the wicked forsake his ways, and the unrighteous man his thoughts: and let him return unto the Lord and he will have mercy upon him; and to our God for he will abundantly pardon.

This verse is full of precious promises from the Lord to the unconverted sinner; which he speaks by the mouth of the Prophet. In the first place he saith,—Let the wicked forsake his ways, yes, let him; nothing to hinder but his own disposition, which is naturally corrupt, but still he had better forsake his way because his heart is not right in the sight of his Maker, therefore something must be done to claim the promise held out in this text. In the verse preceding, appears to be a command: Seek ye the Lord while he may be found, call ye upon him while he is near.

Should I attempt to describe the wicked in all their ways it would take more space in my sheet than would be necessary, for conscience dictates what is sin, or known sins, such as wrath, strife, envy, murder, drunkeness, covetousness, idolatry, fornication, uncleaness, hatred, variance, heresies, railings, and from all such turn away. It is of the greatest importance to turn from all known sins, and we need not be ignorant in this land of bibles; so let the wicked forsake his way, he should not shut his eyes against the light, to indulge in carnal security, nor exclude every ray of hope, the light shines too brightly to be mistaken, for God is angry with the wicked every day. To turn from our wicked ways is not sufficient, for he is to forsake his unrighteous thoughts. Our wicked thoughts when indulged produce wicked ways. Wickedness is conceived first in the heart, and the sinner does not reject it until it becomes full grown, and then it brings forth death; we read that "One sinner destroyeth much good." The sinner is fed and clothed by the same hand as is the saint; yet the sinner is like a troubled sea, whose waters cannot rest.

Under a sense of this truth let the wicked forsake his way, and the unrighteous man his thoughts. After he has forsaken, what shall he next do? The Prophet saith,—"And let him return unto the Lord, and he will have mercy upon him." Now comes the promises,—"*He will* have mercy." Dear sinner, you need not fear, God is infinitely good. We have the greatest reason to rejoice at his declarations: if ye seek me with all your hearts ye shall find. At the recollection of your wicked ways, forsake and live. Lay aside your unbelief and rely on the promises, for God loves the works of his hands, and would not that any should perish, but have everlasting life. If he did not mean what he says, he would not have lengthened out our day of probation until now. But he saith let him return unto the Lord, for very great are his mercies; but not so great as to forgive without repentance or a turning to him, and when you forsake you will incline to turn. Turn ye, turn ye, for why will you die? And to our God for he will abundantly pardon, not *scarcely* but *abundantly*. More than could be expected; more than we deserve, for our just deserts would land us in eternal perdition, where hope cannot come. Repent of your sins, and believe on our Lord Jesus Christ, who will have mercy and who will abundantly pardon, let this animate you and stimulate you to forsake your ways and thoughts, and turn to God! May you thankfully embrace this opportunity to turn. It is my duty to hold up to view the willingness of God to save all that come to him, through Christ the door. This is the object and foundation of our hope.

The Prophet even in this declaration, makes a difference between the two characters upon earth, for he saith *our* God will abundantly pardon. With what propriety can the wicked call him our God? in the sense of this subject before us?

The Saints call him their God, their Saviour, their Redeemer, their King and head, their husband and friend, their spouse, the bridegroom, the Lamb of God which taketh away the sin of the world.

Our God is a consuming fire. What does he, or will he consume? Is it not the wicked? O dreadful thought! Then let them forsake their way and find plentious redemption, and be heirs of grace and glory; and no good thing will he with-hold from them that walk uprightly. All things are yours, whether life or death; all is yours if you forsake and turn to the Lord.

Transporting thought! Who can concieve or form the least idea of the change? To be taken from sin and degradation and raised to be heir, and joint heir with Christ. What a happy change! Look forward then with delight, and sing,—"Worthy is the Lamb that was slain to receive honor and praise forever and forever." O glorious state! the pure in heart are ravished with beholding his glory. Christ told his disciples: In my Father's house are many mansions. There the Saints shall meet from all kindreds and nations, people and tongues, singing redeeming grace and dying love. Why is it called dying love? Because God so loved the world that he gave his only begotten Son to die for lost man. Now let him forsake his way and turn to God. They will sing a new song, and what will it be? "Unto *Him* that loved us, and washed us from our sins in his own blood, and hath made us kings and priests unto God. Honor and glory be ascribed to him that sitteth upon the throne forever and ever."

Dear sinner, reflect one moment and come to the conclusion that as for me *I will serve the Lord.* I will—"Return unto the Lord, and he will have mercy upon me, and to our God for he will abundantly pardon."

ON THESSALONIANS, V, 19.

Quench not the Spirit.

This is a subject of the utmost importance to both Saint and Sinner. This chapter commences with an exhortation to be ready for the coming of Christ; although the Apostle thinks there is no need of his writing unto them, (the church.) "For yourselves know perfectly, that the day of the Lord so cometh as a thief in the night,"—but when *they* say peace and safety—that is they that procrastinate—and say the Lord delayeth his coming, and continue to do wickedly: then sudden destruction cometh upon them. Then will they be in distress, and shall not escape. But brethren ye are not in darkness, that that day should overtake you as a thief, for ye are children of the light, therefore do not sleep as do others that care nothing what the word saith, but watch and be sober, who are of the day, or who believe in the light. Prepare yourselves with the whole armor of faith, hope and love, for God hath not appointed you to wrath but to obtain salvation by the Lord Jesus Christ, who died for us. Whether awake or asleep, we should live for him, and comfort, and edify one another and be at peace among ourselves but you must warn the unruly, and comfort the feeble-minded, support the weak and be patient, and not render evil for evil, but ever follow that which is good; rejoicing evermore, and praying without ceasing, and for everything give thanks, for i^t is the will of God for us so to do. Then comes in this important subject: *Quench not the Spirit.* In the first place the children of God should not do it, because he is our God, and condescends to call us his children, heirs and joint heirs with Jesus Christ and hath given us his Spirit. He hath so formed us that his Spirit can dwell within us, our bodies are the temples for the Holy Ghost to dwell in. What a mercy, that God hath seen fit to give us his Spirit! What a mercy that he sent his Son into the world to save sinners, when we were ruined by the fall.

How dare such, quench the Spirit? It is dangerous to grieve the Spirit at any time for it is unwise as well as presumptious; for God deals in earnest with his creatures. It is he who hath sealed us and given us the earnest of the Spirit in our hearts. It is the Spirit that helpeth our infirmities; for we know not what we should pray for as we ought, for the Spirit maketh intercession for us according to the will of God. Again: But truly I am full of power by the Spirit of the Lord.

Again: For God hath not given us the Spirit of fear, but of power, and of love, and of a sound mind, therefore be not ashamed of the Gospel for it is the power of God to them that believe. In God there is power: in Christ there is power: in the Holy Ghost there is power; therefore be afraid of the power, if we grieve, or quench the Spirit of God. God with-holds the light of his countenance from us that refuse and rebel; and we shall be beaten with many stripes. God is merciful but not all mercy; he is just, as well as merciful—his law is not hard. Let every one tha^t nameth the name of the Lord depart from iniquity. Sin leadeth us to destruction, but a life of holiness, to a life everlasting. If we love God, we shall love his law, and will not dare grieve his Spirit, when it is teaching us, and loading us by its blessed ufluences; for by this Spirit are we taught all truths.

How dare we, when we feel its heavenly influence, to stifle and reject its holy impression, when he was sent to comfort and reprove? I say, how dare *we* say, send by some other, or spare me, trouble me not but let me rest and remain ignorant of thy counsel? The Spirit sanctifies the heart. It is by the spirit that we have access to the throne of grace. By his Spirit he removes our difficulties in the way of salvation; then quench it not for God is angry with the wicked every day, and what is that but doing wickedly? Hence my christian brethren be afraid of grieving the Holy Spirit; for you must grope in darkness, and you know not where you go, and stumble at the stumbling stone; but walk softly, and with trembling steps, or else the Spirit will be wounded. None but God can, or has, brought salvation, and shall we quench his Holy Spirit? Shall we then be so ungrateful, and hard-hearted, and so blind to our eternal interest as to grieve the Holy Spirit of God; whereby we are sealed to the day of redemption.

And what shall I say to the other class of sinners, that is unconverted sinners. I tremble when I look upon this side of the picture for there are so many that shipwreck their souls upon this point. They think that religion is not necessary until death, and the thought of embracing the Saviour is nothing but gloom. The spirit is often reproving such, and convincing them that delay is dangerous; but they say, a little more sleep and slumbering, and sometimes perhaps they do not realize that it is the spirit of truth; and the impression will wear off. But again, and again, the Spirit fulfills his office, by convincing the sinner that all is not well;—and except a man be born again, he cannot enter nor see the kingdom of God, but still he inclines to put far away the evil day. The natural selfishness of the heart operates in various ways; some are too fearful and some too careless about many things; and no wonder if they should incline to put off. Blessed be the Father of our Saviour Jesus Christ that he calls again, and again until we shall know of a surety that it is his spirit that is striving in our hearts, to bring us unto God. Although his heart is at enmity with God, and is not subject to his law, yet the word of God is like a sword; he is becoming more and more convinced that his laws must be obeyed, which causes distress and as the distress increases, his spirit draws nearer, and nearer, and is about coming to the conclusion that without Christ he is undone: he finds no rest, but is like the troubled sea. Then the enemy of souls tells him there is time enough yet, and thus he begins to cast off his sorrows by grieving the Holy Spirit. Guilt flashes in his face, and he cries out— what have I done? He again resolves to forsake his sins, and seek religion with all his heart. Then the working of the Spirit comes in contact with his proud heart, and he fears what others will say at such a conclusion. Then how careful an awakened sinner should be under such temptations? and not quench the spirit. O how astonishing is the long forbearance, and patience of God towards a sinner coming to him, the heavens are clothed in mercy, and thanks to God prevail. How often are they made to cry out—I have done all that I can! when indeed they have not resigned their will.

How critical their situation when eternal life is at stake! God is using the means by which he designs to bring us to Christ but we are rejecting and resisting still. Be careful how you resist· for I fear everytime will be the last, and then what will be the condition of such? Why, weeping and howling for our miseries. How keen the reflection if he should be given over to a hard heart and a reprobate mind.

Dear sinner! be intreated not to grieve or trifle with the operations of the Holy Spirit. As soon as you shall say,—"Go thy way, when I have a more convenient season I will call for thee," (and that season will never be) it is to be feared the grieved spirit will take his flight and O! my heart shudders at such an idea. What! be rejected from the smiles of Heaven, where hope can never come? And dare we be indifferent upon such an event of infinite importance?

Do not be indifferent to your soul's salvation. The time when the spirit is striving with us is the time to accept of offered mercy. When the soul has rejected this offer for the last time, then is he left to his own ways, to fill up the measure of his iniquity, and to treasure up wrath against the day of wrath. Dear soul! shun these dreadful denunciations, and turn to God; for very great are his mercies. I am sure could you look upon the cross and view the love he bears for you, (I am candid and authorized so to say) your heart would melt into love and praise his blessed name.

One thing more, could the sinner believe that the children o God are in distress for their fellow man for they do partake of the same entreating spirit for one another; they are ambassadors for Christ as though God did beseech you by them, or us, to be ye reconciled to God—then would they rejoice, and strive with more dilligence, believing that God or his spirit was in them of a truth: then it would be dangerous for to stifle or quench that impression or belief. It is not so much in the number of times, or in the various circumstances which causes our Lord to with-draw his Holy Spirit, as it is in the knowledge, and wilful rejec-tion of the same. After the sinner is made to believe that this is the last time, and is fully convinced that his spirit is striving to come to Christ, and he discovers Christ sufficient and willing to save, then should he say,—"Go thy way for the present when I have a more convenient season I will call for thee," it is very evident he will never have a disposition to call again! and should he, it is to be feared that he might hear this answer. "I have called and ye refused, I have stretched out my hand and you have not regarded it. Therefore will I laugh at your calamities, and mock when your fear cometh." Therefore be entreated not to quench the tender spirit!

ON ECLESIASTIES, XII.

This chapter commences with an exhortation to the youth, to remember their " Creator in the days of their youth, while the evil days come not, nor the years draw nigh, when thou shalt say, I have no pleasure in them." It is to remember now, not wait until you are ol d, or on a sick bed, or when your senses are not clear, and comprehensive; or deaf, blind, or tottering with enfeebled limbs; but remember *now*, in health and activity, and vigor of mind, before all these infirmities of old age come upon you. "While the sun, or the light, or moon, or the stars be not darkened," while all these things are delightsome to us we should remember him who hath created us, and given these blessings, before the keepers of the house shall tremble, that is, our limbs that were once strong and athletic, but now bow them-

selves through disease: in this there is no pleasure. The grinders too, cease because they are but few. They should remember
their Creator when they eat and drink, for whatsoever they do
should be done with thanksgiving, for teeth are a blessing.
"And those that look out of the windows be darkened." How
common it is for those advanced in years to lose their eye-sight;
and then their joys are deficient, perhaps so blind that they cannot read the word of God, and then they will say there is no
pleasure for us. We are to secure an interest in the Saviour
before all these things come upon us. They shall become deaf,
when the doors shall be shut in the streets; at the same time that
the sound of the grinding is low, and shall rise up at the voice of
the bird, and all the daughters of music shall be brought low. We
do not relish those mirthful scenes in old age which fascinated us
in youth. Those pleasures are gone in a great measure. Also
when they shall be afraid of that which is high. They do not
aspire to high things for they know full well that their time is
short upon earth,—"And fears shall be in the way." They are
not as courageous as in their youthful days, but as they advance,
the grasshopper is a burden. Trifling things appear like mountains, and they cannot surmount them. "And desire shall fail
because man goeth to his long home." Or ere the silver cord be
loosed, or the golden bowl be broken, or the pitcher be broken
at the fountain, or the wheel broken at the cistern,—"Then shall
the dust return to the earth as it was, and the spirit shall return
unto God who gave it." After our limbs and all our members
fail, disease makes its way to the vitals, it is then death feels for
our heartstrings, and breaks the silver cords of life; it is then the
"Pitcher is broken at the fountain, and the wheel at the cistern."
When our blood ceases to flow, then we go to our long home.

Before all these evils come upon us, we ought to remember our
Creator, and make our peace with God:—for all is vanity and
vexation, without an interest in Christ!

This preacher, king of Israel recommends that we should get
Wisdom, which far excelleth gold or silver. He was able to
enjoy all that the world could afford, and it was too small for
him, or any one else. He knew that there were many good
things that might be possessed; but after all it was vanity and
vexation to be compared to Wisdom. He saith,—"All this have
I proved by wisdom; I said, I will be wise, but it was far from
me."

Because the preacher was wise, he taught the people knowledge. He sought to find words which were acceptable and upright even words of truth; he concludes the whole matter by saying, —Fear God and keep his commandments; for this is the whole duty of man. For God shall bring every work into judgment, with every secret thing whether it be good or whether it be evil. Therefore remember now thy Creator in the days of thy youth, while the evil days come not, nor the years draw nigh, when thou shalt say I have no pleasure in them.

ON MATTHEW, XXVIII.

This chapter gives an account of the resurrection of Christ, how the women came to the sepulchre, and as they came to the place, there was a great earthquake, in consequence of an angel descending from heaven. He rolled back the stone, to shew them that he, (Christ) had risen, his (the angel's) countenance was exceedingly bright, and his raiment was as white as snow. And for fear of him the keepers did shake, and became as dead men. And he said unto the women,—"Fear not ye! for I know that ye seek Jesus which was crucified; he is not here, he is risen, as he said," come see the place where the Lord lay! and then he tells them to go quickly, and tell his disciples that he is risen from the dead and that he would go before them into Gallilee, and there ye shall see him, lo! I have told you.

And they departed quickly with great fear and joy, they did run to bear the tidings to his disciples. And as they went behold Jesus met them, saying: All hail! And they came and held him by the feet and worshipped him, then they heard his lbessed consoling voice. Be not afraid: go tell *my* brethren that they go into Gallilee and there shall they see me. All this pleasant interview was with the women. And why? Because they loved him and sought after him, even his lifeless remains that had been deposited in the grave. They (the women) anointed his body with precious ointment, for his burial although they did not understand him at the time, yet they loved him. And O how he loved them and gave himself for them. How kind to send his angel and tell them he had risen. Come see the place where the Lord lay.

What a delightful theme to dwell upon, is the death and resurrection of Christ? Although there is a certain gloom attached to some of its circumstances, that is, to those enemies of the cross. How lamentable that this dying Jesus should not be more upon our thoughts, and we fly to him for refuge!

Let our minds then, be continually upon the cross of Christ, that his death may not be in vain to any of us. The backsliden in heart, when he returns to his father's house, will cite his mind to the cross where he first beheld the dying Lamb nailed to the fatal wood for *his* sins. "He bore *our* sins in his own body on the tree; he is faithful to forgive sins, he is also just, as well as merciful. Here mercy and truth met together; righteousness and peace kiss each other. What sweet harmony in all the perfections of God; or Christ, in pardoning iniquity. The good shepherd lays down his life for the sheep. It is here the love of Christ constraineth us to live, not unto ourselves, but unto him who died for us. The redemption of the soul is precious. If we wish to know the worth of the soul let us look at the cross, and may the Saviour's love be shed abroad in our hearts. The death of Christ is a subject to have constantly before our eyes; it affords consolation in the midst of trials to high and low, rich and poor, and under all circumstances it should be our theme to dwell upon.

Perhaps some think if they view him on the cross at the sacramental table, that that is sufficient, for Christ himself said: As oft as ye do this, ye do shew forth my death till I come, and do it in remembrance of me. It is important to go at his bidding, as did those women thus spoken of. "They went quickly and did as they were told." Should we be ready and willing as they were; no doubt but we should be met also. The pure hearted female would be met as soon as the man, for both are equally alike in their condemnation and justification. I would to God that more women were oftener at the sepulchre, and at the cross and at his feet worshipping and hearing him say,—"Be not afraid, but go and tell my brethren;" he does not hesitate to call those which believe his brethren. And when *they* saw him *they* worshipped him too. He then said,—All power is given unto me in heaven and in earth; then came the commission,—Go ye therefore, and teach all nations, baptizing them in the name of the Father, and of the Son, and of the Holy Ghost, and lo! I am with you always.

ON SOLOMON'S SONG. II, III.

As the apple tree among the trees of the wood, so is my beloved among the sons. I sat down under his shadow with great delight, and his fruit was sweet to my taste.

This shows the mutual love between Christ and his church. I am the rose of Sharon, and the lily of the valley. As the lily among thorns, so is my love among the daughters. As the apple tree among the trees of the wood, so is my beloved among the sons.

How beautifully Christ is described above everything else? He is the chiefest among ten thousand, and the one altogether lovely. His beauty cannot be described. His voice is sweet and his countenance comely. The wise man compareth him to the apple tree, as its fruit is more delicious than any tree of the wood, its shadow was delightful, it was comforting. The church is fed with the fruits of this tree. When the church is low she enquireth after her love. Thy stature is like to a palm tree.

Who is this that cometh up from the wilderness leaning upon her beloved? I raised thee up under the apple tree. Thou that dwellest in the gardens. How delightful for the church when her beloved dwells in the garden where there is all kinds of fruit that is pleasant. A garden enclosed is my sister, my spouse, a spring shut up, a fountain sealed. A fountain of gardens, a well of living waters, and streams from Lebanon. Oh could the church bring forth her fruit and her clear streams of water, that her beloved would praise her and be delighted with her, that she may not be enquiring after her beloved.

But notwithstanding he is withdrawn for a season, she still describes him the chiefest among ten thousand, and all his beauty is held up to view in every comparison that she can invent. This is my beloved and my friend, and may she sit under the shadow of the apple tree with great delight.

Oh that Christ would come into his garden, the church, and say,—Arise my love, my fair one and come away, for lo! the winter is past, the rain is over and gone. The flowers appear on the earth, and the time of the singing of birds is come and the voice of the turtle is heard in our land.

PSALMS, CXIX, 126—127.

It is time for thee, Lord, to work, for they have made void thy law. Therefore I love thy commandments above gold, yea above fine gold.

The Psalmist could appreciate the love ot God and his law above everything else, even gold or silver for that is what men value most, and will hazard their lives, and reputation, and even their souls for wealth; and when they are over anxious for the gold that perisheth, then ought we to make use of the language of the above Psalm. It is time for thee, Lord to work in our hearts and examine our motives, and see if we love the commandments of God above gold, yea, fine gold. When our minds are captivated with the things that perish, it is then we make void the law of God.

O God work like thyself, for thou art a wonder working God, it is time for thee to work or we never can be saved! May the Saints be quickened to love and keep thy law. Rivers of waters run down mine eyes because they keep not thy law. Trouble and anguish have taken hold on me, yet thy commandments are my delight.

I cried with my whole heart, hear me O Lord! I w ill keep thy statutes; again I cried unto thee, save me and I *shall* keep thy testimonies. It is no wonder the people of God are delighted with his law, for it is holy, just, and good. How can it be varied to make it better for us? O how love I thy law, it is my meditation day and night. It is full, it is complete, it is perfect, it is more to be preferred than rubies, yea than fine gold. I opened my mouth and panted, for I longed for thy commandments.

When we cry after a knowledge of the word, the spirit of God will direct us to a portion of the same, that will strengthen us, and comfort us. Thy word is very pure, therefore thy servant loveth it; for thy law is truth. My lips shall utter praise, when thou hast taught me thy statutes. God is perfect and his laws are perfect also.

When the Lord shall work his people will tremble. Why? Because we have made void his law. Can we think he has forgotten what he hath said in regard to his law? Or that his wrath will always sleep? Salvation is far from the wicked, for they seek not thy statutes. The evil doers shall be cut off, they have plotted against the just. The wicked watcheth the righteous, and seeketh to slay him, but the Lord will not leave him in his hand.

What care over them that love his law. *He will* not leave them in the hands of the wicked, but will never leave nor forsake those that keep and love thy testimonies. God is terrible in judgments and in power, how terrible art thou in thy works. Let the wicked perish at the presence of God, although Satan should rage and threaten to destroy, yet are the people of God safe. He will not suffer them to be harmed. Their salvation, and preservation, is not left entirely at the disposal of the creature, for we cannot save ourselves, nor keep ourselves without divine assistance. It is something beside a mere chance that Christ died. It is not an accident that the law was given, and when it is made void, the punishment will not be accidental or perhaps not at all, for the word is gone out and will not return void. Heaven and earth shall pass away but my word shall not pass away. But he that refuses and rebels shall suddenly be destroyed, and that without remedy. Thanks be to God that he has not left us to our own will, but has given us of his spirit to teach us the right way, and helps us to love and obey his commandments for they are life. To love God with all our hearts is more than whole burnt offerings. Wait on the Lord and keep his way, and he shall exhalt thee to inherit the land. When the wicked are cut off thou shalt see it. What a vast difference between the Saint and Sinner.

ON ISAIAH, LXI, 1.

The Spirit of the Lord God is upon me; because the Lord hath annointed me to preach good tidings unto the meek: he hath sent me to bind up the broken-hearted, to proclaim liberty to the captives, and the opening of the prison to them that are bound. To proclaim the acceptable year of the Lord and the day of vengeance of our God, to comfort all that mourn.

By this same spirit the prophet was made to see and foretell the coming of the Mesiah whose garments were dyed with red. He also discovered the condition of the Church that mourn, that they might be called *Trees of Righteousness*. The planting of the Lord that he might be glorified. When he shall come he shall build the old waste places, and the Gentiles shall see thy righteousness and all kings thy glory. Say ye to the daughters of Zion,—Behold thy salvation cometh. And they shall call them *Thy* holy people, *The* redeemed of the Lord, and thou shalt be called *Sought out. A City not forsaken.*

Christ makes mention of the same Prophecy concerning himself, in Luxe iv—18, when he was in the Synagogue, he turned to the same place and read, and then declared that this day the Scripture was fulfilled in regard to himself, he had come to preach the gospel to the poor and the blind, and bring deliverance to the captives, and liberty to them that are bound.

What a glorious deliverance, when we were dead in trespasses ·· ? sins? Who can help making mention of his loving kin.?

ness. Sure they are my people, so he was their Saviour. Although he declared the day of vengeance, yet he will comfort all that mourn.

They shall be called a holy people or the redeemed of the Lord, and thou shalt be called, Sought out. A city not forsaken. Had he not special regard and care for his chosen people there could have been but one cry, and that would be,—Lost! Lost! inevitably lost!

But this was not the case; for they were astonished at his doctrine, for his word was with power. And they said,—Is not this Joseph's Son? He was a Nazarite and his custom was to read in the Synagogue on the Sabbath day, and how careful he was to turn to the place where it was written: The Spirit of the Lord is upon me, &c. And when he closed the book and sat down, the eyes of all the congregation were fastened upon him. So great and powerful were his words, that the devils cried out, saying,—Thou art Christ the Son of God; and they desired to be let alone. The people rose up in order to thrust him out of the city, that they might cast him headlong down the brow of the hill. But he passed through the midst of them and went his way. How many are there who would wish him to depart out of their coasts, not willing to hear from his mouth his powerful doctrines. But it is hoped and believed there are some waiting still at his feet for instruction, and filled with the spirit, and calling him Abba Father. Who is this that cometh from Edom, with dyed garments from Bozrah? this that is glorious in his apparrel, traveling in the greatness of his strength? I that speak in righteousness, mighty to save.

Christ is the center of all our hopes and may we find fresh virtue in his blood. May we pause for a moment, and think what has been done for us. A living way has been opened for us. And is there not reason for deep humiliation of heart? Ought not we to be careful to give him our whole heart and affections. Take heed lest after ye have received the knowledge of the truth, ye wilfully sin, for God leaves nothing to our choice in matters of worship: we have nothing to do with the Iasraelitish worship under the law, but we are now the once purged worshippers, those alone being owned of God, not in the outer court, but in the temple itself.

ON HEBREWS, III, 12.

Take heed, brethren, lest there be in any of you an evil heart of unbelief, in departing from the living God.

This chapter commences by calling Christs' disciples holy brethren, partakers of the heavenly calling; and exhorts them to consider the great Apostle and High Priest of their profession, Christ Jesus, who was faithful to him that appointed him, as was Moses in all his house. But Christ as a Son over his own house, whose house are we, if we hold fast the confidence and the rejoicing of the hope, firm unto the end.

The Holy Ghost saith,—To-day if ye hear his voice harden not your hearts, your fathers tempted me in the wilderness, wherefore I was grieved with this generation and said, they do always err in their hearts. So I swear in my wrath, they shall not enter into my rest, then comes in the words above,—Take heed. But exhort one another daily, that ye be not hardened in sin. For some when they did hear provoked him.

But with whom was he grieved? And to whom swear he that they should not enter into his rest, but to them that believed not? So we see that they could not enter in because of unbelief.

It becomes us to fear lest a promise being left to us, that any should come short of it, for if God spared not the natural branches, the Jews, we must be careful that he spare not us Gentiles.

Seeing then we have a great high priest that has passed into the heavens, Jesus the Son of God, let us hold fast our profession. We should be careful how we profess a belief in Christ, and hold it fast; and let nothing turn our steady feet astray, but continue

I

steadfast in the faith or belief, for he is made a high priest for us. Neither by the blood of goats, and calves, but by his own precious blood, nothing would atone for sin but the sacrifice of himself, by a new and living way which he hath consecrated for us through the veil of his flesh. Therefore take heed, etc. But may it be said in truth, that we are not of those who draw back unto perdition, but of them that believe unto the saving of our souls.

We can scarcely look into the volume of truth without casting our eyes upon some of the precious promises therein contained. It is through faith we stand. Therefore lift up the hands which hang down, and make straight the paths for your feet, lest that which is lame be turned out of the way. Take heed brethren lest there be in any of you an evil heart of unbelief.

Our natural heart is inclining to disbelieve the word; more ready to be hearers of the word than doers. Out of the same mouth proceedeth blessings and cursings. My brethren these things ought not so to be. There must be an evil heart of unbelief lurking within; be not deceived, for what a man soweth that shall he also reap. We should be afflicted and weep and mourn over sin, and humble ourselves in the sight of the Lord—and he shall lift us up. How can we live in pleasure and be innocent? There is a difficulty with us, in that the church of God has leagued itself with the powers of the world, so that they are become one and the same thing to all appearance; and no wonder we are commanded to take heed. No doubt but that the form of Godliness will be satisfying to the natural mind, but rotteness and death within. There are many Antichrists, and this is ominous of the last days, for that reason we ought to give the more earnest heed to make our calling and election sure, lest there be in any of us an evil heart of unbelief in departing from the living God.

It is a crime to depart from the precepts of the Lord. Let us examine the various ways that our adversary takes to draw us from the right way. In youth and activity he fills our mind with vanity, and a desire to rise to a full stature of a man and act for ourselves and manage our own affairs as shall best suit our ambition, and seeking honor and fame, and the aspiring spirit can hardly rest; while those of a diffefent character are lifeless and carless, and sink into unfavorable company where even morality will not have a balance in favor of their conduct;

then both classes have need to take heed and not depart from the living God.

And after we have arrived to more ripe years and character formed, they too are filled with the cares of the world; the love of the same, will choke the word, and it thereby become unfruitful; then take heed, for soon we shall be found departing from God. When we are old and care worn, then also we are in, danger. There is no time from the cradle to the grave but what we are in danger, and actually do at times depart from the path of rectitude, because our natures are corrupt and no good in us naturally. But when I come directly to the text above,—"Take heed brethren," this is spoken directly to the people of God; who have been washed and sactified by the blood of the Lamb, yet there is great danger of departing.

Let him that standeth take heed lest he fall. So great is the care we should have over ourselves. But if we fall shall we rise again? The Apostle saith if we do add to our faith such and such things we shall never fall; that is, if such things abound in us we shall never fall. Let us give more earnest heed that we shall not regret that we have striven to keep the commandments of the Lord.

ON JOB, V, 17.

Behold, happy is the man whom the Lord correcteth, therefore despise not thou the chastening of the Almighty.

This man was found faithful in the sight of his God, and he saw fit to try him in various ways. In the first place while his sons and daughters were feasting, the Sabeans fell upon his oxen, and asses and destroyed them all, and his servants with them. His sheep which were feeding were consumed with those that were tending them. The Caldeans fell upon the camels and carried them away, and slew the servants with the edge of the sword. And again another messenger came and said, thy sons and daughters were eating and drinking wine in their eldest brother's house, and there came a great wind from the wilderness and smote the corners of the house and it fell upon them and they died.

Then Job arose, and rent his mantle, and shaved his head, and fell down, and worshipped God and said: Naked came I into the world, and naked shall I return; the Lord gave and the Lord hath taken away, and blessed be the name of the Lord.

And there was another day when the Sons of God came to present themselves before the Lord, and Satan too presented himself, as he was walking to and fro upon the earth. And the Lord said hast thou considered my servant Job, that there is none like him in all the earth, a perfect and an upright man, one that feareth God and escheweth evil? He was given into Satan's hands for the trial of his faith and love and his integrity; his patience was also tried to the utmost, but in all this he sinned not, nor charged God with folly. His near and dear friends came to comfort and console him, but when they saw him they were speechless, and wept, and for seven days and nights they sat with him upon the ground, for they saw that his grief was great.

And after a lengthy consultation he declared them miserable comforters indeed, and was sensible God had delivered him into the hands of his enemies, and he said his face was foul with weeping, for his kinsfolks had failed him. "Yea, young children despise me, and all my inward friends abhor me: Have pity upon me, have pity upon me, O ye my friends, for the hand of the Lord hath touched me! He was sensible that it came from *his chastening* hand, for happy is the man whom God correcteth. There are many ways in which God tries his chosen ones, for whom the Lord loveth he chasteneth. And why should we be so unwilling to receive chastisement from his fatherly hand? for he does not willingly afflict, but as we are all sinners by nature, so of course we are by practice, in a higher or lower degree. Sometimes our inclinations are crossed and we feel a great reluctance to being in subjection to the just requirement of God. We do not like to meet with disappointments and crosses, but when our will is made subject to his will, then is peace and safety.   It is then we are made to cry,—Unless the Lord had been my help my soul had almost dwelt in silence. When I said,—My foot slipped, thy mercy O Lord held me up.

When dangers stand thick around and Satan as it were, let loose upon us, it is then we call upon God for help and his ear is open to our complaints, were it not for his kind rebukes we should be rebellious still; our natures do not like to feel the rod, but we must wait until our hearts lie submissive at his will, then happy is the man whom God correcteth; therefore despise not thou, the chastening of the Almighty. The wind from the wilderness partook of its own nature. The world is called a wilderness, and while our souls are astray from God we are exposed to all its delusions and errors.

ON PSALMS, CXXXVIII, 6.

Though the Lord be high, yet hath he respect unto the lowly: but the proud he knoweth afar off.

The Psalmist declares he will praise the Lord with his whole heart before the gods; that is, earthly gods, which are made by man. Whether it be gold or silver, iron or clay, it matters not what the people of the world hold in high estimation. God should be praised, for God is a spirit, and he saith,—"I will worship towards thy holy temple, and praise his holy name, for thou hast magnified thy *word*." His word too was precious in his sight, for he saith again: "All the kings of the earth shall praise thee, O Lord, when they hear the words of thy mouth." Although David at certain times strayed, yet he had correct views of Deity, and his heart was often filled with praise; but sometimes he would be brought very low, in consequence of a just sense of sin; yet his confidence was not shaken, for he says, —In the day when I cried thou answeredst me. Though I walk in the midst of trouble thou wilt revive me, thou art my refuge and my portion. Quicken me O Lord, for thy namesake; for thy righteousness sake bring my soul out of trouble." In regard to his confidence he says: I know that the Lord will maintain the cause of the afflicted. For the Lord hath chosen Zion; he hath desired it for his habitation, this is my rest forever. Though the Lord be high he condescends to those of low estate, God looks with an impartial eye. Upon all those that fear his name, will the Son of righteousness arise with healing on his wings. We ought to rejoice that he is high, and also that he will condescend to those of a contrite heart, and that tremble at his word. Who by searching can find out God? yet he reveals himself unto us in his word, and by his spirit. Though he is high we cannot have access to him unless we are humble. Neither can we sing the Lord's song in a strange land. We cannot be blessed, without being confident that he can, and will, hear our supplication. The heavens are thine, the earth also is thine.

But the proud he knoweth afar off. It is pride that keeps us at such an awful distance from God. Pride lifts us up, but not to God, for they—the proud—are afar off. Pride goeth before destruction and a haughty spirit before a fall. A proud look and a lying tongue God hates: and he that is of a proud heart stirreth up strife. The proud have led me greatly in division, but he knoweth such afar off. How important then that we should be of the opposite character, such as he brings nigh by the blood of the Lamb! If I do not remember thee let my tongue cleave to the roof of my mouth. O Lord, thou hast searched me and known me, but not in my pride!

If the Saints stray away and in their course find their hearts lifted up with pride, then may we be assured they are afar off: still they are known; for when they cry unto him with their whole hearts, then he flies to their relief, as a father he pitieth them. How important then that we should keep our hearts from pride: as it requireth diligence to keep the heart, for out of it are the issues of life. We should not shuffle through our religious duties, with a careless, or a proud spirit. O for a better heart to love God more, and serve him better! It should be the constant care of the christian to preserve his soul in a right frame.

This I know is an arduous work. We may pray, and unless we watch, we are none the better. We are made keepers; but our own vineyards have we not kept. We first lost sight of God, and sweet communion with him. Were christians duly humbled under a sense of their proud hearts, they would know one another, at a less distance than many do. But be not discouraged with the difficulties of the way, for whom God loves he loves to the end. And that we may be so happy as to have God know us nigh, and not afar off, is the desire of him who loves us, and gave himself for us. O Lord keep us humble, that we may be found careful to obey thy holy commands.

ON DEUTERONOMY, XI, 16.

Take heed to yourselves that your heart be not deceived, and ye turn aside, and serve other Gods, and worship them.

Moses is exhorting the Children of Israel to love the Lord with all their hearts, and keep his charge and his statutes, and his judgments and his commandments always.

He spoke of his mighty works and his peculiar greatness, the miracles which he did in the midst of Egypt, in the days of Pharoah, and how he destroyed their armies and their horses, and Chariots, and how they were preserved while at the Red Sea, and their enemies were drowned. He related to them what he did unto Dathan and Abiram, how the earth opened her mouth and swallowed them up; and says, your eyes have seen all these things, which he did, and by keeping all the commandments, you may, or will grow strong, and go in and possess the land; and not only possess, but prolong your days in the land which the Lord sware unto your fathers, a land that floweth with milk and honey.

It is also a land with hills and valleys. It is a land which the

Lord your God careth for, his eyes are always upon it. The promise was if they loved the Lord with all their hearts, he would give them rain in its season, the first and latter rain, that they might gather their corn and wine, and oil, and grass for their cattle, that they might eat and be full. Then comes in the exhortation,—Take heed, etc. But he does not stop here: he says his laws must be laid up in their hearts, not only hearts, but their souls, and be bound upon their hands, that they might be continually before them, that they might teach it to their children. It was to be done with diligence, because life and death were set before them, a blessing and a curse: a blessing if they obeyed the commandments of the Lord, and a curse if they did not obey. They were not to offer burnt-offerings in every place, only where the Lord should choose. They were to take heed not to forsake the Levites. He often tells them to take heed not to enquire after the practices of those who worshipped idols; for Moses under God, thought that they were in danger only by asking,—how these Nations did serve their Gods? even so will I do likewise. They were not only commanded to build altars and do sacrifice thereon, but they were to pull down and destroy those that were erected for idolatry. God hates idolatrous worship, ye *shall* overthrow their altars and break their pillars, and burn their groves with fire, and ye shall hew down the graven images of their Gods, and destroy the names of them out of that place. They were to do all this, before they could enter into the land which was promised them. For ye are not as yet come to the rest, and to the inheritance which the Lord your God giveth you. Take heed to yourselves that your heart be not deceived, for the heart is to be established:—for the thoughts of the heart are ruin, and require to be guarded; for if the heart is not right, then shall we turn aside and serve other Gods; not only serve them but worship them also; and that is a crime of no small magnitude: for God hath said,—Thou shalt have no other Gods beside me. There is but one only living and true God and him shalt thou serve. Upon those that keep God's commandments, shall the rain of heaven descend, and cause the heart to flourish and bring forth fruit in abundance. There shall no man be able to stand before thee. Those Nations which were driven out hearkened unto observers of times, and unto diviners, but as for thee, the Lord thy God hath not suffered thee so to do.

He will protect those he loves, for if we keep his commands, he will not suffer us to be moved:—Therefore take heed that ye worship nought but God.

ON JEREMIAH, II, 13.

For my people have committed two evils; they have forsaken me, the fountain of living waters, and hewed them out cisterns, broken cisterns that can hold no water.

God by the prophet Jeremiah, describes the sins of the children of Israel, they were often reproved for their rebellion and love to strangers. Why trimmest thou thy way to seek love? My people have committed two evils, they have forsaken me, and out of that springs innumerable evils, they made themselves Gods that could not save them. But where are thy Gods that thou hast made thee? let them arise if they can save thee in the time of thy trouble. Thine own wickedness shall correct thee· He says how canst thou say I am not polluted, when I have broken thy yoke and burst thy bands? yet hast thou transgressed under every green tree. I had planted thee a noble vine, wholly a right seed; how then art thou turned into the degener⁻ate plant of a strange vine unto me? Should you wash with nitre, and take thee much soap, yet thine iniquities are marked before me saith the Lord!

O generation see ye the word of the Lord. Have I been a wilderness unto Israel? A land of darkness? Yet how often does he call upon Israel to return from her backslidings, and acknowledge her iniquities, and then,—",I will not cause mine anger to fall upon you; for I am merciful saith the Lord." My people have not only forsaken me, but they have hewed out cisterns that can hold no water; they are broken and the Lord with-holds the early and the latter rain.

Truly in vain is Salvation hoped for in any other way, only in Christ. Our cisterns are broken, there is no other name given

under heaven whereby we can be saved; all our good works cannot save us without being mixed with faith in the Lord. Let us
return then unto the Lord for very great are his mercies, and
forsake our many sins that he may heal our backslidings, and
love us freely: and blessed be his name, for his willingness to
save us. Arise and save us, O Lord!

———

ON DANIEL, X, 18.

———

Then there came again and touched me, one like the appearance of a man, and he strengthened me:

And said: O man, greatly beloved, fear not: peace be unto
thee, be strong! yea, be strong! And when he had spoken unto
me I was strengthened, and said,—Let my Lord speak for thou
hast strengthened me.

God saw fit to disclose unto Daniel, what should take place
and what should befall his people in the latter days. He was
much beloved of God and he sent his angel to strengthen him
for he feared God and trembled.

And he said unto me,—O Daniel, a man greatly beloved understand the words that I speak unto thee, and stand upright;
for unto thee am I now sent. After he was prepared he was
made to understand many things that should happen to the
kingdoms, and their overthrow. "The kings shall do wickedly,
and many shall forsake the holy Covenant, but the people that
do know their God shall be strong and do exploits."

Although they seem to be almost overcome by their enemies,
and they shall take away the daily sacrifice and place the abomination that maketh desolate. But they that understand among
the people shall instruct many.

Then he cried and said,—O my Lord what shall be the end of

these things? And he said, go thy way Daniel for the words are closed up and sealed, till the time of the end. But a blessed promise follows: "Many shall be purified and made white and tried. Blessed is he that waiteth and cometh to the thousand three hundred and five and thirty days." God makes use of various ways and means to instruct his Saints; sometimes by dreams, and sometimes by his Holy Spirit in a more powerful manner—his word is already revealed to us—he delights to be sought after by his Saints, and then delights to manifest himself unto them as he does not unto the world. He would not have his children ignorant of the day which is described in his word by his holy prophets, that it should not overtake them as a thief in the night. The shepherds too should be upon the watch to give the alarm, that all might be awaiting for the coming of the Lord. When the soul is relying on Christ, then indeed, dying is but going home, for to be spiritually minded is life and peace:—to walk with God daily is a blessing of no small magnitude: how delightful to feel a hungering and thirsting after holiness. How important then that our souls should reach after God in true devotion, for all we can offer of our natural hearts, is the sacrifice of fools.

It is evident then, that we must be washed in the laver of regeneration, before we are prepared to serve or worship in the sanctuary of the Lord, for nothing is left to our choice in regard to the mode and character of our service. For we are all kings and priests unto God, consequently we should be sanctified and prepared to offer the sacrifice of praise unto God continually; and are we so much exalted, as when we truly magnify his name? for holy worship tends to elevate the soul and lift us up where Jesus is. For the Saints of old were purged and so must we be from dead works by the spirit of God. For this end let us humble ourselves and Christ will lift us up.

Holy God may we feel thy strengthening spirit at our evening oblation, and hear thy voice: be strong! yea, be strong! that we might be greatly beloved of thee!

We know that when he shall appear we shall be like him, for we shall see him as he is, and every man that hath this hope in him purifieth himself even as he is pure. Be patient, therefore, brethren unto the coming of the Lord, be ye also patient, stablish your hearts for the coming of the Lord draweth nigh.

ON MALACHI, III, 16.

———

Then they that feared the Lord spake often one to another, and the Lord hearkened and heard, and a book of remembrance was written before him for them that heard the Lord, and that thought upon his name.

There can much be said in favor of those that fear the Lord. It is with such, the beginning of wisdom, and the eye of the Lord is upon them that fear him, upon them that hope in his mercy. And again: The fear of the Lord is a fountain of life. In the fear of the Lord is strong confidence.

They not only receive a blessing in fearing, but in holy thoughts likewise; for out of the heart proceeds evil, as well as good thoughts. The thoughts of foolishness is sin: and again: How precious also are thy thoughts unto me O God!

When we fear the Lord, we often think of his wonderful greatness and mercy, as well as his judgments; and we will speak often one to another of his loving kindness. When we are in constant fear, our thoughts will be expressed, for out of the abundance of the heart the mouth speaketh, and the Lord hearkeneth and heareth. And it was not that he would or could forget his Saints, that there was a book of remembrance written, but for the sake of our weak capacities, that was inclined to doubt his word. "And a book of remembrance was written before him for *them*, (that is those) that feared the Lord." The lion hath roared, who will not fear? The Lord hath spoken, who can but prophesy? If we fear the Lord it is an evidence we love him, although it is said perfect love casteth out fear.

But this kind of fear hath torment. The Lord taketh pleasure in them that fear him, and those that hope in his mercy. Religion consists in hope, as well as fear and love. It is an anchor to the soul both sure and steadfast. It should be a lively hope that we might delight in the Lord or rejoice. Finally my brethren rejoice in the Lord, and that always, yes and evermore.

The fruit of the spirit is love, joy and peace in the Holy Ghost, we should be poor in spirit that is see ourselves sinners. Nothing can be so delightful as the theme of religion to dwell upon; yet we behold many opposing its reality: sometimes through ignorance, and at other times through wilful depravity and neglect; for there does exist such a union between out natural propensities, and the operations of the spirit of grace, that it may be difficult to distinguish those emotions; as our animal part is affected by the flow of divine things, and continues overpowered by the same.

What a manifestation of the power and glory of God! John discovered in Revelations: "And when I saw him, I fell at his feet as dead. And others that beheld his glory, trembled, and Daniel said,—'And there remained no strength in me.'" And shall we not be afraid of his power? We fear him in love, and we should in revelation; for who can behold God and live? God suffers Satan to transform himself into an angel of light, and then are we subjects of deception. Light is necessary for us to walk by, for we stumble in the night. Therefore we should take more earnest heed, to walk in the light, while we have the light, We may understand much of the scripture and yet be ignorant of the great command enjoined upon us to love God with all our hearts.

The sacred writings are full of directions by which we may know our condition, and when we have a sense of our uncleanness and guilt, we tremble, we groan, we cry out,—Lord save, or we perish; not say my own works have done this, for we are saved by grace, not of works lest any man should boast. The scriptures teach us to try the spirits that we be not deceived, for many false spirits or teachers have gone out into the world, and no wonder we are deceived; for when iniquity abounds the love of many waxes cold. Grace be with all them that love our Lord Jesus Christ in *sincerity*, and then the Lord will hearken and hear, and a book of remembrance will be written before *him* for *them* that fear the Lord, and think upon his name.

———

ON PSALMS, LXVI, 16.

———

"Come and hear all ye that fear the Lord, and I will declare what he has done for my soul."

Let this subject still be continued, for the bible is full and I trust our hearts are not altogether strangers to this fear. In the former text is said,—"And the Lord hearkened and heard," and now it is said,—"Come and hear all ye that fear God and I will declare what he has done for my soul." There appears to be a constant speaking as well as hearing, a declaring too, or telling what has been done for us. When the soul has been brought from darkness to behold the light of God's reconciled countenance, it will exclaim in the language of the text: "Come and hear what he hath done," the soul will leap for joy and cannot be silent. God is greatly to be feared in the assembly of the Saints, and for why? because they speak often one to another and the Lord is with them and that to bless. But as for me, I will come into thy house in the multitude of thy mercy, and in thy fear will I worship towards the holy temple. When the Saints meet together they wish to teach and be taught, and impart spiritual blessings as the Lord has been pleased to impart to them; for coming into *his* house is coming into his mercy, and in the multitude of his mercy. But that is not all,—"And in thy fear will I worship toward thy *holy temple.*" It is required that our worship should be holy, because it is those that fear the Lord that worship him, it is such that say come and hear; who is it that may hear? It is all the families of the earth that may hear what God has done for those that love him.

There are some that come and hear, but *do* not, for their heart goeth after covetousness. The children of Israel sang the praise of God at the Red Sea; God heard them: he guided them through although they oft-times murmured and forgot his many mercies. "He brought me, forth into a large room or place." "In my distress I called upon the Lord—he heard my voice out of his temple." It is evident God hears his children when they cry unto him. But if they break his law, then will he visit their transgressions with a rod—and their iniquity with stripes. Nevertheless my loving kindness will I not utterly take from him, or them, nor suffer my faithfulness to fail. We may fail in all our expectations, but God will not break his covenants: God dwells in Zion and loveth her gates.

Glorious things are spoken of thee—O City of God. Like as a father pittieth his children, so the Lord pittieth them that fear him. Sing unto him—sing praises unto him, talk ye of all his wondrous works. I will sing praises unto my God while I have my being. My meditations of him shall be sweet—I will be glad in the Lord—bless thou the Lord, O my soul! Praise ye the Lord. Who cannot acquiesce in the language of the Psalmist that has ever feared the Lord, and thought on his name, that will not declare what he hath done for our souls.

What a blessed promise in the passage above: "But my loving kindness will I not utterly take from him—nor suffer my faithfulness to fail. It is right that we should be beaten with stripes if we disobey his commandments. The promises of God are yea, and amen to the glory of God. Our salvation must rest upon him, and not on us, poor, blind, helpless, changable, creatures. There is not stability enough in us to obtain a blessing. Grace is our song; and free grace the bottom and top stone; not of ourselves, it is the gift of God.

When we talk of the goodness of God to one another, our heart is enlarged, and ofttimes creates a joy, as well as peace, that is unspeakable and full of blessedness. But what did the Apostle say when Christ walked with them and opened to them the scriptures? did not our heart burn within us? What a blessed effect it has upon us, when we call upon him in prayer, and He inditing our petition; for we cannot think, nor speak, nor act, upright without having his assisting grace. An increase of grace leads us to view more clearly, our moral depravity.

What are all our petitions without holy desires, and faith in the promises?—and what are our praises without gratitude in the heart? If the tree is evil, how can the fruit be good? Neither can the unconverted do service to God, acceptably. We cannot expect it, for the natural heart is a cage of unclean birds.

The work of God then, must not be done deceitfully, but according to the patern shown in the Mount, (or Word;) else he will not be pleased. It is reasonable we should exert ourselves for the truth, for God hath exhalted him to be a Prince and a Saviour for us. The face of the Lord is against them that do evil, and he hateth all the workers of iniquity. What a dreadful thing to have Christ our enemy! If I whet my glittering sword and my hand take hold on judgment, and he will in no means clear the guilty, bind him hand and foot, cast him out where there is weeping and gnashing of teeth, this is a terrible sentence *depart from me!* but we shall see the justice of God so clear, the Saints will say [amen, Allelujah! Who can stand against his great power, for the stars are not pure in his sight. Who is able to stand before the Holy Lord God? How gloomy the contrast from what has been written above: One with lively hopes, and expectations high, waiting for the coming of the Lord Jesus to reveal himself more fully to his Saints; while on the other hand awaits a firey indignation! It is a fearful thing to fall into the hands of the living God, if he is our enemy, his presence is a terror to them that have never had his fear before their eyes. O how shall they escape! O blessed God what more canst thou do? if it was possible for the Son of man to suffer again, sinners would not repent and turn to Thee, but blessed Jesus thou hast died once, for all! And now help us to love and fear thee all the days of our lives, and after death may we drink, in the ocean of thy love, where sin can never enter nor mix with our holy services, but we shall ever sing, holy, holy, Lord God of hosts! Jesus reigns!

ON JOHN, IV, 23.

———

But the hour cometh, and now is, when the true worshippers shall worship the Father in spirit and in truth, for the Father seeketh such to worship him.

We are taught from the sacred scriptures that we are no longer under the law, and that Jewish ceremonies have come to an end. Paul tells us that the law is our school master to bring us to Christ. If it had not been for the law we should not have known sin, neither would it have been imputed, but now are we under condemnation. And instead of going to Jerusalem at set times to worship, because God had promised to dwell in the temple, and to meet with his faithful ones, we are now privileged and blest with the Holy Ghost dwelling in our hearts, whereby we cry,—"Abba Father."

These carnal ordinances, only made way for the establishmen of that spiritual worship, which we enjoy in this life and through eternity, whose kingdom is an everlasting kingdom.

The law made nothing perfect, but the bringing in of a better hope, by which we draw nigh unto God, as Christ has become an high Priest of good things to come, by a greater and more perfect tabernacle not made with hands. Not the washing of divers kinds, nor of meats, nor drinks imposed on them, until the time of reformation—but all things are fulfilled in Christ, all things are finished in the Gospel. For behold I create new Heavens and a new earth. Jerusalem was the place of my rest until she was destroyed in consequence of unbelief and idolatry, and then was that which was spiritual established. And this is the covenant that was made: "After those days saith the Lord I will put my laws into their minds and write them in their hearts.

K

This is the blessed hour spoken of in the above, when the true worshippers shall worship in spirit, for no other is accepted. What a delightful theme for meditation is this! and yet how solemn when we imagine we hear him who has prepared the way, saying,—"O my Father if this cup may not pass away from me except I drink it—Thy will be done!" What love is exhibited towards us! how can such love rest upon such vile creatures all over defiled with sin, as we are. God delights in the obedience of his Son, so he does in our obedience, if he did not, he would not prepare for us a kingdom, spotless and sinless! He became our righteousness; well may we ponder long upon his goodness, and cry unclean. And may we hear the still sweet voice saying, —"Thy sins and iniquities will I remember no more!" To him is the worship of Heaven directed and may we join in the praise of,—" Worthy is the Lamb that was slain to receive power, and wisdom, and honor, and blessing and glory forever." For through him we have access to the Father of Spirits.

Let us rest on his promises and not be destroyed through unbelief, for by faith we stand.

The true worshippers are those that have been purged from dead works; which are under the law but now saved by grace, and the Father seeketh such to worship him. He hath done everything to make us true worshippers. Let us cleanse ourselves from the filthiness of the flesh and walk in the spirit that we stumble not.

The dragon is not destroyed although he has been cast out, his wicked devices are to be feared and guarded against, for in his mouth was a flood of water to destroy the woman, which is the church. But God has protected her from the earliest period to the present time, and ever will, though all hell were raised to oppose it with its utmost power.

Thus the Gentile church is exhorted to stand, having on the whole armor, and not fall through unbelief as did the Jews. Take heed lest there be in any of you an evil heart of unbelief, in departing from the living God.

Lord save from apostacy, and from thy judgments, that must fall upon the guilty. For the hour cometh, and now is, when ' er in spirit and in truth, for the Father seeketh such to worship him.

ON ACTS, IV, 13.

———

Now when they saw the boldness of Peter, and John, and perceived that they were unlearned and ignorant men, they marvelled; and they took knowledge of them that they had been with
Jesus.

It appears that the people were gathered, and those unlearned
men were teaching them, and the Priests and Sadducees were
grieved and fell or come upon them and put them in holds, or
prisons until the next day. Howbeit many of them which heard
believed. The next day all the rulers and scribes and chief-
priests were gathered at Jerusalem to inquire into the matter, for
they had been healing a lame man: they wished to know by what
authority they had done this, or by what power, or in whose
name?

But Peter filled with the Holy Ghost declared to them that it
was by the name of "Jesus of Nazareth whom *ye* crucified," but
who had risen again from the dead. This is the stone which is
set at naught by you builders, they thought that they were
building on the right, or good foundation, but although Priests,
they did not know the power of God, and they consulted what
they should do with these men, for that indeed a notable miracle
hath been done by them is manifest to all them that dwell in
Jerusalem.

But that it spread no farther they must be threatened, and they
told them or commanded them not to speak at all, nor teach in
the name of Jesus. But Peter and John cared for none of their
threats, for they had an eye single to the glory of God. For
said they: "We cannot but speak the things which we have
seen and heard." And being let go they went to their own company and reported all that the chief Priests and Elders said unto

them: and when his company, or his brethren heard, they lifted
up their voice to God with one accord, and said,—" Lord thou
art God which made Heaven and earth"—he referred to David,
who had said,—The heathen raged and the people imagined vain
things against the Lord and against his Christ. And now Lord
behold their threatenings: and grant unto thy servants that
with all boldness they may speak thy word. They did not think
that they were unlearned, but still desired that signs and wonders might be done by the name of Christ. And when they had
prayed; the place was shaken where they were assembled and
they were all filled with the Holy Ghost and they spake the
word of God with boldness. And all that believed were of one
heart and of one soul. And with great power gave the Apostles
witness of the resurrection of the Lord Jesus, which was important, because the Sadducees did not believe in the resurrection of
the dead, nor angels, nor spirits. And great fear was upon
them all. They were bold in the fear of God, for they were
taught by his spirit and who can harm us, if we be the followers
of that which is good? It appears from the writings of the Apostles that there were many in their days that trusted to their
learning, for the world by wisdom knew not God. And by the
foolishness of preaching some are saved, whether learned or
unlearned if attended with divine power. There has always been
a spirit of opposition against the church, for not many mighty,
not many noble are called, but God hath chosen the poor and
despised of this life to confound the wise and mighty, that they
should not trust in their own works, for if we exhalt ourselves we
shall be abased. It is a good hand-maid to religion, but nothing
to be depended upon. Israel was always hated by other nations
And I would ask what is there in the principles of religion that
is not good? The fault is in our own breasts;—a deadly hatred to
God, and his government; we are not subject to his law neither
indeed can be. And when they perceived they were unlearned
and ignorant men they marvelled; no wonder they marvelled,
and so they would now, for the same principle is prevalent, tor
many like to be called Rabbi. They took knowledge of them,
that they had been with Jesus. And O that we might so live
that those around us might be compelled to say the same thing.
That they may not be able to resist the wisdom nor the spirit by
which we speak—help us Lord to be bold as well as harmless in
thy cause.

ON JOHN, v, 39.

———

Search the Scriptures for in them ye think ye have eternal life
and they are they which testify of me.

In this Chapter we are told that Christ healed a man of his in-
firmity which had bowed him down for many years, and that
the Jews upbraided him for doing it on the Sabbath day.

But Jesus answered them,—My Father worketh hitherto, and
I work:—for that the Jews sought the more to kill him.

He still labors with them, and says,—The Son can do nothing
of himself, and,—"That all men should honor the Son, even as
they honor the Father." And again: "He that heareth my
words, and believeth on him that sent me, hath everlasting life.
I can of mine own self do nothing, because I seek not mine own
will." Then he speaks of John bearing witness of him.
"These things I say that ye might be saved."

He further says: "But I have greater witness than John, for
the works which the Father hath given me to finish, the same
works that I do, bear witness of me that the Father hath sent
me;" but he tells them his word does not abide in them, and him
that is sent ye believe not; then he tells them to search the scriptures for it is they that testify of me.

What a oneness between the Father and Son, and then he directs the disciples to be one "Even as we are: my Father in me,
and I in you." How important that we should search the scriptures with a prayerful heart, for out of them we can draw treasures new and old. In them is nourishment for the weak, and
comfort for those that are cast down; reproof for those that are
out of the way, and they are eternal life to those that believe;
therefore search the scriptures and we shall find the stem of

Jesse's rod, the root and offspring of David. Let us search the scriptures for light that we stumble not, and also for love, that we love one another:—for love is the fulfilling of the law. Without love our hearts are yet in the state of nature, and we do not know God: therefore help us to search the scriptures for in them is life.

ON REVELATIONS, XXII.

Behold I come quickly ye servants of mine,
My reward it is with me my call is divine.
Be watching and waiting, for the time is at hand.
To gather together my Saints o'er the land.

Behold I come quickly, now hear what I say:
My Father has sent me, and I must obey. ·
Now put your trust in me and be not afraid,
For I am your helper, and will give thee aid.

Behold I come quickly and blessed is he,
That keepeth my sayings whoever he be,
For in the same manner as I did ascend,
To you I'll come quickly, your ways now amend.

And now my dear brethren: while we wait for Him
May we have on our white robes, that are fine and clean,
That when the bride-groom shall appear for his bride,
Our old filthy garments, may be all laid aside.

Behold|He'll come quickly, may our hearts now rejoice
At the sight of our Saviour, and hear his sweet voice,
Saying, behold I come quickly; O bless that glad name!
May he dwell forever with us, O glory—Amen.

ON READING DANIEL.

———

There was a king in ancient days
Whose heart was darken'd by his ways,
From Babylon he came 'tis said,
Therefore to him homage was paid.

He caused an image to be made,
And thus unto his subjects said:
You must fall down and worship him,
Or my displeasure you will win.

Then to his great men he did say,
Go sound my herald do not stay,
A dedication must be held,
If you obey them all is well.

Whatever time that you shall hear,—
The sound of Lute and Dulcemer,
You must fall down and worship him
Or in the furnace be thrown in.

There were three men whose names we know,
Shaderach, Meshach, Abednego,
Nor were they careful to obey,
The king's command, but still said nay.

Our God is able for to keep
Our bodies from a firey deep
Be it known unto you now,
We will not to your image bow.

The king all in a rage did say,
My mandates now must be obeyed,
So those three men were bound we see,
Because they would not bend their knee.

The king arose all in a haste,
For sure he had no time to waste,
Did we not cast in these three men,
According as we promised them?

The counsel answered true, O! king!
I saw four men walking within,
The fourth is like the Son of God,
He is their strength and rich reward.

'Twas then he made a new decree,
And changed his course as we may see,
Go worship as you think it best,
Your God will save and also bless.

It was not long, before he said,
I had a dream upon my bed,
Which troubled him exceedingly,
And said it was true positively.

These were the visions of my head,
I saw a tree that was not dead,
And it was strong and very great,
So Daniel did to him relate.

The watchers cried aloud to him,
Hew down the tree although a king,
Nevertheless, you leave the stump,
He'll yet yield fruit from that old trunk.

Then Daniel was astonished one hour,
And feared because of his great power,
Tis thee, O king! thou art so strong,
Thy greatness hath to heaven grown.

And they shall drive thee from all men,
A heart of beast be given then,
And after that seven times shall pass,
And you shall surely eat of grass.

And while these words were in his mouth,
There was a voice that issued forth,
Saying, O! king it is for you,
Your body must be wet with dew.

And at the end of certain days,
His heart was fill'd with prayer and praise.
At the same time his reason came,
And blest and glorified God's name.

And now I pray remember me,
As my example you can see,
And shun those Judgments that appear,
Least you may think them too severe.

ON REVELATIONS, I, 7.

Behold he cometh with clouds, and every eye shall see him, and they also which pierced him; and all kingdoms of the earth shall wail because of him, even so—Amen.

John the Revelator was a precious Saint, one that God chose, to commit to his care or reveal things that should shortly come to pass, he was sent to the seven Churches in Asia. His salutation commences thus: Grace be unto you, and peace from him which is, and which was, and which is to come, and from the seven spirits which are before his throne. Unto him that has loved us, and washed us from our sins in his own blood. And hath made us kings and priests unto God and his Father, to him be glory and dominion forever and forever, Amen. Then he declareth to his brethren,—"Behold he cometh with clouds: in like manner as ye saw him ascend, so shall ye see him descend."

He was received up to Heaven in a cloud, and his disciples saw him go, and while they mourned, and gazed they were comforted, for in like manner as ye see him go, so will he return; he once came to redeem lost man and now he will come to glorify. How little our thoughts are occupied on this delightful subject, how little we do realize that he will come. The Jews believed he would come, but did not know him when he did come; but there will be no deception when he comes again, for "Behold he cometh with clouds, and every eye shall see him." His Saints which are scattered over broad creation, will see him and rejoice at his appearance, and those in their graves will come forth to meet him in the air. And not only the Saints, but those that have pierced him, and all kindreds of the earth shall wail because of him. Why will they wail? Because they pierced him by rejection; for he came to save them which were lost, he has wept over sinners and shed his blood for them, and sweat as it were great drops of blood. He has sent his Prophets and Apostles and Ambassadors, but they would not hear them, his angels too accompanied by the Holy Spirit, but they would have none of these things, and no wonder they will wail at his second coming.

Our thoughts do not dwell sufficiently upon the coming of Christ, we are too much like those which say my Lord delayeth his coming and begin to beat their fellow servants.

We are commanded to watch, for in such an hour as ye think not, the Son of man cometh.

He that hath an ear let him hear what the spirit saith unto the churches, he saith, Behold I come quickly, hold that fast which thou hast. He hath long stood at the door and knocked and but few have received him into their hearts!

"Then shall the tribes of the earth mourn, and they shall see the Son of man coming in the clouds of heaven with power and great glory.

Be patient, therefore brethren, unto the coming of the Lord. And again: Be ye also patient, stablish your hearts for the coming of the Lord.

And now, if the brethren were exhorted to be patient, why not now, with the same expectation? for he is now the same object of our affection and hope, as then. We know he has tarried for eighteen hundred years, and both wise and foolish have slept together until now. And what will arouse them? Nothing but the midnight cry: "Behold the bridegroom cometh! go ye out to meet him." It appears that the church has something to do in this matter, for she has been unfaithful in her calling:—but now let her trim her lamps and take oil in them. "For what is our hope, or joy, or crown of rejoicing?" "Are not even ye in the presence of our Lord Jesus Christ at his coming?" He will not forget those whom he gave so heavy a purchase for. He will not leave them comfortless, but will come and reign with them.

Shall we who are expectants of such Heavenly care presume to say,—"My Lord delayeth his coming," and begin to beat our fellow servants, what shall we think of such; but that they will tremble at his approach, for who can abide his coming, or stand when he approacheth, that is to judge the world.

Before this glorious time of Christ's coming, there will be fearful sights, and terrible Judgments, that shall fall upon his enemies. It is compared to great hail stones every one weighing a talent, and men blaspheme God because of the hail. To blaspheme did not render the cause less: No, they had treasured up wrath against this day of wrath!

But the righteous shall shine forth in *his* righteousness, and be made to sit together in heavenly places in Christ.

He says "Ye are dead and your life is hid with Christ in God" and then are we safe? Job saith that those which mourn may be exhalted to safety. "Upon this rock will I build my church and the gates of hell shall not prevail against it."

Who led thee through that great and terrible wilderness and he humbled thee; with fiery serpents and scorpions and drouths where there is no water. Although his promise of safety, yet it is necessary that we should be reproved from time to time, for the natural production of the heart is rebellion against the government of God, and he will make use of such means as shall best please him, and bring us into sweet submission to his will. Not that we shall finally fall to perdition, but fall into sin; and

wound our own soul, but if we abide in his love or commands
we shall never fall, and then when he cometh we shall be ready
to enter into that rest which he obtained for us, by his sufferings,
that when he appeareth we may be like him for we shall see him
as he is. And now, O Lord help us to wait with patience for thy
coming, and not be of that number that shall wail at thine appearance, and call for the rocks to fall upon us to save us from
thy wrath.

———

TO SOLOMON N. PETTIS.

———

I send you here a little book,
  I pray its contents heed,
And gather knowledge in a nook,
  And wisdom when you read.

Full well I know the many snares,
  That for your feet are laid,
And as you tend to worldly cares
  Be careful how you plead.

Be watchful over all your thoughts,
  And also of your ways,
That all the offerings which are brought,
  May end in prayer and praise.

May you like Solomon of old,
  Ask God for the same thing,
Which is more precious than fine gold.
  And you'll his favor win.

May understanding be your guide,
   An Orphan without home,
And when upon your steed you ride,
   Be sure this way to come.

One thing I earnestly request:
   Bad company to shun:
Surely with sorrow you'll regret,
   Do their entreaties spurn.

Accept of this as from a friend,
   For you do know me well,
May I be ever true and kind,
   Though far from you I dwell.

And now I close these few remarks,
   And may they find you well,
These sentiments are from my heart,
   So, Solomon fare-you-well.

LINES.

Now come to Christ whoever will,
And taste free pardon at the rill
While Jesus sits on Zion's hill,
O come to him and drink your fill,
      And love the Lord your God.

If you should say I dare not go,
For I have disobeyed thee so,
Death will come and down thee mow,
Before you willing to him bow,
      And feel his wrath divine.

O! why should you longer delay,
And choose to walk the crooked way?
But look to Christ and to him pray,
That from thy word no more I'll stray,
       And heaven will shout for joy.

Then sing to him who is divine
And say, be all the glory thine,
I am resolved to spend my time,
That I may rest in yonder clime,
       _____ The place prepared for me.

Now pardon Lord our every sin,
And we'll to Thee, our tribute bring,
That our souls be ever on the wing,
Then we will hallelujahs sing,
       Christ Jesus died for me.

Dear Christians all, pray heed the call,
Before you in transgression fall,
Be more like the Apostle Paul,
To shun the wormwood and the gall,
       Which Christ did drink for you.

And when we pass the vale of tears,
Then Christ will drive away our fears,
Our souls should not be in the rear,
But ever prove ourselves sincere,
       In following Christ our Lord.

Then shall we sing without a sigh,
As Christ our Saviour's drawing nigh,
Angels will shout Him from the sky.
Hosannahs to our God on high,
       Salvation through him came.

ON PSALMS, XXXIX, 12, 13.

———

Hear my prayers, O Lord, and give ear unto my cry, hold not thy peace at my tears, for I am a stranger with thee, and a sojourner, as all my fathers were.

O spare me, that I may recover strength, before I go hence and be no more!

The Psalmist said I will take heed to my ways that I sin not with my tongue! for he saw it was necessary to keep his mouth, while the wicked were before him. He was dumb and held his peace: until his heart was stirred, or hot within him; then he spake and said,—Lord make me to know mine end, and the measure of my days; what it is, that I may know how frail I am.

He waited patiently for the Lord, and he inclined unto him, and heard his cry;—he brought him out of an horrible pit and miry clay and set his feet upon a rock, and established his goings, and put a new song in his mouth even praise to God. He was a stranger and a sojourner as his fathers were: notwithstanding he said,—"Lord be merciful unto me, heal my soul for I have sinned against thee."

Abraham also was a stranger and sojourned; and after Sarah's death he mourned and wept for her, and said before all the people, that he was a stranger and a sojourner, and wished for a burying place amongst them, and bought it. And again in Hebrews we are reminded of the same. The whole tenor of scripture and our own experience, go to establish the fact, that we are strangers and Pilgrims here below; and we say by our own profession, that we seek a country, even an heavenly one, wherefore God is not ashamed to be called our God; although our feet get turned out of the way, and we cry unto him, yet he is not ashamed to be called our God. Were he strict to mark iniquity against us who could stand?

O Lord hear my prayer, and give ear to my cry for I am poor and needy, but thou givest liberally, yea, thou art more ready to give than earthly parents are to give gifts to their children. Let thy loving kindness and tender mercies continually preserve me, for innumerable evils have compassed me about: be pleased O Lord to deliver and make me to know my end, and be a stranger and pilgrim. Mark the perfect man and behold the upright, for the end of that man is peace, but my wounds are corrupt because of my foolishness. O spare me, that I may recover strength for we are helpless and stand in need of thy divine assistance—God dwells in Zion. After giving the dimensions of the land and its borders the Prophet closes by saying: "And the name of the City from that day shall be, '*The Lord is there.*'" Shall it never be said that the Lord is in *this place?* O Lord pity our condition and visit us, for except thou dost build the house the people work in vain. Help us to deny ourselves of such things as administer strength to the flesh, such as Idolatry, Hatred, Variance, Emulations, Wrath, Strife, Heresies, Envyings and such like, that we shall not fall a prey to apostacy, for many shall fall away in the last days. But help us to cultivate the fruit of the spirit, such as Love, Joy, and peace—Long-suffering, Gentleness, Goodness, Faith, Meekness, Temperance:—against such there is no law. O the depth of the riches, both of the wisdom and knowledge of God, how unsearchable are his Judgments, and his ways are past finding out. For of him and through him, and to him, are all things to whom be glory forever—Amen.

He that hath ears to hear let him hear. Behold I come quickly. Worship God.

REFLECTIONS IN A STORM.

Behold! the clouds arrayed in solemn order. Hark! hear the
    sound,
While lightnings flash from pole to pole, The orbit round.

While rain and hail descend in stormy mass; We tremble sore,
For fear, Alas! (our natures cannot help) we fear, The day is o'er!

And while we gaze upon the elements around, The wind doth
    blow,
The trees lie prostrate fallen on the ground, All in a row.

Methinks I hear some one behind me ask: Is this the way?
The Arch angel sounds his trump at last, All in dismay!

Look yonder! who is that all clothed in white, Glorious in splen-
    dor?
In Majesty divine, and beauty bright! Who can but wonder?

What brought him here, but love divine? Can earth contain
    him?
And as I shrink before his awful presence, I heard him say:

I've come to gather all my saints to me, For them I died,
Through tribulation deep they've passed you see, Thus he replied.

L

CORRESPONDENCE, ETC.

—

Lenox, Ashtabula Co., Ohio, 1847.

MY DEAR MRS. K:

It was but yesterday that I heard of your affliction, and my mind was so much exercised upon this subject that I dare not refuse writing you a few lines to show the sympathy I have with you in the loss of your dear little Mary. Her beautiful form is before me as I last saw her at our house, constantly. And now dear sister, what I wish to impress upon your mind is, that you should not weep or mourn for her. No doubt you realize from whose hand she came, and by whom she was taken way, and feel assured that the recent rending of the tender fibers of your heart strings can only be healed by the consolation of the Holy Spirit, for whom he loves, he chastens. We believe the kingdom of heaven is composed of such. How often dear sister are we reminded of our frailty, and what insignificant atoms we are in the ocean of life. Let the bitter tears of an affectionate parent be dry, she will not return to you, neither desire thou that she should; for she has escaped many trials and difficulties which she must otherwise have passed through, had she been spared to riper years; do not weep for her, but consider the hand of the Lord hath touched you, and rejoice that he purgeth you to make you bear much fruit. O my friend do not say my all is gone, for many dear friends are left you yet; therefore lift up your head and rejoice that you are so kindly recognized in love; can we realize the richness and sweetness that is produced by such severe disappointments, coming from the hand of our heavenly Father! Could we clearly anticipate the joys which are laid up for all those that serve our Lord and Master: how happy should we be when he makes his appearance upon earth! May we be found watching and waiting for his coming that we enter not into temptations, and that we may hear the blest sentence, come ye blessed of my father, enter into the joys of my Lord.

Yours with due respect,

ABIGAIL HOUSE.

———

Lenox, April. 1847.

MY DEAR BROTHER D:

It is a long time since I felt it my duty to write to you, and when I came to the conclusion, then my courage would fail me, and had it not been in consequence of the visions of the last night I should still have remained silent.

I thought you were in this place desiring to spend a few days, and you called on me for conversation and for certain reasons, we could not converse together as we wished, and we sat like Job's three friends for some time without speaking, at length we both commenced writing, but no one knew our communications. When I awoke my former impressions came to my mind. Now pardon me my brother for taking the liberty of addressing you as one in whom I have the fullest confidence—as a lover of God and also of his children.

My mind was early led to study the doctrines of the Apostles, and primitive churches, and as far as I could understand, its order was ravishing to my soul, and I felt to yield everything to its influence.

When I was but a youth I forsook all my young companions, and many who were more advanced in years, for the sake of this blessed gospel, and I have nothing to regret, only that I did not yield sooner and live more to its rule. And here I am obliged to stop on account of the falling tear, for my zeal enkindles a flame in my bosom that cannot easily be extinguished.

I united with a few in number that were disposed on account of the love they bore toward their Master, and I was willing to be one of that number, and share with them in evil as well as good report. My heart was often made glad in their company, ror they were nearer to me than anything else on earth:—but after the elapse of a few years they wished to be like their neighbors, having the form of Godliness without the power thereof, and from such we are commanded to stay away—after much labor and being told I was possessed of a devilish spirit, the union was somewhat broken, and I withdrew from them; and after, lived quite a number of years alone,—still adhering firmly to the doctrines I was so early taught from the scriptures of divine truth. Yea! divine I say, because nothing of a carnal nature could teach us to separate from worldly things. Christ has declared that his kingdom is not of this world, consequently we ought not to blend them together, for in their natures they are entirely different:— one is darkness, and the other is light—one is selfishness while the other is true benevolence; one is pride, the other is humility of heart—we know the fruit of the spirit is love, joy, peace, long suffering, gentleness, and such like, neither can the carnal man discern the things of God, or the spirit of God, for they are spiritually discerned. There we see God has made a difference, ever since he made a covenant with Abraham, that there should be a distinction between the Jew and Gentile nations:—so in the Gospel day, Christ has come a light into the world, and unbelievers love darkness rather than light because their deeds are evil. By this we can see there is no analogy between the two kingdoms. In the gospel day we are commanded to be not unequally yoked together with unbelievers, for what part hath he that believeth with an infidel? A christian church is an assembly of persons who believe in Christ, and worship the true and living God, and accepts of nothing but spiritual worship:—and it should be rendered according to the word. It is evident that the baptism and the Lords supper were instituted for the benefit of the church to prove her obedience, and love to her head, and that it should be refused to unbelievers, and the church should stand independant of the world in everything pertaining to the kingdom of God:— for the natural heart is at enmity with God; is not subject to his law, neither indeed can be. It is not capable of doing one act in accordance with the divine command.

And now dear brother since the Gospel teaches us such pure doctrines what shall we do? shall we abide by it, or shall we set it aside, and say we will not be ruled by such principles. I have

sacrificed every friend for this principle however trying. That
the Lord may carry me safely through is my prayer,
Yours in Christian Love,
ABIGAIL HOUSE.

Lenox, Ashtabula Co. Ohio, April, 1847.

DEAR BRETHREN:

While reading the Memoirs of Elder
David Marks, page 404, I noticed in his discription of Woodstock
in the town of Oxfork, Brock District, he makes mention of a
set called Christians, and thus he says: "Among their distin-
guishing peculiarities is the order of their meetings. When
they assemble for worship they all sit together and do not allow
those they consider impenitent to mingle with them. On such
occasions they have no one selected to preach to them but any one
who chooses may speak, or pray, or engage in any act of worship
to which his views of duty may lead him. They have separate
meetings in which they preach to the world, but these they do
not call meetings of worship."

Pardon a stranger for taking the liberty to those whom I trust
love and serve our Lord and Saviour Jesus Christ, while many
profess to love the holy cause of God, make it extinct by joining
with the wicked world in their most solemn exercises:—which
God has commanded us to separate from. I have often trembled
at the idea of the church and world joining hand in hand when
their motives and views are so entirely different. It is rising of
thirty years since I embraced the religion of our Lord and Saviour Jesus Christ, and from that time, I have been led to
believe that the natural heart is opposed to all that is good, neither can its possessor worship God in an acceptable manner, and
for this reason I have been obliged to separate from all churches
and stand alone and bear my own responsibility as I understand
the scriptures; and meet the frowns of many who profess Christ;
but I have vowed to the Lord and I cannot go back, come what

may, I must follow the Apostles doctrine, although alone,
Some years since there was such a people in the city of New
York. I would to God there was such a people in this region of
country! I am sure I should be delighted with such a sight:
and although the waters of Lake Erie roll between us, yet my
heart is made to rejoice at the intelligence before described.
Will you have the goodness to inform me more fully of your
sentiments of doctrine, and especially in regard to the new birth
or change of heart, and likewise of ordinances. Such as Baptism and the Lord's Supper, and also the support of the ministry, and their character—for the church has most grossly departed from her primitive state of holiness—in love and
good works, thinking it of little consequence whether we obey
the rules of the Gospel or not—having forgotten that we were
purged from dead works—and should not live to the flesh, for
they that live after the flesh shall die. It is the willing and
obedient which eat the good of the land:—but they that refuse
and rebel shall be destroyed, for the mouth of the Lord hath
spoken it.

I have thought much of you for some time past, and have
wished it was in my power to make you a visit. As I am a
stranger to any one in your country it will be quite uncertain
whether this communication will reach you, if it should, please
have the goodness to return an answer, and you will greatly
oblige your friend, although a stranger,

ABIGAIL HOUSE.

P. S.—Can you give any information in regard to the colored
people in your country, that have escaped from bondage? I understand there is a colony of them not far distant. Be so kind
as to inform me of their condition: we would follow them with
our good wishes, and such things as they need to make them
comfortable, as we are preparing some clothing for them,

Yours,   A. H.

O! ye shepherds, look about you,
  Feed the strong support the weak,
They had better be without you,
  If their wealth is all you seek.

"THE RIGHTS OF WOMEN."

———

"The rights of women, what are they?
The right to labor and to pray,
The right to watch while others sleep,
The right o'er other's woes to weep,
The right to succor in distress,
The right whom others curse, to bless,
The right to love while others scorn,
The right to comfort all that mourn,
The right to shed new joy on earth,
The right to feel the soul's high worth,
The right to lead the soul to God,
Along the path our Saviour trod,
The path of meekness and of love,
The path of faith that leads above,
The path of patience under wrong,
The path in which the weak get strong:
Such women's rights, and God will bless,
And crown their champions with success."

Have the courage to obey your Maker at the risk of being
ridiculed by man.

Kind words do not cost much.

What is the difference between man's own righteousness and
his own light in religion? They are strictly the same thing.

Lenox,——

DEAR BROTHER:

        Some years have elapsed since we have met in social meetings or in the prayer circle; those were happy hours; those indeed were golden moments, long to be remembered; but dark clouds have changed the religious atmosphere, and we must expect many more for we live in a world of change. Our very dispositions change: some times for the better it is hoped, but our natures are the same fountain of uncleanness. It is true our affections undergo a change when they are placed on heavenly and divine things. Then the fruit thereof is holiness, and by and by we shall be changed from grace to glory. Tell me brother W., is the spark yet alive in your bosom? or are you in the dark? I have reason to hope better things of you. In the first place God's promises are sure, whom he loves he loves to the end. A mother may forget her offspring, but God will not forget those he has purchased at so dear a rate. And again:—"No one shall be able to pluck them out of my Father's hand;" for their names are written in the Lambs book of eternal life.

    In the second place we think we have seen the evidence of such a hope. We may be so inconstanced that our faith will not be clear, temptations may surround us, and becloud our Sun, so that its warming influences may not be so clearly felt, and we may be left to doubt our own condition, not on Christ's part, but on our own. But the Apostle tells us to add to our faith, virtue, etc—and then says if these things which he hath mentioned, be in us, and abound, they make us so that we are neither barren nor unfruitful:—and if we do these things we shall never fall: that is, never fall into sin, but walk in the light that we stumble not. What is christianity but that which Christ was while on earth. He is a king, and we are his subjects—his kingdom is not of this world like himself; neither should his children partake largely of the vanities thereof. All the virtues of the heavenly life are the virtues of humility. I desire with all humility to be taught and instructed in the ways of holiness. On the other hand,—Is not the light departed from us, and driven us into the wilderness? If I never more see you may we be

found not in our own righteousness, but in the righteous ness
of Christ not having spot nor wrinkle nor any such thing,

And believe me as ever, your friend in the truth,

ABIGAIL HOUSE.

———

Lenox, Ashtabula, Ohio, etc.

My DEAR FRIEND:

I received yours of the 5th of May, saying your health was as
good as usual, and that your cares were increased in consequenc
of building a house, which will add very much to your toil and
labor, and you know it requires great effort to keep the body
healthy as well as the soul, but when our physical powers are
put on the stretch, then our mental faculties are absorbed too
much; because we are so constituted that matter and mind have
an influence over each other.

We are generally too anxious to make preparation for the
flesh, and neglect the more weightier matters, such as judgment
and the love of God; these things ought we to do, even if we
leave the others undone. We very much desire to have houses
to dwell in, and forget that we have, or can have, a house not
made with hands *eternal* in the heavens, that is worth running
a race for:—but in a race *one* obtaineth a prize: and the Apostle
tells us, "So run that ye may obtain." We cannot accomplish
much good without making exertions and when we are exhorted
to make our calling and election sure, it means to double our
diligence; to exert ourselves, to strive, and let no time be lost
until the crown is secured that fadeth not away.

What a blessing that we have such a price put into our hands
to get wisdom. For the fear of the Lord is the beginning of
wisdom, in getting this treasure there is no danger, we run no
risk it is sure; it is certain, not so with earthly substance for it
takes to itself wings and flies away.

Let me hear from you again, and learn your prosperity.
When you are prospered do not be lifted up for that is a
crime. I trust ere this time you have learned the wiles of Satan!

he tries to worry even if he cannot destroy. He is very suc-
cessful in both. Why is it that we are not more on the look-
out for his satanic windings? It is because we are so slothful in
regard to our eternal welfare, and think it will be easier and
better with us by and by, but we may be assured he will stick
by us to the loss of everything; therefore let us arm ourselves
and when he comes with his temptations, be able to say, "Get
thee behind me Satan." My respects to your family, and believe as ever,   Your Friend,
                                                ABIGAIL HOUSE.

————

Lenox, ——

MY DEAR BROTHER AND SISTER IN THE FAITH:

I received
your communication with pleasure, and it was like cold water
to a thirsty soul. Never shall I forget the kind instruction I
have received from you, nothing is more cheering than to learn
that you are walking in the truth, and that your care toward the
church aboundeth. You no doubt feel the responsibility resting
upon you as you should, having such a charge committed to
earthen vessels, and I hope you will ever be faithful, and prove
yourselves good soldiers for Jesus, who is your captain, king,
and head.

And may you dear sister, as an help-mate assist in all your
calling, teaching the younger women to be sober, chaste, and
lovers of their own husbands; help them by your example to
adorn themselves in modest apparel, not in plaiting the hair
nor wearing of gold but of a meek and quiet spirit, which in
God's sight is of great price. Women anciently did much for
the cause of God; and why should we not now? The Prophet
said woe to the women that art at ease in Zion, and where are
we discharged? The Apostle tells us that they are all one in
Christ Jesus, male and female, bond and free, Jew and Gentile.

Christ talked with the women, and his holy spirit comforts
us now:—he appeared to them while at the sepulcher, he will
manifest himself to us at his feet or at the cross, where he deigns

to meet with his Saints. How beautifully he made himself known to Mary, while she stood weeping at the place where they had laid him? and because she could not find him, she desired him—the gardener as she supposed—to tell her where they had laid him. He said unto her, Mary! as she turned herself, she knew him, and said Master, where dwellest thou? If we will search after him he will be found of us, and we must look for him where he is, not where he is not.

Let men and women be workers together with God, and he will assist in all our hopeful undertakings. He is *more* ready to give *good gifts* unto us, than earthly parents are to give to their children. O what a kind Father! Why should we be so loth to call upon him for every good gift?

Did we realize that we were poor, and blind, and naked, and that he stood rea ly to give us durable riches, and had eye salve for our eyes, and would clothe us with his righteousness, when we truly desired it, then would our tongues be unloosed, and we should sing glory to God in the highest, peace on earth, and good will to man, for he is worthy of all praise.

How hard to be denied the privilege of conversing with you, instead of writing, but I must submit by hoping that you will be sent like Timothy of old, to the refreshing of the Saints.

Many waters cannot quench love, neither can the floods drown it, when God's love enkindles a flame in our bosoms, we say to our cares as Solomon in his songs,—" I charge you by the roes and Hinds of the field, that ye stir not up, nor awake my love, till he please." Just so it is with us now, we ought to watch our temporial concerns, that the s pirit is not choaked, or disturbed, so that when we arise to open the door he may be found, and not say, have you seen him whom my soul loveth? Draw us with the cords of thy love, and we will run after thee. How kindly does our Saviour bear with our infirmities, notwith standing he woos and beseeches with us, to be reconciled to him, for he has taught us in his word, that there is no other name given under heaven, whereby we can be saved—then let us forsake every idol, and to him bow. I hope I shall hear from you ere long, that my joy may be full, for what greater consolation than for the children of God to mingle their spirits and voices in harmonious strains of praise to him who hath washed us in his own precious blood.

We then have no time to lose, but for everything give thanks whether we eat or drink, all should be done to the glory of God, and while we are permitted to stay upon earth, let us consider that we are but strangers and pilgrims, and this can be understood by the humblest minds.

The word describes the church as being driven into the wilderness, and does she yet remain there? Or is she coming up out of the wilderness, leaning upon the breast of her beloved? Come what will, let us be resolved to serve the Lord with meekness and fear. knowing that it is his good pleasure to give us the kingdom through our Lord and Saviour Jesus Christ.

Yours in much Love,

ABIGAIL HOUSE.

Who are these arrayed in white
   Brighter than the noon-day Sun?
Foremost of the sons of light,
   Nearest the eternal throne.

These are they that love the cross,
   Sufferers in his righteous cause,
Nobly for their Master stood,
   Followers of the dying God.

COMPOSED BY JOHN ROGERS.

———

Give ear my children to my word,
  Whom God hath dearly bought,
Lay up his laws within your heart,
  And print them in your thoughts.

I leave you here a little book,
  For you to look upon,
That you may see your Father's face,
  When he is dead and gone.

Who for the sake of heavenly things,
  While he did here remain,
Gave over all his golden years,
  To prison and to pain.

When I, among my iron bands,
  Enclosed in the dark,
Not many days before my death,
  Composed this little work.

And for example to you, youth,
  To whom I wish all good:
I send you here God's perfect truth,
  And seal it with my blood.

To you my heirs of earthly things,
  Which I do leave behind,
That you may read and understand,
  And keep it in your mind.

That as you have been heirs of that,
   Which one shall wear away,
Commit no sin in any wise,
   Keep his ten commandments!

Abhor that arrant whore of Rome,
   And all her blasphemies,
And drink not of her cursed cup,
   Obey not her decrees.

Give honor to your mother dear,
   Remember well her pain,
And compensate her in her age,
   With the like love again.

Be always ready for her help,
   And let her not decay,
Remember your father all,
   Who should have been our stay.

Give of your portion to the poor,
   As riches doth arise,
And from the needy naked soul,
   Turn not away your eyes.

For he that doth hear the cry,
   Of those that stand in need,
Shall cry himself and not be heard,
   When he doth to speed.

If God hath given you increase,
   And blessed well your store,
Remember you are but in trust,
   And should relieve the poor.

Beware of foul and filthy talk,
   Let such things have no place,
Keep clean your vessels in the Lord,
   That he may you embrace.

You are the temple of the Lord,
  For you are dearly bought,
And they that do defile the same,
  Shall surely come to nought.

Be never proud by any means,
  Build not your house too high,
But always have before your eyes,
  That you were born to die,   ·

Defraud not him that hired is,
  Your labor to sustain,
But pay him well without delay,
  His wages for his pain.

And as you would that other men,
  Against you should proceed,
Do you the same to them again,
  When they do stand in need.

Impart your portion to the poor,
  In money and in meat,
And send the feeble fainting soul,
  Of that which you do eat.

Ask counsel always of the wise,
  Give ear unto the end,
And ne'er refuse the sweet rebuke,
  Of him that is your friend.

Be always thankful to the Lord,
  With prayer and with praise,
Begging of him to bless your work,
  And to direct his ways.

Seek first I say the living God,
  And always him adore,
And then be sure that he will bless,
  Your basket and your store.

And I beseech Almighty God,
　　To replenish you with grace,
That I may meet you in the heaven,
　　And see you face to face.

And though the fire my body burn,
　　Contrary to my kind,
That I cannot enjoy your love,
　　According to my mind.

Yet I do hope that when the heavens,
　　Shall vanish like a scroll,
I shall see you in perfect shape,
　　In body and in soul.

And that I may enjoy your love,
　　And you enjoy the land,
I do beseech the living Lord,
　　To hold you in his hand.

Though here my body be adjudged,
　　In flaming fire to fry,
My soul I trust will straight ascend,
　　To live with God on high.

What though this carcas smart awhile,
　　What though this life decay?
My soul I hope will be with God,
　　And live with him for aye.

I know I am a sinner born,
　　From the original,
And that I do deserve to die,
　　By my fore-fathers fall.

But through our Saviours precious blood,
　　Which on the cross was spilt,
Who freely offered up his life,
　　To save our souls from guilt.

I hope redemption I shall have,
  And all that in him trust,
When I shall see him face to face,
  And live among the just.

Why then should I fear death's grim look!
  Since Christ for me did die,
For king and Cæsar, rich and poor,
  The force of death must try.

When I am chained to the stake,
  And faggots girt me round,
Then pray the Lord my soul in heaven,
  May be with glory crowned.

Come welcome death the end of fear,
  I am prepared to die,
Those earthly flames will send my soul
  Up to the Lord on high.

Farewell my children to the world,
  Where you must yet remain,
The Lord of hosts be your defense,
  Till we do meet again.

Farewell my true and loving wife,
  My children and my friends,
I hope in heaven to see you all,
  When all things have their end.

If you go on to serve the Lord,
  As you have now begun,
You shall walk safely all your days,
  Until your life be done.

God grant you so to end your days,
  As he shall think it best,
That I may meet you all in heaven,
  Where I do hope to rest.
            M

Dear Mrs. C.

      You inquire, how it is that I am so familiar with Domestic Animals? In the first place, I answer: I have a great and not only great, but very great bump of Philoprogenitiveness and that is not all. I was early taught kindness to brutes, which has not only produced kindness, but has resulted in excessive fondness. And I have often thought, even if people did not like them, how they could be so cruel! When I look upon the innocent calf, or the tender lamb, I say whose mind so depraved, or heart so hard, as to inflict unnecessary pain upon *them*, or those that have grown to mature age—they are dependant upon man for their sustenance: they are helpless, and power was given to man to rule over them, and he should be careful what measure he metes out to them. The beasts inhabited the earth before man was made, and of course have the same right as ourselves. Although man holds the government, he also must bear the responsibility: they were made subject to him, but never to abuse. Man has a higher intellect, and is made in the image of his maker. Fear was implanted in the brute creation, that is, fear of man—but brute animals were never commanded to love and fear God with all their hearts. They were made for the end, for which they were designed, not for torture, but for the service of man, and are blessings that should be received with thanksgiving. When they have labored day after day, should they be forgotten? or should they through shameful inattention have their meals neglected, or cut short through covetousness? God made grass for cattle, and herbs for the service of man. He has made provision for both. When man puts more upon them than they are able to perform and inflicts cruel blows, let such remember the rod is for the fool's back, and he will surely be punished.

When I take a view of these things no wonder my mind is tender toward them and my spirit grieved within me to tenderness. Let the father then instruct his son while young, and never look on one act of cruelty with any approbation or allowance, but mark the offence with timely and diligent correction! No time should be spared or means neglected, to cultivate the tender mind, for very true is the old adage: "As the twig is bent the tree inclines," and before the heart gets hard by habit, and before it runs into revenge the reform should be made. And let the mother *deny* her babe, that knows no better than to worry and inflict the tender offspring of those we have domesticated in our houses; she should protect them from the violence of the heartless child; she should not only teach but restrain.

Though I have been excessively fond of seeing them in their in their own playful form, yet I have reproved myself, and resolved again, and again that these should not be my chief delights, and that they should not have that part of my affection that belonged to Deity.

I have been astonished to see mothers approbating in their lovely daughters the reading of vain and foolish novels, and the indulging in parties of amusement, and never teaching them kindness! They should be instructed in the cares of domestic life, to be kind and gentle to those under their care.

Thus you see my dear friend why I indulge in such a course, and for a long time have come to the conclusion that it is right. First, because God is well pleased, and commands acts of kindness and benevolence to be manifested toward man and beast, for a merciful man will be merciful to his beast. Second, because they are made very happy on the score of fear. Fear hath torment in us, and why should it not in them likewise? When they are filled with fear, they incline to stray, and perhaps do mischief; when, otherwise, they would have been docile at home; and above all a clear conscience is much to be desired. That the worm is not suffered to commence gnawing in this world which will never cease in another. Oh dreadful thought! Oh solemn change!

May the Lord forgive all such as have abused his mercies through ignorance, and all such as have been more wilfully disposed. May our ears never more be saluted with the groans of the hungry and wounded, nor our eyes with beholding the poor emaciated, and blind, and lame, and galled creatures that came from their Makers hand without blemish—for when he made the world and all things in it, he pronounced them very good. But man's rebellion has brought sorrow, pain and death;—and nothing will liberate one' animal part, but the sentence pronounced in the garden. We have all partaken, for in Adam we have all died: but thanks be to God for the remedy.

If this does not satisfy your enquiries, please give me information, and I will write you again.

Love to all, and believe me your friend,

Lenox.   ABIGAIL HOUSE.

———

Lenox, Sept. ———18-

DEAR SISTER:

You say, you think that had you lived in the days when Christ was upon earth, you could not have done as they did at his crucifixtion. It is very likely that you would not have done as some of them did, for many of them were unbelievers who did not believe what the Prophets had told them concerning the Messiah. They thought him to be a king, or earthly Prince, that should deliver them. But they would not think, if he was such a character that he would spring from such an humble family; neither be born in a manger where the oxen were fed: therefore they would not have him to rule over them, consequently they were filled with unbelief and cried out,—Away with him! crucify him! crucify him! and release unto us Barabbas.

It makes me shudder while I reflect upon the various ways in which I look on and see him crucified in our days of light and knowledge, when we have tasted that he is good: we have felt his spirit to witness with the word, that we are his through redemption, and still we can hear his holy name blasphemed. Isaiah saith: "Ye that make mention of the Lord keep not silence."

There is much for us to do, that love his name. We should

often reprove such as take his name in vain, for God hath said he willnot hold him guiltless that taketh his name in vain.

We deny him when we disobey his commands, when we think our way is just as good. And many times we think it better: being much easier, it will not require as much self denial as the rule he hath laid down in the Gospel. We deny him in omiting to read the scriptures. They are given to us for our comfort, and to guide us on our way that we stumble not. If we walk in the spirit, we walk in the light. The spirit and the word agree. We grieve him by neglecting those examples which he has set us; for it is our business to honor and glorify his name while here. It is our duty to be agreed as touching various points in our supplications, and we should meet on the first day to commemorate his death and sufferings,—it should bring to mind how they—his disciples—took down his body, and wrapped it in *clean* linen and laid it in a new sepulchre. This he did for us: —and is he there yet? No! blessed be his name! he is risen to make intercession for us.

Moses was constantly instructing and reproving the Jews in the law which was given to him on Mount Sinai, that they should not omit one of his commandments; but do exactly as he had told them on penalty of his chastisements which he declared should fall upon them. They should be cursed with burning fevers and with consumptions, and with blindness and astonishment of heart, and their lands with drouth;—they should be cursed in the city, and in the fields; he saith: "Take heed, and hearken, O Israel, this day thou art become the people of the Lord thy God, thou shalt therefore obey his voice." These were all types and shadows of the real substance, which we have had, and still we are unbelieving. Should we say,—how shall we know these things since the fathers have fallen asleep? The Lord Jesus whilst here on earth said it was needful that he went away, for then, he would send the comforter. And that bears testimony that his word is truth, for his holy Apostles were inspired by the Holy Ghost, and we have the witness in our hearts, daily that these things are true.

And now a new commandment have I given unto you, that ye should love the Lord your God with all your hearts, and your neighbor as yourself, love, now is the fulfilling of the law.

The children of Israel were often reminded from whence they came; from a land of enemies, a land of bondage, and the Lord brought them out with the strong arm of his power, and nothing but his Almighty power could save them from their grasp. But God made a covenant with Abraham, that there should be a seed that should serve him; and this blessed promise reaches to us Gentiles.

"This is the covenant that I will make with them: after those days saith the Lord, I will put my laws into their hands, and in their minds will I write them." By a new and living way which he hath consecrated for us, through the vail, that is to say, his flesh. Let us draw near with a true heart, in the full assurance of faith to obtain those things promised to us in the Gospel, exhorting one another, and so much the more as we see the day approaching.

Let me hear your views more fully upon this subject, and tell me what you think of Hebrews, xi, in regard to faith, wherefore we receiving a kingdom, which cannot be moved—let us have grace whereby we may serve God.

Yours in Christian union,

Abigail House.

Dear Friend:

Did you ever think what a beautiful chain of circumstances and prophesy the Bible contains in regard to the first and second coming of the Messiah how he was to come, and through what lineage, and how many there were that represented him:—or were typical of him in many instances? Moses was a lively type, how much care for the children of Israel. And when he smote the Egyptian, it was then intended he should deliver his people, and even before that, when he was in the bullrushes and found, and nourished by the king's daughter. It was that same Moses that was called unto the Mount to talk or receive the commandments from God, to deliver to the people to represent the two covenants, to Jews and Gentiles,—"For a new commandment I give you which is love." The bush that was on fire, and was not consumed, shows that God will again restore his chosen people to their own native land, although they have been in captivity for many years;—yet they are not forgotten; nor consumed as a Nation, but will be grafted in again to the good Olive tree!

When we are broken off through unbelief (which many of the Gentiles will be) then will they be received through the preaching of the Gospel, for God is able to graft them in again, they were to separate from other nations and be a distinct people, forbidden even to marry; and so it is in the Gospel day, but how grossly have we departed from his commands in marrying ourselves to the world. Christ is our bridegroom, and head, and the church is married to him by vows that she will be to him and no other.

Christ saith: "Behold I am married unto you," that being the case what will be the consequences when she departeth from the living God? Again how Moses interceded for his people that they should not break one of God's commandments, on penalty of not enjoying the goodly land, that flowed with milk and honey:—so the promises in the Gospel are that we shall inherit eternal life, if we love God with all our hearts, souls, minds and strength.

The other Prophets too refer to Christ, Jonah's case in particular, when swallowed by the fish, he remained in him three days and nights, and so was Christ three days and nights in the heart of the earth. Jonah expected to see the destruction of Ninevah because the Lord had told him to cry in the ears of its inhabitants, that within a set time that great city should be destroyed! and, after many trials, he went and delivered his message, and unexpectedly to him the people repented, and God spared them at that time; but their repentance did not at all reflect on that noble Prophet's veracity. Isaiah saith unto us, "a son is born," etc., and other predictions of the Saviour's coming and indeed all the Prophets were agreed in this blessed event, and time would fail me to enumerate the many passages of scripture in regard to his coming to reign with his Saints, for all pointed to Christ and his church. In these we discover the character, the nature, of the love of the Son of man, although it was said, God at a certain time repented that he had made man upon the earth for their imaginations and thoughts were evil continually yet he has gone on, it is true, dealing in love and mercy. There is no confidence in all that were made, in regard to man, but in him God saith—that is Christ—am I well pleased; and in reply he saith: "Lo! I come to do thy will, O God."

Had not man rebelled there would have been no need of this sacrifice. "He was made sin for us, who knew no sin that we might be made the righteousness of God in him," and thus we are adopted into heirship with the Son. "For an inheritance incorruptible, and undefiled, that fadeth not away reserved in heaven for us." How blessed to rely on such security to be kept by the power of God against the power of darkness.

And now dear friend is this your hope and crown of rejoicing? If so where ought we to be living? And where is the church living? in heaven and is her conversation there? Does she give light to the world, or is she grovelling in darkness, not knowing whither she goeth? O believe me, for surely we shall not go unpunished.

I should like to hear from you on this subject: For they that fear the Lord spake often one to another, and for our encouragement the Lord hearkened and heard. Give no offence.

Believe me your friend in the Gospel,

Lenox.   ABIGAIL HOUSE.

———

MY DEAR FRIEND:
As soon as I heard of thy affliction I felt to inquire of the Lord why is it thus, that some are so grievously scourged, while others are left to go on, and fill up the measure of their sins. It soon occurred to my mind what is said in scripture,—"Whom the Lord loveth he chasteneth," he also is pleased when they repent and turn to him. It brings to mind the case of Solomon, after he had built the house of the Lord and done so much for the name of the God of Israel, and walked in the steps of his father David—and more than excelled him in wisdom, that the Queen of Sheba came to inquire and see his

greatness which far surpassed what she had heard, and she was compelled to exclaim: " Happy are thy men, happy are these, thy servants which stand continually before thee, and that hear thy wisdom." "Blessed is the Lord thy God, which delighted in thee, to set these on the throne of Israel forev r." But Solomon loved many strange women of those nations which God had forbidden—and turned his heart after their Idol Gods, thus showing that his heart was not perfect. And the Lord was angry and said he would surely rend the kingdom from him, When he heard that, he called the Elders of Israel together, and spread forth his hands toward heaven and said,—" Lord God of Israel, there is no God like thee in heaven above, nor on earth beneath." His prayer was very interesting and forcible; he desired his supplication might be heard in behalf of his people, that if they should sin, let their crime be of what sort it may. "Then hear thou in heaven, and forgive," for he acknowledged he only knew the hearts of the children of men—for he it was that did separate them from among all the people of the earth to be his.

God cannot look upon sin with any allowance neither will he pass by our iniquities, he will hide his face from us, and that is to be feared as much as though we possessed a kingdom. Let us strive then my friend to walk in his commandments, and live. Let us thank him for all his fatherly love and kindness, for he knows what is best for us, do not murmur nor complain, although you are grieved and cast down, trust in your head and be cheerful.

Yours in Christian Patience,

ABIGAIL HOUSE.

———

DEAR GIRL:

After hearing from you on the decrees of God, I thought if it were as you say that we cannot help doing just as we do, and what need is there in trying? Yet we do feel ourselves under some moral obligations to adhere to the rules laid down in the Gospel, for when we come short of its true meaning, we will charge God with folly, or more than that, with injustice, and partiality.

Our hearts rise in opposition to his government, and that will show us that we are fallen and rebellious, and have also a disposition to dethrone the Almighty. But what if we do? What then? Can we by our belief change his decrees? Or if we curse, what then? Are we any the better? Hath not the potter power over the clay to make one lump unto honor and another unto dishonor? Shall the thing formed, say unto him that formeth it, why hast thou made me thus?

Whether our views are correct or not, God is the same, and our business is to submit to his will, for he is just. It is not only our duty, but it is our joy and privilege to acquiesce in his divine law, for God is love, and he that abideth in God abideth in love. It is enough for each one to bear his own iniquity. Perhaps you will say that God requires more than you can perform, I think not; for the fulfilling of the law is to love him with all the heart, and our neighbor as ourself: and the latter you think is as hard as the former. You may ask who is my neighbor? It is not always him that hath joined fields, but him that doeth his Master's will; him that is God-like: such should we love, and when we love like that, we shall do our neighbor no harm. "For love worketh no ill to his neighbor." I would recommend that you should read the scriptures, and that will show you your fallen estate, and also the remedy. "Whoso believeth on the Son hath eternal life." Take courage then dear girl, there is a refuge where you may flee and be safe: and that is the *name* of the Lord. Press into the kingdom, for it has come nigh unto you.

Yours with the best of wishes,

ABIGAIL HOUSE.

DEAR SISTER:

I have just read the fiftieth chapter of Jeremiah concerning the fallen condition of Baylon, and the judgements thereof, because she had destroyed the place where the Lord did dwell, the house she had built unto his great name. God's anger was kindled against the proud, and when the king of Babylon heard the prophesy of Jeremiah, his hands waxed feeble and anguish took hold of him. At the noise of the taking of Babylon, the earth is removed, and the cry is heard among the nations.

See the contrast: "In those days, and in that time saith the Lord, the children of Israel shall come, they and the children of Judah together, going and weeping, they shall go and seek the Lord their God. They shall ask the way to Zion, with their faces thitherward, saying, come let us join ourselves to the Lord in a perpetual covenant that shall not be forgotten." "My people have been lost sheep, their shepherds have caused them to go astray, so they had forgotten their resting place." The children of God forgets, but he never forgets those he loves—their "Redeemer is strong, the Lord of hosts is his name." Although Israel is a scattered sheep, and lions have driven him away, yet shall he be restored, for the Lord hath declared it, though their land was filled with sins of various kinds, he has not broken his covenant. "The Lord hath brought forth *our righteousness.*" What shall we learn by "our righteousness" for we read that our righteousness is as filthy rags and so I believe, therefore is it not Christ? "Come and let us declare in Zion the work of the Lord our God."

When Jerusalem was in affliction she remembered her pleasant things of old—so it is with the people of God in this day, when the rod is laid heavy upon them: they will cry out,—O! that it were with me as in months past; then they remembered the *pleasant* things of old. But how are the mighty fallen, fear and a snare is come upon us, desolation and destruction, the gold is become dim, and the fine gold changed. Remember O Lord

what is come upon us, consider and behold our reproach. The
joy of our heart is ceased. "Turn thou us and we shall be
turned, renew our days of old."

Write me soon on this subject more fully, and oblige your
friend and a true well-wisher to the cause.

ABIGAIL HOUSE.

———

DEAR BROTHER:

After reading the visions of Ezekiel concerning
the Sanctuary, and especially the description of the temple, and
the ordinances thereof, the Lord entered into the inner-court
and his glory filled the house, and the prophet fell upon his face.
And the Lord said unto him: "Son of man, mark well, and
behold with thine eyes, and hear with thine ears, all that I say
unto thee, concerning all the *ordinances* of *my house* and MARK
well all the laws and especially the *entering in* of the *sanctuary*." He was commanded to say to the rebellious house of
Israel,—"O ye house of Israel, let it suffice you of all your
abominations. In that ye have brought into my sanctuary,
strangers uncircumsized in heart and flesh to pollute it."

Thus saith the Lord God,—" *No stranger* uncircumcised shall
enter into my Sanctuary which went astray from me after their
idols—they shall even bear their iniquity. But such as kept
the charge of the sanctuary when the children of Israel went
astray, it is they that shall come near and minister unto Me."

Thus we see it is the sanctified which keep the charge, and go
not astray that caused the Lord to dwell there, and established
the name of the city,—"*The Lord is there*." Where, dear
brother shall we go in the sanctuary of the Saints where it can
be said,—The Lord is there? Perhaps you will say come to our
chapel and there you will find him—and another will say no,

you will find him with us. In this way the scripture is fulfilled,
where it saith,—"Lo! here, or lo there is Christ we are to believe
it not," for we have gone so far astray that we may, or are
liable, to take the shadow for the substance. I ask, is it possible that the genuine christian does not know the sweet whispers
of the holy spirit and its operations? Or is it because all classes of
uncircumcised in heart and ears, have entered into the sanctuary
with the presumption of ministering to his holy name, that has
caused Deity to withdraw his reconciled countenance, and
forced him to say as he did to Judah after their revolt.

To what purpose is the multitude of your sacrifices unto me?
I am full, etc. When ye come to appear berore me, who hath
required this at your hands to tread my courts? Bring no more
vain oblations, incense is an abomination unto me.

"The new moons and Sabbaths, the calling of assemblies, I
cannot away with; it is iniquity, even the solemn meeting. Your
new-moons, and appointed feasts, my soul hateth, they are a
trouble unto me, I am weary to bear them. And when ye
spread forth your hands, I will hide mine eyes from you; yea.
when ye make many prayers I will not hear; your hands are full
of blood."

" Wash you—make you clean—put away the evil of your
doings from before mine eyes, cease to do evil—learn to do
well."

There is no chance for dissembling, God will find us out, he
knows every thought, and every motive of the heart.

"Although the daughter of Zion is left as a cottage in the
vineyard, yet shall she be remembered as the City of Righteousness. The faithful City. But she must be redeemed by judgments."

"O that we might return unto the Lord, for very great are his
mercies, he saith,—Let us reason together, though your sins be
as scarlet, they shall be as white as snow, though they be red
like crimson, they shall be as wool " We have every encouragement to walk in the ways of holiness. "If ye be willing and
obedient, ye shall eat the good of the land," but not so with
those who refuse and rebel. "They shall be devoured with the
sword, for the mouth of the Lord hath spoken it. No one shall
escape without repentance, not even the shepherds. "A voice
of the cry of the shepherds and an howling of the principal of

the flock shall be heard, for the *Lord hath spoiled their pastures.*"

"How shall we escape if we neglect so great salvation." Let gentleness and meekness be the constant features of our hearts that when provocation cometh we may find ourselves calm and resigned to the will of Heaven, if it should come even by the hand of our enemies. I confess myself to be a miserable sinner, and have great need of God's help and mercy, to carry me through this vale of tears, but 1 know he delights in pardon, and if we confess and forsake our sins, we shall find mercy.

Let us make one more effort to live so that God may dwell in us to the cleansing of our hearts and ways, so, that he may visit us by his spirit. Then shall we be satisfied when we are like him, or more like him. It is my sincere prayer that he will not cast us off to the disgrace of his cause.

Let me hear from you soon, and believe me as ever,

Your unworthy Friend,

ABIGAIL HOUSE.

DEAR SISTER:

Whilst meditating upon faith, I am led to believe, we do not realize properly its nature. When we pray, we must not doubt, but that we shall receive, and if we have faith, without works, then are we not profited.

Even so faith, if it hath not works, is dead being alone. By faith Moses led the Israelites through the wilderness. Through faith kingdoms were subdued, and many others, too numerous for me to mention. Read for yourself in the eleventh of Hebrews how they all died in faith, looking and waiting for the promises.

The Apostle tells us,—"If a brother or sister be naked and destitute of daily food, and one of you say unto them, Depart in peace, be ye warmed and filled, notwithstanding ye give them not those things which are needful for the body what doth it profit? Why nothing of course. Our faith is made perfect by works. Ye see then how that by works a man is justified, and not by faith only. For as the body without the spirit is dead, so faith without works is dead also. Is any sick among you, let him call for the Elders of the church and let them pray over him, etc., and the prayer of faith shall save the sick.

Elias also prayed that it might not rain, and it rained not. And he prayed again, and the heavens gave rain.

How unprofitable are our lives without a degree of that faith, that works by love and purifies the heart. "Our life what is it? even a vapor as the flower of grass we shall pass away." Those that endure trials and temptations are counted happy, and for our encouragement the Apostle saith,—"Be patient therefore, brethren unto the coming of the Lord. Be ye also patient, stablish your hearts, for the coming of the Lord draws nigh."

And now dear sister shall we be found in faith? Do we anticipate when our Lord shall come of being caught up together with him, and those that have long been asleep, to meet him in the air, and so be forever with him?—O it is too great! for such poor, unworthy worms of the dust. Be comforted my dear sister with the thought, and remain faithful.

ABIGAIL HOUSE.

————

MY DEAR FRIEND:

It is a long time since I have heard from you, and I hardly know where to write to you, it may chance to find you and it may not; if it should, it will serve as a token of friendship, which is of importance to old acquaintances. Formerly, I have been much delighted in your company, and can sincerely wish it could be again received with the same enjoyment, but should we never be permitted to enjoy each others society again, let us hold fast that affection that is deep rooted in our minds. I found nothing wanting in you, but what we term a change of heart, or being born again, to which you have often said you were a stranger: I hope ere this you can say through grace divine, God is your portion, and you will not fear what

man can do unto you. If God be for us, who can be against us?
We know our natures are in opposition to true holiness, for that
reason a warfare takes place that should always be kept up in
good earnest and our carnal minds, brought into subjection to
him who is all, and in all.

Tell me my dear Mrs. S. how it is with you, can you say all
is well? Are you dreaming of heaven in consequence of your
good moral character? a good character is of importance, but if
that is all, rest not contented until you have found that peace
which is like a river, that makes glad the City of our God.

Write me as soon as you receive this, for I have thought of
you much of late,—O could I reach your hand once more! My
heart would leap for joy, but if I never more see you, accept of
my thanks for all your kindnesses to me. I shall never forget
them. Give my best respects to your daughter, tell her to
remember her Creator in the days of her youth, and remember
she must give an account of her youthful vanities. Still let me
say to her, that youth is the best time to seek religion, and
serve the Lord before we get hardened in sin,—and the sweet
influences of the Holy Spirit have less effect upon the mind.
Remember me to your husband and may you go hand in hand,
through this wilderness world, and at last be so happy as to
reign with Christ above, which is the sincere wish of her who
pens these lines; and believe me as ever,

Your Friend,
ABIGAIL HOUSE.

ON READING II OF KINGS, 4.

———

It fell on a day, as Elisha pass'd by,
There was a great woman that unto him cried,
And so in his way, she prepared him a bed,
And as oft as he pass'd, he called and eat bread.

She said to her husband, now I do perceive,
This man is so holy, that him i'll receive,
I'll set in his chamber, a table and stool,
Sure this will I do, if he calls me a fool.

It fell on a day as he partook of his fare,
What shall I give for all her kind care?
Go, call her Gahazi; she came to the door,
A son you shall have, and not any more.

It fell on a day, when the child it grew sick,
Carry him to his mother and be very quick,
He said to his father, my head, O my head!
He sat until noon, and then he was dead.

She call'd to her husband, do send me I pray,
One of those young men, and do not say nay,
For I must go where the man of God dwells,
Why it is neither new-moon; but she said all is well.

She started with speed and led him not slack,
Thy driving for me but let the whip crack,
He saw her a coming, and said to his servant:
Go meet her and tell me, she'll give you her errant.

N

I pray to tell me, and that without guile,
Is it well with thy husband? Is it well with thy child?
And she answered the man it is all very well,
I never will leave you, but live where you dwell.

When he returned back, he walked to and fro,
He then stretched himself upon the child so,
That he sneezed seven times and opened his eyes,
He said to the shunammite, now take thy praise.

A. H.

ON READING MATTHEW, 26.

Come all who love the Lord indeed,
And seek his counsel for to plead,
May you be brought his word to see,
May it be wine upon the lee.

We read what Christ said to his Saints,
That they must watch without complaint.
Can you not watch with me one hour,
To save yourself from Satan's power?

When he came back his soul was pained,
For he found sleeping yet again,
Saying—sleep on now and take your rest,
Surely this way is not the best.

He went again and he pray'd,
He fell upon the ground and said,—
O father if it is thy will
I'll drink of it for to fulfill.

Now they that laid hold on him,
And led him to the Priest's within.
Where Pharisees of high degree,
And hypocrites as you may see.

Then the high Priest did rend his clothing.
What further proof need be disclosed,
For we have heard his blasphemies,
Say, who is it, that smiteth thee?

Now Peter sat upon the ground,
A damsel also came around,
And said thou surely art the man,
Therefore do not deny again.

Immediately the cock did crow,
And that made him tremble so!
He wept because he had denied,
His Lord and Master,—thus he cried:

O Lord forgive for I have sinn'd,
Let me be shadow'd with thy wing,
May I forever faithful be,
Till death and through eternity.

A. H.

———

REVELATIONS, I, 7.

———

Behold He cometh with clouds and every eye shall see him!

Behold now He cometh with clouds from on high,
And all that have pierced him shall lift up their eye,
And wail because they, his spirit have denied,
Ah! sinner, beware, the King then replied.

I am Alpha and Omega, the beginning and end,
How can you reject your very best friend,
I pray you take warning, and do not refrain,
For as sure as you do, you will lose all your claim.

Not so with the Saints, for he saith unto them,
You have stood for my truths in spite of all men,
Now you that overcometh, I'll give you to eat,
Of the tree which hath life, and also hath meat.

Although He had somewhat against some of them,
Yet He'll not reject them, though they've been to blame,
He truthfully said to those without fears,
Be careful to listen, all you that have ears.

Be watchful and strengthen the things that remain,
For I have not found all your works just the same,
You must repent of them and be very quick,
Or I'll remove from you, your own candlestick.

Remember therefore what thou hast received,
And hold fast those things you have learn'd in my creed,
All you that overcometh a robe of pure white,
Shall be given to wear, by day and by night.

Behold I come quickly, hold fast that thou hast,
Be a faithful true witness, or you'll sink at last,
O may the true fire in your bosom get hot,
And each one be willing to stand in his lot.

                                                    A. II.

MY DEAR SISTER IN CHRIST:
When I last saw you we were conversing upon the subject of Christ's second coming. You thought it meant his coming in the hearts of his people by his Holy Spirit, I was compelled to differ in sentiment with you, as I understand the word. The Apostles have occasion in their exhortations to make mention of Christ's love to his Saints, and to encourage them on their way, he often cheers them like this:

2 Thessalonians ii. "Now we beseech you brethren by the coming of our Lord Jesus Christ, and by our gathering together unto him, that ye be not soon shaken in mind, or be troubled neither by spirit nor by letter as from us, as that the day of Christ is at hand. Let no man deceive you by any means, for that day *shall* not come, except there come as a falling away first, and that man of sin be revealed; the son of perdition. Who opposeth and exhalteth himself above all that is called God, or that is worshipped so that he, as God sitteth in the temple God, showing himself that he is God, etc."

1 Thessalonians xiii. "To the end he may stablish your hearts, unblameable in holiness before God, even our Father at the coming of our Lord Jesus Christ with all his Saints. iv—16 For the Lord himself shall descend, from Heaven with a shout, with the voice of the Arch-angel, and with the trump of God: and the dead in Christ shall rise first. xvii. Then we which are alive, and remain shall be caught up together with them in the clouds, to meet the Lord in the air, and so shall we ever be with the Lord. xviii. Wherefore comfort one another with these words."

Again: Titus 2—xiii. "Looking for that blessed hope and the glorious appearing of the great God and our Saviour, Jesus Christ."

Revelations 20. Describes the first and second resurrection John saw thrones and they that sat upon them, and he saw the —"Souls of them that were beheaded for the witness of Jesus, and which had not worshipped the beast, neither his image, and they lived and reigned with Christ a thousand years.

Again: James 5. Be patient therefore brethren unto the

coming of the Lord. Behold the husbandman waiteth for the precious fruits of the earth, and hath long patience for it, until he receives the early and latter rain.

Be ye also patient, stablish your hearts, for the coming of the Lord draweth nigh."

And now dear sister, while I cast my eyes over these sacred pages my heart is filled with astonishment, to see the goodness and forbearance and long sufferings of God to his children, which are so undeserving of his mercies, and when the blessed Saviour said it was needful that he should go away that the comforter should come, I cannot but ask why should he take any notice or have any care for us? But I must stop that inquiry and give thanks to his most glorious name, that he does take any notice of such poor unworthy creatures. I ought to say,—Come Lord Jesus, come quickly. My heart should be so filled with the love of God, that it would cause me to watch, and be sober, until he makes his appearance. It is true that the Apostles, and ancient Christians were looking for h s immediate descent upon the earth, for it was said,—In like manner as he ascended so shall he descend, It is also said that he will come like a thief in the night, and blessed is he that will be found watching. One day with the Lord is as a thousand years, and a thousand years as one day. If Christ will reign upon the earth with the Saints there must be terrible judgment that will fall upon the wicked, and why are we not receiving them from time to time? Again: It is said,—The dead in Christ shall rise first, and we that are alive shall be changed in a moment, in the twinkling of an eye and be caught up. Can we realize his goodness? and are we of that number that will call the King of Saints from his throne to earth again? He once came to redeem lost man, and now he sits to intercede for his Saints, and at the time appointed he will come and receive those who have shed their precious blood for his name, and have denied themselves of every ungodly lust—and have crucified the deeds of the flesh—neither have they done sacrifice to Baal, nor Baals God's.

When I look upon Christ's atoning blood, my righteousness is but filthy rags; yes, filthy rags.

These are but a few remarks on a theme of immense importance. I am soon lost in my own nothingness, and the wisdom and the forbearance of God are beyond our comprehension.

But who does not regard his preciousness to save. He is a God of Justice too, and that we should appreciate; for we at times feel to deal out as we think, justice to our fellows: but God hath said,—Vengeance is mine and I will repay. I acknowledge I have degressed from my first position. I might add many more passages upon our Saviour's second advent, but your views are that he is already come. I think he is yet to appear, and I delight to trace him from the manger to Calvary, from thence to the tomb where he lay, in accordance to the divine will;—he then arose and ascended on high, and led captivity captive and gave gifts unto man. And what were they? He gave the Holy Spirit, he also gave us titles of Kings and Priests unto God— and that is not all, he calls us children, and if children, then heirs of an eternal inheritance which fadeth not away. And now what more can he do? Are we not undeserving? Will anything short of this answer us? Methinks I hear you answer No! with a sigh; feeling your dependance upon his grace, for help and safety.

He has not gone and forgotten his Saints; for he said I go to prepare a place for you:—and if I go and prepare a place for you, I will come again and receive you unto myself; that when I am there ye may be also.

I will not leave you comfortless, I will come to you: because I live 'ye shall live also. O! how closely are those that believe united to the Son of God! He saith again: "I am the vine, ye are the branches," and we cannot bear fruit except we abide in the vine. May God of his infinite mercy cause us to hold out faithful to the end, that we may be saved, not in our own worthiness for that cannot be, but in his alone.

For him to return to earth, is his manifested love; which he has promised to do, and I believe he will do it. And let us wait for the time draweth nigh. Give me your mind more fully, as we have had but a short opportunity upon the subject.

And believe me as ever your friend (too unworthy to be a sister) but believe in the Gospel of our Lord Jesus Christ. Grace bewith you.

ABIGAIL HOUSE.

SISTER C:

Once more let me stir up your pure mind on the subject of the law having a shadow of good things to come, and not the very image of the things, can never with those sacrifices which they offered year by year, continually, make the comers thereunto perfect. In those sacrifices there is a remembrance every year, it is impossible that any other blood should take away sin. Then he said,—Lo, I Come to do thy will, O God. By this offering he hath perfected forever them that are sanctified. Then was there a new covenant made. After those days, I will put my laws into their hearts, and in their minds will I write them. And their sins and iniquities will I remember no more.

This being the case we have all boldness to enter into the new and living way, and draw near with *true* hearts, in full assurance of faith, and hold it fast without wavering, and then are we to provoke one another unto good works, by assembling ourselves together and exhorting one another so much the more as ye see the day approaching. If we sin wilfully after receiving this knowledge of the truth, there remaineth no more sacrifice for sin.

Is it reasonable or suitable that we should return to the law of ordinances? for we are no longer under the law but under grace; we are now brought nigh by the blood of Christ.

God will strip us of all the glories and honors that are not ascribed to *his* name. We must enter into him by a new and living way. The law of worship now is entirely different: with the heart man believeth unto righteousness, and with the mouth confession is made unto salvation.

Israel was a type of the Christian Church in many respects. It was the Priests that worshipped in the inner courts, and so is it now: for all that "Believe are Kings and Priests unto God." And again: "Ye are a spiritual house." Why will we reject the new for the old? And why do we desire to be again in bondage? for then are we debtors to the whole law, circumcision and everything; according to the pattern; there were no non-essentials then, nor are there at the present time. We read of outer worshippers, and what shall we say in regard to such? Can they worship to divine acceptance? What an insult to the spirit of truth to bring in those whom God refuses! "Take heed lest we sin!"

And now, dear sister where are our hopes? Can we look over our past lives and see anything that will justify a belief that we are of that number whom God is the Lord? When we look at our natures, all is darkness and death, but when we lose ourselves in the promises of God, it is then that light springs up in the soul. O God create within us a clean heart aad put a right frame of spirit within us, for without thy grace we are undone! help us to trust more deeply in thy merits than we ever have done! holy Father help us to sink more and more into thy will!

My dear sister, let us study more earnestly the scriptures for they are given us, for our rule to measure ourselves by; and and the Holy Spirit to witness with the word for they too agree!

May our hearts be knit together in love always abounding in the truth for our God is a consuming fire.

I must confess I wander quite too far, as I was speaking of the law and carnal ordinances. Paul was accused of setting forth of strange Gods, because he preached unto them Jesus and the resurrection, when he was passing by and beheld upon their altar (the Athenians) this inscription: *To the unknown God*—his spirit was stirred within him, when he saw the city wholly given to idolatry. And the times of this ignorance God winked at, but now commandeth all men everywhere to repent. Ignorance is a sin and is noticed by the Almighty—1 Cor., x—xiv. "Wherefore my dearly beloved, flee from idolatry." Peter speaks of abomniable idolatries—and what agreement hath the temple of God with idols? "Thou that abhorest idols dost thou commit sacrilege?" "Little children keep yourselves from idols." It is evident it is our duty to worship the living and true God, and he will accept of the free and sincere offerings of the heart. May we accept of the holy sacrifice which has been made for us. "A new and living way not under the old dispensation, the law, but Christ which is our head, Amen.

Yours with sincerity,

ABIGAIL HOUSE.

MY MUCH BELOVED BROTHER IN CHRIST:

I have read carefully that portion of scripture you referred me to, Ephesians 1—2. They are rich truths indeed. For we are his workmanship created in Christ Jesus, unto good works, which God hath before ordained, that we should walk in them, as we have been made nigh by his own precious blood. Now therefore, ye are no more strangers and foreigners but fellow-citizens with the Saints, and of the house-hold of God. And are built upon the foundation of the Apostles and Prophets, Jesus Christ himself, being the chief corner stone which groweth unto an holy temple in the Lord, in whom ye also are builded together, for an habitation of God, through the spirit. What consolation and comfort in reading the blessed word. I need not repeat the word, for you have been made acquainted with it by the same spirit, by the effectual working of his power. I often think of the promises, and some times my heart is made to leap for joy, when I read the prayers offered by our Saviour to his Father for the Apostles; in St John 17: "Neither pray I for these alone, but for them also which shall believe on me through their wound." He also saith: "I pray not thou shouldst take them out of the world, but that thou shouldst keep them from the evil." But when he speaks of the world, what a lamentable sound!

"O *righteous Father*, the *world hath not known thee*;" he adds, I pray not for the world, but for them which thou hast given me." Notwithstanding the care and the love which was manifested to his Saints, yet they were scattered and left their blessed Saviour to suffer alone, although he had overcome the world, yet he tells his Disciples in me ye might have peace. In the world ye shall have tribulation but be of good cheer I have overcome the world. Dear brother let our hearts rejoice that *he* hath overcome the world: that we by the same spirit may overcome also; that we may be one in spirit as Christ and his Father were one; the Saints must partake of the same spirit or be none of his, I would that we were more and more moulded into his likeness, and less conformed to the wicked world. Be ye transformed by the renewing of his word.

Once more let me say if our eternal *all* depended on our own exertions, or ability to save, we should still remain in darkness; for our natures are darkness itself. No rays of divine light but what comes from God, for we cannot think a good thought without being indebted to divine favor; for Christ saith,—" Without me, ye can do nothing."

We may strive till all our efforts are lost, and not one ray of hope appears, until Christ who is our life shall appear with healing in his wings, who is mighty to save.

When we are dead to the world and alive to Christ, the Apostle tells us,—For ye are dead and your life is hid with Christ in God. Then my dear brother are we not safe?

"Who saith is able to pluck them out of my Fathers hands!" This is our hope. What we have committed into his hands he will keep. But some will say is there no fear of deception? I answer there is, but by reading the word with prayerful attention we may know our condition, for love is the first principle in the soul, and if we love God with all our hearts, we shall manifest the same love to his Saints, let them be where they will. Not because they love us, for the Pharisees do the same, they draw nigh unto me with their mouth, and honoreth me with their lips, but their hearts are far from me, in *rain* they do *worship me, teaching* for *doctrines* the *commandments of men.*

We can discover from all the sacred pages the difference between him that feareth God, and him that feareth him not. But there is no need that I should write this unto you, for you are acquainted with the windings of Satan, or you would not have referred me to this portion of scripture. May we be grounded in the truth and built up in the same spirit, and walk in the light of his countenance. May our feet be guided in the paths of peace and virtue, while thousands are walking in the downward road that leadeth unto death, and we will ascribe all the praise, and glory to him that ruleth in the hearts of the children of men.

I feel grateful for your kind care towards me, as the scripture saith, "Care one for another and so fulfill the law." Write me again and be assured it will be thankfully received.

Yours in Christian Union,
ABIGAIL HOUSE.

Lenox, Sept.——, ——.

MY DEAR YOUNG FRIEND:

      I cannot forbear sympathizing with you in the loss of one of your youthful numbers. God has seen fit to call one and leave another, and when it will be your turn none but God knows! Had he reversed the call what would have been your condition? would you have been where hope could not reach your case? if so, why will you delay seeking an interest in the blessed Redeemer who is ready and willing to save all that come unto him? Short of this you cannot be happy:—neither is there salvation in any other. If you die in your sins, where Christ has gone, you cannot reach him. You have not lived even to this age, without having felt the need of having your sins forgiven. Your cry was no doubt,—God be merciful to me, a sinner! where now are those ardent desires, those fervent breathings after forgiveness? O that you would turn to your former anxiety about your soul, and grieve no longer the Holy Spirit; for all is yours, only believe. When you first saw yourself a lost sinner what was your cry? Methinks I hear you say, it was,—"God be merciful to me, a sinner." If you have not found pardon still cry and struggle on, until you find him "whom your soul loves" and then hold him fast and not let him go. God hath declared that his spirit shall not always strive with man. Be not deceived for what we sow that shall we also reap; if we sow to the flesh we shall reap corruption, but if to the spirit, life everlasting. "Choose you *this day* whom you will serve." Do not say because I am young there is time enough; before you are aware the ax may be laid at the root of the tree, and you be a cumberer of the ground. Do not trifle with death for it will surely come and perhaps like a thief in the night. Turn then my dear girl from the ways of folly, and give up all for the sake of him who died for you, be no longer his enemy, fly for refuge to the hope set before you in the Gospel. Eternal pain awaits every unbeliever, but that you may feel the importance of seeking while the day lasts, before the night of death shall overtake you, when no one can work, is the desire of your unworthy friend and well wisher.

ABIGAIL HOUSE.

My Dear Sister:

As the winds blow, and as the foliage changes its beautiful green to a pale red and yellow, so our frail bodies are returning to their native dust, and shows our decay. As our eyes are often beholding those we respect and even love, laid in the silent grave, we say: How long O Lord before our change shall come? The answer is,—"Be ye also ready." If we knew the time the thief would come, we would not suffer our house to be broken. Watch therefore, for ye know not the hour when the thief will come!

The Saints are the salt of the earth, and when one is fallen asleep in Christ, we have reason to mourn on our account, and rejoice on theirs for they have no more sorrow, nor pain. Some are taken in their bloom and spring of life, and others in summer —or manhood, in all their honor and greatness, while others are handed down to old age, which resembles fall and winter; when their snowy locks are whitened for the grave. So the sands run in our glass till the last particle falls, and then we are gone, gone, forever and forever.

Say my dear sister are you ready now to cross this narrow flood, or are you trembling while you see others standing on the brink of everlasting joy or pain, just ready to have their fate fixed, where hope can never come; if out of Christ. "As the tree falls so it will lie—for there is no work, nor device, nor knowledge in the grave whether we go."

Could we realize the unalterable change, I am sure we should be more sober and watchful. And then why do we not? for, sure we are taught by the word; and our own observations and experiences correspond. Nothing will, nor can liberate us from sin but death, and yet how we fear to enter there! O may we find by happy experience, that perfect love casts out all fear, then the arms of love are ready to receive us, and angels ready to beckon us away.

How blest are they who still abide—close sheltered in thy bleeding side. None but Jesus can do us any good. " O for a closer walk with God" is the desire of *my* heart, and I have no doubt but it is the cry of yours.

Pray for me! And believe me dear sister, as ever your true friend in the Gospel.

ABIGAIL HOUSE.

———

Lenox, Sept. —, ——

MY DEAR LITTLE S:

You are so far from here I cannot see you, and I think of you much, and should I write a few lines accept them from a friend:—for you know, when you were still smaller I delighted myself in your company:—as a child your prattles were amusing, and the thought would often occur, what will he be when he arrives to manhood? but the time has not yet arrived, and if your life should be lengthened out until that period, I hope I shall hear no evil of you;—as a lad, you stand high; and I am glad; for it is in youth that the character is formed, and how important that it be founded on right principles. Be thankful then that your instruction has been of the right kind;—had not your parents seen the folly and evil of sin, they would not have known how to instruct their children.

Nothing my son can eradicate those principles but the influence of bad company:—and that, I hope, you will always shun. Let the precepts and examples of your father be set before you, and bind them about your neck. When Solomon was shewing how his parents instructed him—he saith: "For I give you good doctrine, forsake ye not my law." For I was my father's s n, tender and only beloved in the sight of my mother. Enter not into the paths of the wicked, and go not in the way of evil men. Avoid it—pass not by it—turn from it—and pass away. In doing this the Lord shall be thy confidence, and shall keep thy feet from being taken. And as you advance in years read often the 6 and 7 chapters of Proverbs. "My son keep thy father's commandments and forsake not the law of thy mother—if thou be wise, thou shalt be wise for thyself." Look at the contrast: "Who so walketh uprightly shall be saved, but he that is perverse in his ways shall fall at once." "As the whirlwind passeth so is the wicked no more:—but the righteous is an everlasting foundation."

"The way of the Lord is strength to the upright: but destruction shall be to the workers of iniquity." Again: "The way of the wicked is an abomination unto the Lord; but he loveth him. that followeth after righteousness." Who of us will not prefer the way of wisdom." For her ways are pleasantness and all her paths are peace." Who so seeketh wisdom seeketh understanding."

While you remain in the slippery paths of youth, shun its alluring charms of vice and folly, for they will sting like an adder. I hope your religious instruction and your timely heeding the same, will save you from the vortex of woe; how it will rejoice those of your ancestors and put new vigor into all such as feel an interest in your future and eternal welfare. May you grow from youth to manhood, and from manhood to old age—and when you are called to be here no more, may you go down to the grave like a shock of corn fully ripe:—that it may be said, he has died as he lived, in peace.

It is not strange I take a great interest in the rising generation, for as they crowd us off the stage of life, I wish our places might be supplied with those that shall reverence their Creator, and all such as love him.

Do you not wish you loved our Lord and Master? Methinks you are desiring to know the way of life and salvation, but do not know how to obtain it.

O that you could look to him this moment as a precious Saviour and feel his loving presence! I hope if I should be able to see my dear young friend before long, he would be pleased to tell me he had obtained this blessed salvation!

Let your inmost soul cry out,—"Nothing but Christ can do helpless sinners good," he can wash and make you clean, open your heart and let the King of Glory in. Jesus is precious while I write; I hope you will come, and your sister with you, and make us a visit, and then we can converse more fully upon this great and important subject; how plain that youth is the time to serve the Lord. Let God have your first thoughts, and be very watchful over little sins, in that way you fulfill the word. "Keep thy heart with all diligence for out of it are the issues of life." Write me on the receipt of this, and believe me as ever, your constant friend.

ABIGAIL HOUSE.

Remember me to your father and mother, and sister.

MY DEAR YOUNG MISS G:

I was glad to hear from you, by the way of Mrs. ——, who told me many things in regard to your affairs, and among the rest, that you were inclining towards matrimony,—and I would have no objection to that you know, if the man is worthy of your affections, and I presume he is or you would not suffer your attachment to be placed upon him; for you are aware it is for life. Does he possess principles of a divine nature? or are they only strictly moral? from what I heard, his character is good:— if not, do not incline or accept the offer, but shun him as you would an enemy. Is he a gambler, or a tipler, or a Sabbath breaker, or dishonest in his deal, or over anxious for money? or is he unkind to the poor, and above all—is he cruel to the beasts under his care, which the Almighty has entrusted to him? If you can learn he has none of these leading traits of character, join your fortune with his and you shall have my best wishes and not only mine, but community at large, will acquiesce in your noble choice. If he is truly pious choose it rather for kindness is the characteristic of a Saint. Humanity mixed with benevolence is a prominent feature in the christian religion. Can you realize how many times in the course of life, you may stand in need of Christian forbearance, when the cares of a family are pressing upon you:—you will then seek the kind arm of protection, and long suffering, to sustain you under every circumstance. Let me entreat you then to be kind yourself and avoid all occasion of discontent. Let your feet abide at home, and manage your household affairs with prudence and economy, eating your bread without idleness, bringing up your domestics in the fear of the Lord. You will no doubt feel your responsibility as one that must give an account of all that you do, considering you are on probationary ground, and believing that whatsoever is bound on earth is bound in heaven. My dear girl, if you think I am taking too much responsibility, or liberty, pardon me, and I will for the future be more careful. I feel an interest in *your* welfare and in that of the rising generation at large. As soon as convenient, come and visit us; we shall all wish to see you and your ——.

Remember me to your mother, and believe me yours,

ABIGAIL HOUSE.

Lenox, October 5.——

MY MUCH BELOVED BROTHER IN CHRIST:

My mind to-day has been cited back to your boyhood when the Spirit of the Lord was striving with you, and melted your heart into tenderness, and the tears of repentance followed in quick soccession, down the pale cheek of (almost) despair. O what a struggle my poor soul was in for fear you would reject the kind offer of mercy, and that so you would be lost!—lost—forever! O how many make shipwreck of their souls in such a critical moment as this!

It pains my very heart while I write. But we have great reason to rejoice, for the comfortable hope we indulge, at the present time; for it is through grace we are saved.

Nothing my dear brother rejoices me more than to hear you are walking in the truth. It is a long time since I have most earnestly desired that Christ should found again in you the hope of glory. I know we have our ups and downs, tossed and worried with temptations of various kinds:—but I rejoice to-day, that you are found faithful, and once more harnessed for the work God designs to you do. Doubly accursed are those who know their Master's will and do it not;—for the sin of ignorance, is winked at, not passed by without any notice, but observed, according to the crime. Therefore, my brother,

O

let us be careful that our lives correspond, with our best judgment, that will make the penalty more tolerable: for if we wilfully offend, the promise is many stripes. Will the day ever arrive with me of which the Apostle spoke? "He that offendeth not in tongue, the same is a perfect man, able also, to bridle the whole body." I know for one, I have spoken many times unadvisedly with my lips.

I have no doubt but I should have much more cause for joy and rejoicing, did I not feel the need of so much confession! but he that confesseth and forsaketh *shall* find mercy.

I must acknowledge my many and great obligations to you for all your kindness to me, I have found an increase of faith since I last saw you, and may I still continue to grow in grace and in the knowledge of our God. When the power of faith comes, the strongholds of Satan give way. I fear for many in this place yet; but I do not feel that struggle which I formerly have, for there is a number which I believe never will feel the drawing of the Holy Spirit again! O what a condition such a soul is in! "Not one gleam of hope appears!" O that they had been wise, before it was too late!

Well then let us call on those who have not rejected for the last time, and entreat them not to put far away the day of Salvation! For the sake of such let us draw near the throne of grace, and ask God to pardon their sins. How often have I feared we should never be in social meetings again: but there is one consolation: We can both read the same blessed word of truth, which is given for our rule to walk by—and in it is comfort and reproof. My soul is grieved that I have not more ardor and zeal for God when he has shown himself so kindly to me, and not only to me, but to the whole human family.

All things are now ready, in the language of the Gospel, and Jesus will save to the uttermost all that come to him believing. What a pleasure to meditate and contemplate, on the riches of divine things:—how strengthening to the soul to look forward with increasing delight, at the Christian's prospects: that when toils and temptations are over they will "Receive a crown that fadeth not away." Methinks when you read, you are saying,—Glory to God in the highest!

I know there are duties enjoined on the Christian that are too often neglected:—and the one which occupies my mind the most is: "The night on which our Saviour was betrayed, He took the bread and broke it, to show what he was about to suffer for our sakes and gave thanks and said,—'Take eat, this is my body which is broken for you. This do in remembrance of *me.*'"

After the same manner also, he took the cup, when he had supped said,—"This cup is the New Testament in my blood, this do ye, as oft as ye drink it in remembrance of *me.*" For as often as ye eat this bread, and drink this cup, ye do show the Lord's death till he come. And what next follows is but lightly observed:—that is self-examination, for "he that eateth and drinketh unworthily, shall be guilty of the body and blood of the Lord." O my soul what a crime! He eateth and drinketh DAMNATION to himself not discerning the Lord's body. For this cause many are weak and sickly, and many sleep. O my dear brother, how often I am made to shudder at the careless and gross abuse, of so sacred an ordinance. No wonder the churches are sickly, and not only sickly but dead; never viewing the consequences, but dreaming of heaven; and what will their disappointments be? Should they say,—"Have I not prophesied in thy name, and in thy name done many wonderful works? Yet *God will say* I know you not, Depart! But how blessed and happy are the Saints in doing *this* till he comes. Why? Because he saith as I live, ye shall live also. In like manner as ye saw me ascend, so shall I descend, for where I am, there shall ye be also.

How evidently he loves his Saints, when he said,—"I go to prepare a place for you, for where I am, there shall ye be also."

He leaves this as a token of *his* remembrance of us. May we not listen to the "Lo! here's and lo! there's" but keep our eyes upon the one object of our affections, and love him with all our hearts, and our neighbor as ourself.

I wish I was more dead to the world, and then should I be more alive to Christ. What is all the world to us without him? Why, it supplies our natures with food and raiment but nothing can satisfy the immortal mind but to know we are born of God: for "In him all fullness dwells; without him we can do nothing." The love of the world bringeth death, but the love of Christ, brings life and peace, and joy in the Holy Ghost, and this love casts out all fear of future punishment and all that man sees fit to inflict upon us, for it is perfect love. Let us then my brethren persuade as many as we can, to embrace the Saviour, that they may be filled with this love. O how loth the human family is to receive that, which is the best for them, and also they *indeed* are lost without it. Call upon them as an ambassador o. Christ, as though God did beseech them by you, to be reconciled to him. How much there is to be done, and what little time to do it in; therefore let us "Work while the day lasts for the night of death will soon overtake us, wherein no man can work."

Yours in Christian bonds,

Abigail House.

My Dear Girl:

It is but recently that I heard of your affliction, and I feel to sympathize with you deeply, you can hardly realize your loss yet, for every day you need a mother's counsel and kind care, such as no other one can administer to you. I write from experience; I have drank of the same cup of affliction—and it was bitter indeed, for I was much younger than yourself. After many trials with a step-mother I was led to believe there was a reality in religion, but how to obtain it, I did not know. Happily after many struggles, and conflicts I was made to see myself a poor undone sinner. Not till then did I see the need of a Saviour, which caused me to cast all my cares upon him, and then I found him precious to my soul. He was better to me than all earthly friends: besides nothing else could make up the loss.

Now my dear girl, have you been thinking of this way, to make amends for your grief? If so, I rejoice but shall be more joyful when I learn you have found him, of whom Moses and the Prophets wrote. I hope your mind may never be turned aside after vain things, which will sink you lower and lower; then you will be less inclined to seek after holy things. Let me say to you my dear, you never can have a better time:—youth is a blessed time to serve the Lord, before men grow cold, and harder in sin. Their affections are more easily wrought upon, and the cares of this life are not so numerous. How important then, that we should make it our first business to secure an interest in one who is better to us then earthly friends. I most earnestly wish, that you would be like your namesakes of old. It was Mary that chose the good part that should never be taken away. It was Mary that washed her Lord and Master's feet, with her tears, and wiped them with the hair of her head. It was Marys that stood at his crucifixion to see what was done with his body, and it was they that went early to the Sepulchre and found not the body, and went and told the disciples he was risen. It is true the disciples did not at first believe them, but went with them and found it was even as they had said. So likewise should women be active in the cause of their Redeemer, love his name, his nature, his every act.

His name is most precious while I write; I love the narrow path and my delight is to walk in it. Yes, Glory to His holy name! I know it! Are you not by this time saying,—O! that I knew the place where I could find him. I too would fall down at his feet and cry: unclean! unclean! I hope soon to hear that my dear Mary, has obtained this precious salvation; you must come just as you are. Jesus is ready to receive you without money or price. Look at his bleeding side, his hands, his head, his feet hear him cry it is finished. Fear not then—he died for you; only believe that he can, and will save all that come unto him. Come now. To-day if you will hear his voice, harden not your hearts. There are no lions in the way that will harm you: they may roar and strive to frighten you, yet rely on his willingness and mercy to save:—trust in his grace and you will find pardon. Do not deny, but open the door of your heart, and let the king of Glory in, may the Lord bless you in your prayers, when you feel to say,—"Father all I have is thine." "Had I ten thousand hearts, Dear Lord, I'd give them all to to Thee; Had I ten thousand tongues they all should join the harmony." O how can I be denied for your sake! and for the sake of him who died for you. I would to God that all believers were more ready to give them-selves into his hands. Be humble, O my soul and let me praise thee! and keep me from a dull spirit that I may rejoice in the rock and God of my salvation.

May I be an instrument in God's hands of stirring you up to more speed! If you feel you are not safe, give yourself no rest, until you find that rest and pardon promised in the Gospel. Bear with me if I ask again, are you in earnest in seeking the

Lord; if so, your cry is "God be merciful to me a sinner."
And "Lord save, or I perish." Have you confidence in God?
Has he power to save? Do you pray when you are at leisure?
please answer my questions and may the Lord have mercy on
your soul! is the desire of your unworthy friend and well wisher.

ABIGAIL HOUSE.

Remember me to surviving friends.

———

MY MUCH BELOVED SISTER:

   I had almost dispaired of hearing from you, as it had
been some time since I wrote, but last evening as I was about to
retire a lad came in and handed me a letter. I took it and hasti-
ly broke the seal, and found it written by your own hand. I
read it, and it was like cold water to a thirsty soul. You say
you have been sick and nigh unto death, and that you felt no
reluctance in changing worlds: That indeed was a good state of
feeling, and much to be desired in sickness or in health; you
also say your Son T— has become pious, and that creates within
you joy unspeakable; and no wonder, for I feel as though it was
a great cause of rejoicing; we read there is joy in heaven, over
one sinner that repenteth. You informed me of the death of our
friend Mrs. G., but did not say whether she died in peace. If
there had been any alteration in her life, I presume you would
have made mention of it. She was kind hearted and I was fond
of her society, and nothing wanted but a new heart, I have spent
many a pleasant hour with her.

  It brings to mind the words of the poet:

> "Former friends, how oft I have sought 'em,
> Just to cheer my drooping mind;
> But they've gone like leaves in Autumn,
> Driven before the dreary wind."

So our friends are dropping one after another, and soon it will
be said of us, they are gone: Do you dear sister, feel as anxious

as you formerly have done for the things of this life? I think you will answer: I do not. You have two good reasons why you do not—first because the Lord has blest the labors of your hands to a comfortable supply. Second, because he has taught you the vanity of all below the Sun, and that everything is subject to a failure. If we have food and raiment we ought to learn contentment; for what can we enjoy more in this life? Where ever our treasure is, there will our hearts be also. And whatsoever is bound on earth is bound in heaven. I hope we shall be more diligent as we advance in years, in the ways of holiness and be better fitted for life or death as our Master shall see fit or make such use of us as he shall think proper.

Again: You say your minister, Mr. P. is about to leave you, that he has got another call. I would ask what is his call? a place where he can get a greater salary? Or have the people treated him so ill that he is obliged to shake off the very dust of his feet as a token against you!

There is something quite singular in such movements. *All* our ministers call themselves Paul, and in one sense they wish to be or hold to his doctrines, that is where he says: They that preach the Gospel shall live of the Gospel but not like him when he labored with his own hands that he should not be chargeable to any. For though I preach the Gospel, I have nothing to glory of, necessity is laid upon me, and woe is unto me, if I preach not the Gospel, for if I do this thing willingly, I have a reward; what is his reward? Why verily, when he preached the Gospel he might make it without charge and not abuse his power in the Gospel. He did not use this power lest he should hinder the Gospel of Christ. So careful was he in this great matter, he chose to suffer, rather than to take wages, and then goes on to say: For such are false Apostles, deceitful workers, transforming themselves into the Apostles of Christ. And no marvel, for Satan himself is transformed into an Angel of light—therefore it is no great thing if his ministers also be transformed as the ministers of righteousness whose end shall be according to their works. After speaking more fully of his sufferings and the last the care of churches. Our ministers care only for the one, of which they are made Pastor. I have heard some say, that they would not preach unless they could have a support; it is feared they know nothing of the dispensation which Paul referred to. I tremble for their disappointment, when they will claim an entrance--and

begin to tell over what they have done, why, they have prophesied in Christ's name, and cast out devils, and done many *wonderful* works; by this we see they are not transformed, they are
hirelings, and care not for the flock. We will all say that is
not our minister, for he is a good man, he visits all the people
of his parish, rich and poor, and is very attentive to strangers,
and the sick.

That indeed is very good, in and of itself:—but if they do this
for the sake of gain, God knoweth there is no true standard, that
Satan will not imitate. Christ has said that many false spirits
have already gone out into the world to deceive; and these very
deceivers say "We have taught in our streets." It is also said,
we have ten thousand teachers, not many fathers. If there were
many false teachers *then*, how many are there *now?* It is impossible to enumerate, but by their fruits ye shall know them.
They must not be like Eli's two sons, which said—or his servants
—"Give flesh to roast for the Priests, for we will have flesh of
thee;" notwithstanding all the people could say, they would answer, nay, thou shalt give it me now! if not I will take it by force.
When we see the spirit of Belial we should fear.

Do not let us cast off all, because many have turned aside after
Satan; but keep an eye on the chart, that does not vary to
accord with our circumstances: it stands forever true!

There is great responsibility resting upon the servants of the
church, if they are called by the higher power; and if called by
man, then are they men pleasers, and care but little for the
consequences.

Perhaps you will say enough, for the present, and I think so
too; for it is a subject of great importance, and we must all give
an account of the deeds done in the body, whether good or bad.

Will you have the goodness to send me those tracts you made
mention of, and I will return them the first opportunity. Write
me of your progress in the divine life, for many cares tend to
choak the word which *should* dwell in us richly.

Give my best respects to your children, and believe me as
ever your friend and companion,

                                        ABIGAIL HOUSE.

What though this world deceitful prove,
    And earthly friends and hopes remove,
    With patient uncomplaining love—
        Still would we cling to Thee.

I understand, brother G— is rather on the decline; it is to be feared he will not recover, let us pray for him while Jordon's waves around him roar. His wife is very calm.

A. H.

———

MY RESPECTED FRIEND:

I was of late thinking over old acquaintances, and whether you remained the same in regard to your belief in religious things, or rather moral sentiments. You used to say that if a person lived a moral life that was sufficient, and all that was required. Let me say to you my dear sir, that, is right as far as morality and virtue are concerned, and I would now earnestly urge that both Saint and Sinner should adhere closely to the moral law, and should we violate that, in various ways, are we the sufferers? for instance: If we are intemperate in any thing, such as taxing our natures with over much exercise, we suffer in that, or immoderate drink, then our nerves and reason suffer in consequence of that. If we are too strongly excited with angry passions, that not only causes suffering in ourselves, but those around us, even excessive mirth is not convenient for us, but has a tendency to stir up the same passion in others; for every spirit begets its own likeness, and each sin has its own bearing upon ourselves and others.

Thus you see that nature and nature's laws are too often violated and causes more or less suffering, and we pay the penalty in proportion to the offence. But there is a divine law when broken causes true repentance, and tears of grief and sorrow which is felt alone by the inner man, and without this heartfelt sorrow for sin, the penalty can only be described in the word which saith: "He that sinneth shall die and the wrath of God abideth on on him." It is *enough* to have the *wrath* of *God* upon us. I am compelled to believe from scripture and from my own experience that God works upon the hearts of the children of men in such a way as to make them acquainted with themselves in showing to them that they are sinners, and that their hearts are in opposition to his divine law. Were it not so, we should not feel a condemnation resting upon us. The Holy Spirit is doing its work upon our hearts. "Convincing us of sin, of righteousness and of Judgment to come." "Of Judgement because of unbelief." Our hearts are naturally unbelieving, and are putting far away the evil day. I hope these lines will find you a true believer in the Gospel. I will write you again soon, for I have spent my time and paper. In haste.

Yours in Friendship,

Abigail House.

Remeber me to your family, especially to your aged mother.

—

MY AGED MOTHER IN ZION:

Suffer me to address you as one whom I love in the faith: Your thread of life has been lengthened out to a great age and for many years you have been a believer in the truths of the Bible: which has caused your knowledge to be increased, and your long experience has taught you, that man is frail and that everything below the sun is subject to a failure. Disappointments have abounded in all your humble walks of life; and from time to time you may have thought that there was no sorrow like unto yours. I would not say that trials of all descriptions have found their way in your cup; you have not had an inebriate for your husband, nor a gambler, nor a profane swearer, nor many other vices to which men are exposed, and above all one who has broken the marriage covenant and given occasion for excessive grief. From many of these things have you been spared, both in your husband and children, and children's children as well.

It is necessary that we should keep up a constant warfare in our minds, as the flesh lusteth against the spirit, and the spirit against the flesh; for they cannot agree—one follows the law of nature, while the other follows that of grace.

May your life still be spared to instruct more of the rising generation, to be humble and holy; to be virtuous and without blame; teach them to be courteous and kind, liberal; to the

Saints, and others as much as in them lies; in fine, teach them to love God and they will love one another, for love is the fulfilling of the law.

It is brought fresh to my memory, how many times I have seen you pleading for poor sinners, at the throne of mercy. And I too remember seeing the penitential tear drop in quick succescession down the cheeks of the blooming youth, and many of those I trust were wiped away, by the soft hand of mercy, and the accepted ones made to rejoice in the God of their Salvation! But my mother, shall we ever experience such a time again? of the outporings of God's spirit upon our friends and neighbors? Many of our fathers and mothers have fallen asleep in Jesus, for that reason and others, our strength is made weak. May our cry still be, Lord revive us! O revive us!

Although your head is taken away and old age and disease are upon you, yet I trust your confidence is in him who careth for the widow, who are widows indeed. He never will leave those that put their trust in him—

"Even down to old age all my people shall prove,
My sovereign, eternal unchangeable love.
And when hoary hairs shall their temples adorn,
Like lambs they shall still in my bosom be borne."

How glad I am that the promises are extended thus far, and O how I wish we could rely more upon them, and never doubt his willingness and power to save! He gathers his lambs in his arms, and carries them in his bosom, and gently leads those that are with young. You know my aged parent, in the church of Christ, what it is to be in distress for those who are not far from the kingdom of heaven;—how gently you were led on by the Holy Spirit, how much wisdom you stood in need of, what carefulness! yea, what fear, yea, what vehement desires! It can truly be said that such are gently led!

But probably that time is over with you; you must now bear with your natural infirmities such as are incident to old age, pain and disease, and soon death will follow. "The sting of death is sin," but there is a victory to be obtained, and I hope you will shout: "O death where is thy sting! O grave where is thy victory!" It is through Christ we sing the song of redemption.

O how much you need your husband's care and council! Old people require the tenderest care, they may, and do lose their relish for many things, but their affections do not deminish towards those who treat them kindly; their limbs and health and eye-sight, and memory may all fail, yet love never fails, with those who ever had a heart of gratitude. Should your life be spared until you are helpless, I hope you will have kind friends. Your children partake so much of their mother's disposition, that I am inclined to think you have nothing to fear, sometimes, near relatives are the most obstinate and cruel!

I presume you would not say you wished for another life to live it. I mean a natural life, you no doubt wish you had lived a better life, and that I think all Christians can say with propriety, as we have a law in our members, which was against the law of our minds; and we are like the Apostle when he cried out,—"O wretched man that I am! who shall deliver me from the body of this death!" When he would do good, evil was present with him, and so it is with us:—thanks be to God who giveth us the victory through our Lord Jesus Christ!

Shall I ever have the privilege of taking you by the hand again? I do not know that I can expect it. If I never more see you in the flesh, the time is soon coming when our spirits will mingle, increasing in love and joy, it is hoped—and where no sin will interrupt. Sin destroys much of our communion with God.

How much reason for mourning over our unfaithfulness and ingratitude to him who has so much care for us. I have thought for a few days past of the love of Christ. Who of us are willing to die for our enemies! such as revile us, and speak all manner of false things against us, or that take our property, or injure us at all;—we dislike them;—and many times hate them, instead of loving and forgiving them as it is our duty to do. "If thine enemy hunger, feed him, if he thirsts give him drink." etc. But who of us will die for our friends? Shall we be so sluggish still, and never act our part? Come holy dove, from the heavenly hill, and sit, and warm our hearts. This ought to be our constant cry, for more love and light; more self-denial, more knowledge of ourselves, more hatred of sin, and less conformity to the world. I am heartily sick of myself, and wish I could sink more and more into the divine will, and sail in the ocean of pure blessedness, where joy and peace are not so often disturbed by the wicked devices of Satan, and the indwellings of our own corrupt hearts. But I must forbear, as I do not expect to be free from any natural propensity to sin: therefore pray for me, as long as life shall last, that I may be one that shall hold out faithful unto the end, while many make ship-wreck of faith, and their souls draw back, and God hath no pleasure in such.

Yours in the bonds of Union and Love,

ABIGAIL HOUSE.

———

MY DEAR YOUNG FRIEND:

I received yours of the 25th, and will make no delay in answering your kind letter, which came to hand last evening. I could scarcely sleep after reading that you were very thankful that I cared enough for you to write you on the subject of relig-ion. It ought to be a subject of constant acknowledgment of God's mercy and care over us, that he does lengthen out our lives to seek and serve him.

You say your mind has been exercised more of late about your future welfare, and that you do not feel safe in your present condition. I am glad you are thinking, and continue to think, until you are constrained to say that God is love. Should you have a clear view of yourself and the sufferings of Christ for those who despitefully used and persecuted him, you would be astonished and cry out as above, surely God is love! Do not let any thing turn your steady thoughts aside; but read the scrip-tures more frequently, and as frequently be in your closet; keep yourself from vain company, for that will cause the spirit to depart; for Christ's spirit inmost, is a solemn spirit. It requires solemnity to go to the throne of grace, and doubly so when we behold our lost and undone condition. How indeed, can we be cheerful, when every moment we are exposed to death and aftedeath the Judgment? How then, my dear girl, can we be cheerful? or where is the time for amusement?

I must stop here, and confess, I am ashamed while I warn others, that I myself spend negligently so many of my precious moments. But do as I *say*, not as I *do*. There is *one*, whose examples are far better to follow. Follow *his* and you will be safe.

I intend to see you before long, if the Lord wills as I have but a short time to write. If I should fail, have the kindness to write me again. Let me impress this on your mind, that delays are dangerous, and I will still hope when I see you, that you will be able to say: "I have found him, whom my soul loveth." And I will say: "Hold him and do not let him go." O the joys of a young convert! when they can say: "He is the chiefest among ten thousand, and the one altogether lovely."

Yours in friendship,

ABIGAIL HOUSE.

DEAR SIR:

Our Nation wears a gloomy aspect on the account of her being at war, within her own borders; her strength is failing as she becomes disordered, not that she has come to arms but the spirit of rancor, which is to be feared will amount to serious difficulties,—and how can we bear to see our once happy and independent Nation in confusion and Anarchy? It reminds me of the Jewish Nation:—they were once the people God delighted in, and as they commenced worshipping other gods, besides the living and true God, they met with his disapprobation, although the law was given to them by Moses, and Moses received it from God, on the Mount, and the very first and greatest command was: "Thou shalt have no other Gods before me."

"Thou shalt not take the name of the Lord thy God in vain."

"Remember the Sabbath day."

"Honor thy father, and thy mother."

"Thou shalt not kill."

"Thou shalt not commit adultery."

"Thou shalt not steal."

"Thou shalt not bear false witness against thy neighbor—nor covet anything of his."

But before Moses came down from the Mount, they had made themselves an image, for man *will* worship something; and what was the result? Why Moses threw down the tables of stone, on which these laws were written, and that by the finger of God, for he could not endue their dancing and merriment; and called to know who was on the Lord's side—and all the sons of Levi came to him, and he told them to gird on their swords, and slay every man, his brother, and the same day there fell about three thousand men. Thus we see how God hates in both Jew and Gentile, the spirit, and also practice of idolatry.

When our fore-fathers first set their feet on Plymouth rock they did not feel like falling down to worship Gods of gold, nor wood, nor anything made by men's hands, but him only that brought them over the briney deep, the same hand that led the children of Israel out of bondage, that they had so soon forgot: And who of us hath not broken his law? and are we justified? We think the Lord hath fought our battles in by gone days, that we might inherit this, our American soil. Our blessings have been abundant; our land has produced milk and honey. Men servants, and maid servants, and sheep and oxen, and if it were not for the sin of Slavery, I should still hope our Nation might be spared. But when we see idols set up in our churches, as Daniel calls them abominations where they ought not to be, we must look for desolation. God's spirit cannot dwell with idols, God dwelt in the temple until images were brought in— the Jews were very zealous for their law, and so are we:—we still are desirous of our form of worship, whether we have his holy spirit to guide and direct us or not; and that may be an idol. Our ministers preach against all other sins more than idolatry. Coveteousness is idolatry, for he that loveth his goods or money to excess is a coveteous person, and idolator. We may idolize our minister, our churches, our sect, (if popular,) our families, and in fine everything we love better than our Creator himself, is specious or rank idolatry. The scriptures gives us a knowledge of men in the latter days. For men shall be lovers of their ownselves, covetous, boasters, proud, blasphemers, disobedient to parents, unthankful, unholy, without natural affections, heady, high-minded, traitors, fierce, despisers of those that are good, ever learning and never able to come to the knowledge of the truth, etc.; and their folly shall be manifest, and proceed no farther, corrupt minds, reprobates concerning the faith. And now is not our community filled up too much with such characters, and will not God punish us for all our sins? and " Will his judgment always sleep? or will he be avenged on such a Nation as this?" Let these things sink down into our hearts, and reform one and trust the event.

Yours,

ABIGAIL HOUSE.

LINES.

Arise, O Lord with strength divine,
And save a Nation which is thine,
From ruins brink, just at this time—
    Appear for her relief.

We see the rod hang on our land,
Ready to fall at thy command,
And may we all take the alarm—
    Before it is too late.

The yoke is forced upon our necks,
Its galling weight it doth perplex,
And know not what will be the next—
    Perhaps the battle cry.

"O save our Nation!" is our song,
Though we are many thousand strong,
Yet nothing can avenge the wrong,
    Without thy helping hand—

If we like Israel of old,
Suffer thy wrath, which has been told,
May we like them be ever bold—
    And conquer through thy name.

This Nation 's towered in thy sight,
Because she trusted in thy might,
Therefore, we pray, take not thy flight—
    Nor leave us in dispair,

Long have we lived in thine embrace,
And many mercies we can trace,
To *Thee* in every clime and place—
    With over-flowing love.

Still may our hearts to thee o'er-flow,
With grateful praise while here below,
And if our foes should down us throw—
    We still will cling to thee.

Therefore great sovereign we will pray,
That we may walk the narrow way,
Should our vile natures lead astray—
    Thou only can forgive,

Should Slavery's arrant power yet crush,
Our once free Nation in the dust,
We like the Jews will say we must—
    Weep o'er this happy land.
      P

Down sat by Babylon's cold stream,
With heart-felt sense in the extreme,
From careworn cheeks t e tears did teem—
    In past remembrance sweet.

But thou canst still our cause defend,
And may we on thy grace depend,
Be thou alone our guardian friend—
    And we desire no more.

We thank thee, Lord for peaceful days,
Our lot was cast under thy rays,
O! fill our hearts with prayer and praise—
    The glory shall be thine.

Though Kings and Presidents proclaim,
The people's rights they do disdain,
In pride and selfishness to gain—
    Honors they shoul not share.

        A. H.

HIMSELF HATH DONE IT!

Himself hath done it, all—O! how those words,
  Should hush to silence every murmuring thought!
Himself hath done it—He who loves me best,
  He who my soul with his own blood hath bought.

Himself hath done it—Can it then be ought,
  Than full of wisdom, full of tenderest love?
Not one unneeded sorrow will He send,
  To teach this wandering heart no more to rove.

Himself hath done it—Yes, although severe,
   May seem the stroke, and bitter be the cup,
Tis His own hand that holds it, and I know
   He'll give me grace to meekly drink it up.

Himself hath done it—O! no arm but His,
   Could e'er sustain beneath earth's dreary lot;
But while I know He's doing all things well,
   My heart His loving kindness questions not.

Himself hath done it—He who 's searched me through,
   Sees how I cleave to earth's ensnaring ties;
And so He breaks each reed on which my soul,
   Too much for happiness and joy relies.

Himself hath done it—He would have me see
   What broken cisterns human friends must prove;
That I may turn and quench my burning thirst,
   At his own fount of *everlasting* love.

Himself hath done it—Then I fain would say:
   Thy will in *all* things evermore be done;
E'en though that will remove whom best I love,
   While Jesus lives I cannot be alone.

Himself hath done it—precious, precious words;
   Himself, my Father, Saviour, Brother, Friend:
Whose faithfulness no variation knows,
   Who, having loved me, loves me *to the end.*

And when, in his eternal presence blest,
   I at His feet my crown immortal cast,
I'll gladly own, with all his ransomed Saints,
   Himself hath done it—all, from first to last.

THOUGHTS ON DEATH.

—

What is death? It is the separation of soul and body. It is the laying down our corruptable part, to dissolve into its native dust, and our spirits to return to him who gave them; the body is sown a natural one and is raised a spiritual body, for flesh and blood cannot inherit the Kingdom of Heaven—therefore it must be dissolved in the grave, and then raised in a situation fitted to dwell with Christ forever, and forever, or sink beneath his wrath, for as the tree falls, so it will lie, for there is no work, nor device, nor knowledge in the grave, whither we go.

When we sow our fields, we expect the seed sown, to die:—as the Apostle saith: "Thou fool, that which thou sowest is not quickened except it die. For this corruptible, must put on incorruption, and this mortal put on immortality." Death is called the last enemy, because our natures struggle for the last time. It is also called the gate of endless joy to the Saint. There is a sting in death from which our natures recoil. "This sting of death is sin, and the strength of sin is the Law;" but there is a victory to be obtained over death: ("O death where is thy sting? O grave where is thy victory?")—did the Saints but realize that when they were unclothed, they could as is supposed see their former associates, and the ancient Saints, and not only them but the Lord Jesus Christ;—but now we see through a glass darkly, that is our flesh. Why will we dread or fear to enter into Jordon's cold streams; or stand on the brink shivering? fearing to launch away? It is no wonder we tremble when we have our senses, and see ourselves standing as it were, in both worlds and hearing the angel say that time with us shall be no longer; we can hardly help looking back on our unprofitable and sinful lives, and say: How can we be saved? No other way, only in and through the blood and righteousness of our Saviour, the Redeemer of mankind.

Shall we not give glory to the name of Jesus, for opening up a way whereby we can be saved from eternal destruction? May our souls enter into a survey of Divine Providence, or grace, towards us; for while we were undone by sin, God looked upon us with a pitying eye and said, *live!* O thou spirit of wisdom, and love, and pity, accept of a thank-offering from a heart not altogether ignorant of thy mercies. HE hath forgiven me ten thou- and offences. Open thou my lips, and my mouth shall show forth thy praise. O that thou wouldst search me and know my heart, and let me break forth into a song of praise! Let our thoughts be often on death, that when we feel his cold hand pass over our extremeties first, and then reach for our vital part, we may be calm and our minds serene in the trying hour, and trust in him who does a l things well. He has said in his word he will never leave nor forsake such as put their confidence in him.

He knows that it is not good for us to live always here. It is declared that we are strangers and pilgrims here below, and it is a blessing to the Saint, to lay down this tabernacle of clay, which is full of pain and disease, which are the seeds of death, and when it is grown, or arrived at maturity, then comes the sentence: "Thou shalt surely die." The flaming sword is set in the garden to prevent from "Partaking of the Tree of life and living forever." Thus we see that disease and death are affixed to our mortal part, and there is no escape.

But to the sinner this is sad indeed! for there is no change in the grave; as the tree falls so it lies; an increase of sorrow and pain, the worm that never dies is gnawing his guilty conscience, and in dispair, waiting for a fiercer doom. O sinner, that you should flee from the wrath to come! Strive to enter into the straight gate and narrow way that leads to life, which will secure you from that storm w hich will fall upon all those that reject him, who has died for us—is the desire of her who writes this.

ABIGAIL HOUSE.

•

MY DEAR SIR:

   For a long time I have felt it my duty to say some_
thing in regard to the abuse of animals. My heart has been extremely pained when I have seen unnecessary pain inflicted. In
the first place I would speak to the mother, for to her care is
committed the tender infant; they grow active, and want amusement: she with a heart of ambition, and domestic cares gives her
restless child a helpless kitten. The child lays hold of it by the
throat, for it knows no mercy, and of course can show none.
The mother hears its pitiful moans, but does not come to relieve
it from the child's giant grasp, and she too, is aware if she does,
she will only shift the cries from the kitten to the child. As a
son advances in years, his father, perhaps, takes him into the
field, to divert him. His ox, or horse does not quite suit him,
and he inflicts heavy blows upon it, not thinking the child takes
any notice of him:—but ere long the son siezes the whip, and
like his father shows his authority. The father is pleased at this
appearance of manhood and soon lets him carry the ruling instrument; and not without wielding it often. Thus he goes on
from step to step until he becomes expert in managing the team,
to his father's acceptance.

  In all this time his parents should inculcate kindness, teach
him that every stroke causes pain and discontent. The parent
should spare no pains in cultivating the tender mind to be humane; as the natural mind is rather brutish. Perchance the
humane father has a refractory son, who refuses to give heed to
his most noble commands; and sport himself with cruelty. He
should be watched very closely, and if arguments will not do,
chastise him, as he does the brute, for if he grows up cruel, the
amount of suffering that he may cause, cannot be told.

  I would that this subject was more agitated and that community would strive with the parent to teach those that are advancing into manhood, the nature of kindness.

He who gave us life and breath, gave us the beasts of the field for our special benefit, and he who abuses them must be called to an account: and many I fear, have never taken it into consideration that God takes notice of the brute, and of the treatment which they receive; but let us consider first the horse:

Perhaps there is no creature amongst our domestic animals, that affords as much comfort and pleasure as the horse, and perhaps no one called to pass through more suffering; he performs his task with apparent cheerfulness and faithfulness; he labors in the field, on the road, in machines, and in fine, where his master pleases to put him. But if he refuses the work, not understanding what is required, or perhaps through fear, there are many drivers that have but one alternative, and that is, to compel them speedily to comply. But the horse too has a will, and is ruined at once, for such business. It is probable that had the master been more careful and patient, he (the horse) might have performed his task with kindliness, mixed with some awkwardness.

If our business requires haste, the horse is ready to comply with our request, and often delights in speed, and notwithstanding his willing mind, how often is he urged forward by the driver beyond what he is able to go, for the purpose of telling what his horse can do:—time after time, performing double he should do. His limbs begin to fail and he is sold to another, more indiscreet than the former, who finding that he cannot perform his labor sells him to a third, and he perhaps a man of intemperate habits:—and who does not pity a drunkard's horse?

The horse is made capable of carrying upon his back as well as drawing. He generally is willing to do that. There are exceptions to all rules; but I am willing to make this assertion, that, ninety-nine times in a hundred, the beast can be made to obey, and perform, better without such severe chastisement, than with it. They are whipped for trifles, yea, for nothing only to gratify the foolish passions of a race. Ah! foolish, did I say, more than that; they are cruel, and accursed!

It can hardly be said that any other creature is capable of so many kinds of abuse as the horse. Over-worked, over-drove, cut short of his meals, the lash is quite too often used; and when he is examined, he has but one eye, and perhaps none, that serves him as a guide; his head afflicted with sores, with extreme lameness of every description, all denote abuse.

On the other hand, how beautifully he carries himself and with what alacrity he moves and obeys the kind word of his driver, when he is full-fed, and he performs his work with pleasure; and those that ride feel quiet, and composed. And did the young man but realize the beauty of a moderate gait, and the satisfaction which a young lady has with such a partner, I am sure they would be oftener found on the side of safety, and their mother too would feel much better with such a performance.

The next is the docile cow, we cannot touch all their afflictions. In the first place, when they are young they ought to be kindly treated, as they are perfectly ignorant of what is wanted of them. The humane man will be patient, and use the judgment that is given him *above* the brutes; while others render themselves far *lower* by their hasty ungoverned spirits, and so render themselves not only brutal but ridiculous. The cow is not only willing, but glad to be rid of her burthen of milk, and perhaps she has good cause for her stepping, or even kicking, as it is all the way which she has to manifest her pain, and is not that enough, instead of laying on the rod? We ought to use due diligence to effect a cure. Men ought to look to their interest as well as humanity. If he cruelly belabors his cow, she will fail of her milk soon; for she is in constant fear which does affect her quality of milk, and she is also unhappy. She gets tired of standing in one position long at a time—and flies too, are annoying her, by stings, which she cannot resist, combined also with fear. In view of all which, who will not pity the poor cow?

And again: Some are unthinking when they take from her, her offspring, the God of nature has so formed her that she should love her young, and the most of them will run all hazards for its sake, when they think it in danger. And how she will mourn at her loss! and the tender calf when he is borne away perhaps for slaughter with his feet tied, which is painful, and he suffering with hunger and fear, knows not what his fate is, or will be, if it cries, no fond mother to answer or relieve it. And should not man be careful how he uses those under his care? The cow is of infinite value, a blessing from GOD.

I am aware that the tempers and dispositions vary in animals, as it does in the human family, and it requires wisdom and skill, and prudence, and patience, to manage. Power was given to man, because he was made a little lower than the angels, and possesses a higher intellect, that was made in the likeness of his Maker, will in some measure be like him, or ought to be. Some may be so thoughtless or so haughty, as not to concern themselves about such trifling things, and feel no resposibility. While others expect to give account for all these things, as small as they may appear to others.

Thus we see as many dispositions as there is creeping things on the earth, and all rightly understood, might be of great use.

Next, the dog which is of but little use, is subject to much abuse, he is not to blame for being a dog, nor for being ours; but we are to blame for getting him, and then not using him well. There is no creature amongst our domestic animals that manifests so much affection and attachment to his master, as the dog. It matters not what kind of weather, he is always on hand to go at his bidding, and come at his call, wet and cold, tired and hungry, he is not thought of; and if he is, it is with a frown or kick—but not so with all, for some will share with their master in their meals. A benevolent spirit should prevail in our hearts, and lives, and indeed if the heart is tender such acts will flow out.

I have heard some men say that they liked to kill creatures. I do not know how any one can delight in taking life, for the pleasure of taking it; but necessity compels men to do it, and they should do it as humanely as possible, and I have thought that little boys should not be present as it tends to make them hard-hearted and to delight in torturing small insects, when *all* should be taught the contrary. It is our duty to make everything as docile and happy as we can and teach the same to our children, and to others at every opportunity.

I hope dear sir, from these few lines your mind will expand and take the subject into consideration, and do much good. That it may be agitated more and more as the world advances to a close, is the desire of your friend.

ABIGAIL HOUSE.

OF SOLOMON.

Solomon the preacher, was king over Israel in Jerusalem, and when he had a sense of his own unworthiness and the perfection of God, he exclaimed,—Vanity of vanities, all is vanity!—and not only vanity, but vexation. He said there was nothing new under the Sun. One generation passeth away, and another cometh, but the earth abideth forever; he said, I communed with my own heart, Lo! I have come to great estate, and have gotten more wisdom than all they that have gone before me in Jerusalem. He gave his heart to know wisdom. "For in much wisdom is grief, he that increaseth knowledge, increaseth sorrow." He thought to satisfy his mind with mirth and pleasure, but this also he said was vanity. He gave himself to wine and folly: all was vanity. He built houses and planted vineyards; and gardens, and orchards, and trees of all kinds of fruit; he made pools of water, he had much cattle, and servants, and maidens; he got men and women-singers, and musical instruments of all sorts: he got him gold and silver in abundance, and whatsoever his eyes desired he obtained, for his heart rejoiced in all his labors. Then he looked on all the works of his hands, and behold, all was vanity, and vexation of spirit. Then he turned himself to behold wisdom, and it exceeded folly, as far as light excelleth darkness.

Therefore he said he hated life; because his work was grievous, under the Sun: all was vanity. He did not know who should possess his wealth after him whether a wise man or a fool; that was vexatious to him: and his heart took no rest in the night.

For God giveth to a man that is good in his sight, wisdom and knowledge, and joy, but to the sinner he giveth travel, this also, is vanity.

He also said there was a time for everything under the Sun.

And how true, when he said,—He hath made everything beautiful in his time. He had learned from experience that man
should eat and drink and enjoy the good of his labor, for it is the
gift of God. He saw under the sun the place of judgment, that
wickedness was there: and the place of righteousness, that iniquity was there. Then he said in his heart, God shall judge the
righteous and the wicked,

Moreover he said that man and beast all went to the same
place. That is in returning to dust;—but he said the spirit of
man goeth upwards, while the beast goes downwards.

Thus he continues: So I returned and considered all the op-
pressions that are done under the Sun, and behold: the tears of
such as are oppressed, and they had no comforter: their travel
was vexation of spirit. And everything he saw, surely was vanity. He not only preferred wisdom, but recommended it to
others—although he saith there is a just man upon earth, that
doeth good and sinneth not:—yet his counsel is to get wisdom,
for it is better than rubies and more to be desired than gold, yea
than fine gold.

Sometimes we are destroyed by our own wisdom—he makes
mention of this likewise: Be not righteous over-much, neither
make thyself over-wise; why shouldst thou destroy thyself? Be
not over-much wicked, neither be thou foolish; why shouldst
thou die before thy time? But true wisdom strengtheneth the
wise. This wisdom have I seen under the Sun and it seemeth
great unto me.

He told the young man to rejoice in his youth, and to let his
heart cheer him in the days of his youth—but remember that
God would bring him into judgment for all things. Therefore,
remove sorrow from thy heart—and put evil away from *thy
flesh* for childhood and youth are vanity.

And one thing more he had found to his sorrow that was more
bitter than death; the woman whose heart is *snares* and *nets*,
and her hands are bands:—who so pleaseth God shall escape
from her, but the sinner shall be taken by her.

Lo! this only have I found, that God hath made man upright,
but they have sought out many inventions.

After this, he put forth songs which are called Solomon's.

He goes on to describe the love Christ bears to his church, and
in return, the church loves him with all her heart—although she
discovers her imperfections by saying: "I am black but come-

ly." Draw me, we will run after thee," and further saith "Mine own vineyard have I not kept, but still his name is as ointment poured forth, therefore do the Virgins love thee." After losing sight of her blessed head, she exclaimed: "Tell me, O thou whom my soul loveth, where thou feedest, where thou makest thy flocks to rest at noon." The flocks were fed, both young and old "beside the Shepherds tents." Christ has made it the duty of his under Shepherds to feed the flock of God. And while the king sitteth at his table, "My spikenard sendeth forth the smell thereof." When man is in his place, subject to his head, which is Christ; all things are in order, fair, and beautiful. "A bundle of myrrh is my beloved unto me." The nature of religion is pleasantness, and kindness and love.

"Behold thou art fair, my beloved, yea pleasant."

And again he saith: "I am the rose of Sharon, and the lily of the valleys—as the lily among thorns, so is my beloved among the daughters." The christian is like lilies among thorns; liable to be choaked with cares of this world, and its conformities.

Not so when they sit down under his shadows and partake of his fruit, love, joy, and peace, then the soul enjoys great delight. "He brought me to the banqueting-house and his banner over me was love." When a soul is filled with the love of God, it cannot bear to be disturbed, they cannot be willing to lose sight of this sweet enjoyment; and saith,—"I charge you! O ye daughters of Jerusalem, by the roes and by the hinds of the field, that ye stir up not, nor awake my love till he please." A little unnecessary conversation sometimes, will disturb our love in Christ. Sometimes one thing, and sometimes another, for he is like a roe, or a hind, he cannot stay with those that do not love him, with all their hearts.

My beloved spake and said unto me: "Rise up my love, my fair one and come away." And O that we could hear this blessed voice oftener, and be more ready to obey! To come away from our vain delusions, and leave our hopes, and our all centered in Christ the head of the churches. "The winter would soon be passed, and the singing of birds would come, and flowers appear on the earth, and the tender grapes give a good smell."

But when these tender grapes, the fruit of the vines are in any way injured, they will cry out: "Saw ye him whom my

soul loveth? but it was but a little that I passed from them—the
watchman—but I found him, whom my soul loveth." "I held
him and would not let him go." Joy again, springs up in the
heart, and we resolve that we will ever hold upon him, let
what will take place. Our hope is firm, and faith sure. We
feel strong like the horses in Pharaoh's chariot. "Every man
with his sword upon his thigh, for they are expert in war."
It is necessary that christians should have on the whole
armor, and also be shod for the race that is set before them.
"Looking unto Jesus the author and finisher of our faith.
Christ doth, at times, see the church in her purity. "Thy
teeth are like a flock of sheep, even shorn, which came
up from the washing; whereof every one bear twins.
And when he sees their comeliness, he desires her company,
and says: "Come with me, from Lebanon, my spouse look
from the top of Amana and the lions den. When she speaks
truth in righteousnees, then her lips drop as the honey-
comb—she is like a garden enclosed, a spring shut up, a
fountain sealed—a well of living waters and streams from
Lebanon." Solomon agrees with the Apostle when he saith
that his word should be like a well of water, springing up
into everlasting life. O that the church would arise and invite
their beloved into the banqueting-house, and let his banner
over us be love.

"Awake! O North wind, and blow upon my garden, that
the spices may flow out." Let my beloved come into his
garden and eat his pleasant fruit. How readily does he hear
and answer the cries of his children. He is more ready to
give good gifts than earthly parents are to their children; hear
the answer! I am come into my garden, my sister, my spouse:
I have gathered my myrrh with my spices—I have eaten my
honey-comb with my honey, I have drank my wine with my
milk, eat, O friends! drink, yea drink abundantly! O beloved!"
Where is the Christian that does not have his ups and downs—
his time of light and darkness, to try his love, and faith, and
patience, and his courage. All this is necessary to become useful, and see our own imperfections, but the soul is never at ease,
while its Saviour's face is hid; but will inquire of many it sees,
especially of those that watch over it for good, if they have seen
anything of him whom it loveth: but there were watchman an-

. ciently, as well as now, that did not care for the flocks. "The watchman that went about the city found me, they smote me, they wounded me, yea, the keepers of the well took away my veil from me." And what next can she do? she has been about the city and made all possible inquiry, and has been treated with neglect and abuse: but one thing more she can do. "*I charge you, O ye daughters of Jerusalem* if you find my beloved that ye tell him that I am sick of love.

Some will answer: "What is thy beloved more than another beloved?" O thou fairest among women, what is thy beloved more than another beloved that thou dost charge us? Why: "My beloved is white, and ruddy, the chiefest among ten thousand." Then how beautifully she describes him, although he has withdrawn a little for a moment, yet she loves him, and enumerates his beauties, as far as words can express, and adds: yea, he is altogether lovely. "This is my beloved, and this is my friend, O daughters of Jerusalem!"

This awakens an inquiry in the breast of others: Whither is thy beloved gone? or turned aside, that we may seek him with thee? Why, he has gone down into his garden to the beds of spices, to feed in the garden, and to gather lilies. Who is she that looketh forth in the morning, fair as the moon, and clear as the sun, and terrible as an army with banners." "I went down into the garden of nuts, to see the fruits of the valley." It is important that we should go down very low, before we can find him whom our soul loveth; then before we are aware, "Our soul is made like the chariots of Ammi-nadab."

Her faith will be increased, and she will take hold of the boughs of the palm-tree, and invite her associates to go into the field, where there is work enough to be done, and be early to the vineyards and see if the vine flourishes.

"Who is this that cometh up from the wilderness leaning upon her beloved?"

O that the church would come out of this wilderness world, and lean upon I im who has done so much for his church that cannot separate his dying love. No! the waters cannot quench it, nor the floods drown it.

O "Thou that dwellest in the gardens, the companions, hearken to thy voice: cause me to hear it."

"Make haste, my beloved and be thou like to a roe, or to a young hart upon the mountains of spices."

After all this, Zion will still revolt, more and more; still backslide, and serve God with her lips only. He wants no vain oblations, and will not hear.

O how is that faithful City of Jerusalem become a harlot? How ready would he come and purify her from dross, and take away all our sins? "Return unto me, O backsliding daughter, for I am married unto you, saith the Lord of hosts."

ABIGAIL HOUSE.

———

MY DEAR SISTER:

I can hardly refrain from going to see you this morning, but situated as I am, I will converse a little with my pen, however childish it may appear. As I passed the lovely picture of our Saviour; it so ravished my heart, that I could scarcely keep from kissing it, and I do not wonder Mary kissed his feet for she saw his beauty; and who can forbear saying: "He is altogether lovely; he is the chiefest among ten thousand; his mouth is most sweet; yea, he is *altogether lovely*. This is my beloved, and this is my friend."

When we look at the nature and character of our blessed Jesus, how it will make our hearts leap for joy. He does care for his Saints; he will come again, and receive them to everlasting happiness; and while I am contemplating on the subject, I can almost exclaim,—Come Lord Jesus, come quickly! and I ought to feel it entirely, for what on earth is so pleasing, and so satisfying, as to know and feel that we have reconciliation—that God is at peace with us, and that our ways are acceptable with him. And O why do we not strive more to do these things he requires of us, and do it with more cheerfulness? It is because we lose sight of his beauty. Let us read his word oftener, and with more care:—it will guide our feet into all truth. Our dear Saviour himself said: "It is enough for the Disciple to be as his Master and the servant as his Lord." He tells them to fear not! If they have called the Master of the house Beelzebub, how much more they of his household? We must be careful not to deny him, for if we do, he will deny us. Let us meditate more fully on the subject of the love, he bears to us, for we must know that if he did not care for us, he would not have suffered as he did, and have said, where "I am, there shall ye be also!"

I cannot think he has paid such a price for those who believe on him and then trusts them to take care of themselves, for they can do nothing without him. And they ought to ask council of him about all they do or say, for the nearer we are to him, the more beautiful he appears:—his very name is sweet. No wonder the poet hath said:

"Sweetest of all names is Jesus, how it doth my heart inflame."

I could never bear to hear his most excellent name made use of in sport or jest.

I sincerely wish I was more humble under his goodness, for his loving kindness and tender mercies are great, let us strive in our prayers to be more like our Master. "Peter said they (the disciples) had forsaken all, and had followed thee,"—then Jesus said unto them,—"Verily I say unto you, every one that hath forsaken houses, or brethren, or sisters, or father, or mother, or wife, or children, or lands, for my name-sake, shall receive an hundred fold in this life, and shall inherit everlasting life.' When I turn my eyes within, all is darkness and death. Not so when I view Christ by an eye of faith, and think the promises are mine as much as though there were no one on earth beside myself. When he told me to seek first the kingdom of Heaven, I thought that was for me, and when I read in John iii: God so loved the world, that he gave his only begotten son, that whosoever believeth on him should not perish, but have everlasting life;" that too was for me. I often felt myself under condemnation, and the only remedy was to believe on our Lord. All the threatenings were against me! And while we were under the law we were exposed to the penalties and wrath of God. And when we saw ourselves undone by sin, and that in our natures, we are truly unclean, and no way of escape from impending woe, but to believe on him who died for us—how hard to be changed—how hard to be born again—how hard to pass from death to life! It never can be done without divine assistance. And when we have the evidence of this, then the scene is changed from darkness to light, from the power of Satan to the living God.

Then indeed the promises are ours to the joy of our souls. The Lord is our sun and shield; the Lord will give grace and glory, and no good thing will he with-hold from them that walk uprightly, and *such* are led by the spiri. of God, and then are they adopted into heirship with the Saints, and joint heirs with Jesus Christ. And what then my dear sister; are we safe? Their robes are washed in the blood of the Lamb—and God shall wipe all tears from their eyes; they that sleep in their graves shall arise and shine as the stars in the firmament of Heaven; this is our expectation and our hope, and let us gaze with the eye of faith on our portion, and O that we might live as becometh heirs of such an inheritance! O my beloved sister, with what solemnity we shall recollect the sins which made our Saviour mourn and drove him from our face, our thoughts will be distracting. I know these things weigh down and prevent the believer from looking up and desiring the coming of our Lord! O that the love and power of God might be more manifest in the Saints, to show that we are looking for such things, and may, eternity be stamped on all our actions.

Therefore as much as in us lies, let us gird up the loins of our minds and be sober, and watch unto prayer, that we may through faith hope to the end, for it is written, "Be ye holy, for I am holy."

Let us give heed to what is written in this also: "Now is our salvation nearer than when we believed."

A little evil put off or away does not answer—but the cry is: "Come out, O my people and be separate and touch no unclean thing, and I will receive you, saith the Almighty."

We had better make no profession of religion than to disregard the commands of our great law giver. We cannot serve two Masters, I know by experience, in this condition it cannot be said that "Ye are the light of the world," surely his image should be visible to beholders. "Men do not light a candle and put it under a bushel; but let your light so shine before men that they may see your good works, and glorify your father which is in Heaven." Here is the believer's ground to work upon; then his faith will be increased; and here only is our peace.

He has not called us into his vineyard, there to work or not, just as we please, but to do the work of the day in the day, as he hath appointed. He requires no more than we can do, his bur-

Q

den is light when we get a glimpse of his beauty, and hear his
voice. When "He goeth down into his garden of lilies, and
where the pomegranates bud."

"We are kept by the power of God through faith unto Salvation—not of works lest any man should boast." There is no
boasting in religion.

And now to return to the subject on which I first commenced,
that is, his ravishing beauty. I have seen him in the visions o.
the night; and my imaginations could hardly paint out so lovely
a being. The inquiry will soon run through our minds, how
could the Jews crucify one of so much beauty? I suppose they
saw no form or comeliness in him;—but said away with him!
crucify him! Their hearts rose in opposition because they believed not on him. I came near saying had they known him,
they could not have done it;—but when I cast my eyes around.
I see that even the believing Gentiles do grieve and wound him,
notwithstanding they have tasted of the good word; and here I
must confess again, that I have done many things I ought not to
have done, and left undone many of those I ought to have done
—and I feel from time to time to say: "It is no more I, that do
it, but sin that dwelleth in me."

When we repent under a heart-felt sense of our sin, and unworthiness, he looks again on us with a pitying eye and saith:
"I forgive—go and sin no more!" But O how many times is
he wounded in the house of his friends. He knows us to be
"Poor and miserable, and blind, and naked—and he has told us
to come to him, and buy without money or price." All is his,
and all we have to give to him is ourselves, and give up our former sins, and live in honor to his name. We must suffer for his
name and for the sake of his Gospel. O! I think sometimes I
have not suffered enough to bear the name of a disciple.

I wish to feel more of a hungering and thirsting after holiness,
and that I may be kept from out-breaking sins, and not bring a
wound upon his blessed cause; and O! Lord keep my heart from
secret faults. I have nowhere else to go:—he is my confidence
and my *all*. Help me dear Sister, with your prayers, that I may
walk the narrow way, for I am aware that many snares are laid
for my feet; and O how apt I am to turn aside! and not only
wound his cause, but my own soul also. May we ever keep his

kindness and his willingness to save before our eyes, which
makes him so lovely and so beautiful.

Yours in Christian tenderness,

ABIGAIL HOUSE.

MY DEAR SISTER:

After the lapse of years, I resume my pen, think-
ing you will answer this: after hearing from me afresh. I do not
accuse you of unkindness or forgetfulness; it is only the want
of a little leisure time, for I am bold to assert, we shall never
forget the pleasant hours we have passed in each others company. Not only pleasure, but real comfort in exchanging our
views and feelings which has produced a regard and fellowship,
that cannot be easily eradicated, or hidden, even by our domestic cares.

Enough of that. What shall we say now? What is our condition now? Are we striving still to walk in the straight and
narrow path, which leads to joys on high? I must say to you I
have the evidence that God's promises are true, for he saith, He
never will leave nor forsake those that trust in him; he does
dwell in Zion; he does hear the young ravens when they cry; he
does come to our relief; he will not leave us comfortless, nor
suffer us to be tempted above what we are able to bear; but will
make a way for our escape. "I hear the voice of my beloved
say: Rise up my love and come away." "For lo! the winter is
past, the rain is over and gone—the flowers appear on the earth
—the time of the singing of birds has come, and the voice of the
turtle is heard in our land." "The fig tree putteth forth her
green figs, and the vines with the tender grapes give a good
smell."

"*Let my beloved come into his garden and eat his pleasant
fruits.*"

"The immortal Vine of Heavenly root,
Blossoms and buds, and gives her fruit;
Lo! we are come to taste the wine,
Our souls rejoice and bless the vine."

"And when we hear our Jesus say:
Rise up my love, make haste away;
Our hearts would fain out-fly the wind,
And leave all earthly loves behind."

WATTS.

My dear Sister is it so with your sitting under his shadow with great delight? is his word sweet to your taste? do you see that beauty in his character which you did in your early love? You no doubt know what a wintry season is, as well as the one just described. How comforting after a long and dreary winter to her the sacred turtle dove proclaim the new the joyful year. I wish I could see you and tell you the beauties I behold in the Gospel's clearest glass. O let not my Lord depart until he has washed and cleansed my heart and made it a fit temple for the Holy Ghost to dwell in; how quick all earthly pleasures flee, when he unveils the beauties of his face. It out-shines all created things. May this stir up a sweet remembrance of former days, whereby you may be enabled to cry Abba, Father! May the day star from on high visit your heart, and lead you into still waters, where you can bask in the ocean of divine bliss. May your Sun so shine that you will have no cause of stumbling; for when we walk in darkness we are apt to tumble: and O what stumbling, and blundering creatures we are; and as the poet hath said:

"O that we might blunder right!"

I still feel as though our natures were opposed to God, and all that is good. When we are in deep trials and afflictions, he leaps and flies to our relief. Dear Sister let us,

"Praise our Maker with our latest breath, and when our
voice is lost in death,"

May we praise him still. "May nothing be able to separate us from the love of God, which is in Christ Jesus our Lord."

May we mount up on wings of faith, higher and higher, until we shall rise beyond the power of Satan, our arch enemy, and then shout victory to our great Shepherd, and head, and lay our crown at his feet. O glorious hope! "It doth not yet appear what we shall be, only we shall be like him, for we shall see him as he is."

Remember me in your prayers, that I may never fall, and believe me as ever your friend,

ABIGAIL HOUSE.

LINES.

The law and Prophets were till John,
Since then man has the Gospel plan,
The true Messiah was the man—
    That was expected here.

An angel was to Mary sent,
While she was standing in her tent,
She asked him closely what he meant—
    That he should come to her.

Fear not said he! be not afraid,
For I am sent to give thee aid,
And say to Joseph, take the maid—
    Her innocence you'll prove.

The "Son of God," he shall be called,
To save his people great and small,
From Satan's power of sin and thrall—
    And Jesus is his name.

O! that we could our Saviour meet,
Fall down and worship at his feet,
Then supplicate the mercy seat—
        He'd wipe away our tears.

O blessed hope!   O glorious day!
How oft we'd feel to praise and pray,
Or fly on wings of love away—
        To our eternal home.

Lord send thine angel for to keep,
Our souls from falling in the deep,
Prepare us Lord, that we may meet—
        Thee, in the air of bliss.

May we press on both day and night,
Our heavenly journey with delight,
And love his name with all our might—
        Then happy we shall be.

May we behold thy smiling face,
Then streams of mercy we shall taste,
And that will keep us in our place—
        Or we shall stray from Thee.

Thus we'll be found in Zion's ways,
And unto God we'll sing his praise,
While Angels smile around and gaze—
        Such notes they ne'er could sing.

Soon we shall mount on wings of love,
Where Gabriel stands with harps above,
And shout hosannahs, for the dove—
        Did rest on him who saves.

Of all the friends he is the best,
Come all that weary, and find rest,
That you prepared, be for the next —
        Through faith in his dear name.

                                        A. H

MY DEAR FRIEND:

How beautiful and interesting a theme is it to dwell upon the name of Jesus? My heart thirsts after the Gospel of our Lord and Saviour Jesus Christ; nought on earth so delightful and refreshing as his word. It is life and power: how I wish we could understand more of its doctrine and adopt it more readly, for our rule of practice. Let his righteousness be our guide.

We are, many times, too careful to establish *our own* righteousness through ignorance; and go about to establish the same, and do not submit ourselves to God. For Christ is the end of the law for righteousness to every one that believeth; Jews and Gentiles all one in Christ. There shall come out of Zion the *Deliverer!* O how many great and blessed names are attached to him. Why? because all power was given unto him, and he deserves our highest praise, and let us praise him and search the scriptures what little time we have to live.

WHAT CHRIST IS CALLED IN SCRIPTURE.

He's called a Sun, he makes our day,
To light the Pilgrims on their way
They need not stumble, but should say—
　　He is our light divine.

He's called a Star, whose brilliant light,
Guides the wayfarer even at night,
They gaze, and gaze because 'tis bright—
　　At length a cloud appears.

He 's called a King, he reigns supreme,
And all his subjects, worship him,
Crying, holy, holy, for he brings—
    Salvation to our race.

He's called a Counsellor of peace,
That we may in his love increase,
And make our jarring natures cease—
    He smilingly draws near.

He 's called a Rock, the corner stone,
The same he builds his church upon,
No winds, nor storms can beat her down—
    While her foundation stands.

He 's called a Tree, whose cooling shade,
Shelters the Christian when he 's made,
A struggling effort and hath said—
    To Zion I am bound.

He 's called a Root, how firm he stands,
Deep in the earth, mark well the land,
Though Asia's winds may dash the sand—
    Nor worms can it destroy.

He 's called a Branch, who's lovely fruit,
Nourishes those, while in pursuit,
The church's task it well doth suit—
    And strengthens them withal.

He 's called a Vine, around he coils,
The tender fruit lest Satan spoils,
The spreading branches and the soil—
    O Lord protect thy Saints!

He 's called a Door, and open stands,
With out-stretched arms and also hands,
Ho! every one on sea and land—
    May enter while there 's room.

He 's called the Way, the Truth and Light,
We'll strive to enter with our might,
Lest gloom and darkness both unite—
    And sink us in despair.

He 's called a Shepherd, and he'll keep,
Close by his side, his wandering sheep,
He neither slumbers nor doth sleep—
    But bears them in his arms.

He 's called a Lamb, O blessed name!
Who came from heaven to earth to save,
And washed away our sins and gave—
    Forgiveness through his blood.

He 's called a Fountain, let us bathe,
In the pure stream of love, and raise
A song of shouting and of praise—
    To our deliverer's name.

He 's called a Lion, shall we fear
When his great strength surrounds us here?
No—surely we'll to him draw near—
    His name shall be our song.

His name is Jesus, our best friend,
On him our hopes of heaven depend,
Through grace we'll shout glory, Amen!—
    And own him Lord of all.

Come sinners all, both great and small,
Come listen to the Saviour's call,
Before death comes, or you will fall—
    Where hope can never come.

THE SECOND PART.

Thy name is great, O Lord of host!
Father and Son, and Holy Ghost,
Dear saviour we have nought to boast—
    Only thy precious blood.

Thy name is great, we must confess,
Our guilt and our unsteadiness,
We feel indeed our way to press—
    As thou hast given command.

Thy name is great Counsel divine,
We would desire pure love like thine,
And carefully improve our time—
    Which swiftly runs to waste.

Thy name is great, and we can see,
Thy power in wind and hail and tree,
In mountains, hills, and also sea—
    And insects of all kinds.

Thy name is great, plant of renown,
O pity us and do not frown,
Forbid that we thy cause should wound—
    While we sojourn below.

Thy name was great, when thou did'st say,
To Peter as he made his way:
Towards thee, Fear not, have no dismay,
    Believe and trust in me.

Thy name was great, when thou did'st break,
The bread for thy Disciples sake,
Lo! I am with you and will take—
    You, to myself above.

Thy name was great, while on the cross,
Because thou saw that all was lost,
Without thy blood though much it cost—
    For man, poor fallen man.

At thy great name, when the earth did quake.
The rocks did rend, the mountains shake,
All things in nature signs did make—
    When thou gavest up the Ghost.

Thy name was great, when thou did'st tell,
Thou would'st prepare a place, to dwell,
For thy dear Saints for it is well—
    For them to intercede.

Thy name is great, and all must bow,
Their knee to thee, and we may now,
Find pardon if our souls lie low—
    At the Redeemer's feet.

Thy name is great, we 're lost in thought,
For in thy word we oft are taught,
To comprehend thee, we cannot,
    For sin has made us blind.

Thy name is great, O Jesus! why
Shall we forever sink and die,
Help us to cry and also try,
    Thy mercy to obtain.

Let thy sweet name fill us with love,
That when thou comest from above,
We 'll shout to see Thee, Lamb like Dove,
    Remember all thy Saints.

Thy blessed name, my heart shall praise,
While I attempt thy fame to raise,
Help me to sing in fitting lays—
    The glories of thy name.

My Dear Friend in Old Age:

As the winter is passed and gone, and spring comes with all its beauty, how it reminds me of my fallen nature. Once a child, and helpless from that to youth; gay and cheerful, and perhaps vain. From that to riper years, and more active in life; soon old age comes on, and infirmities and cares increase, and we give way for others. Our knowledge and judgment pass away; intellect and memory fail, and our substance, wealth if we have any, is conveyed into other hands, and nought but the old stump, is left. What can there be desirable in old age, or any other age, if it were not for the expectation of a brighter day? There are, it is true, in all stages of human life, some pleasing enjoyments, which attach us to earth—and no time nor state, exempts us from trials, and death. But having well grounded hope, we can say: Blessed be old age, as we are nearer ripe for the grave, and glory heaves in view; although our eyes are dim, that we cannot look out of the windows, and the grinders are few, and fears shall be in the way, and the grass-hopper shall be a burden and all these things which are incident to the aged. Yet there is something in it which animates and buoys up the spirits of such, because nature has its proper course. The Sun, Moon, and Stars, all move in their order, and the seasons, Spring, Summer, Autumn, and Winter, all have their beauties and luxuries. He that made heaven and earth said there should be seed time and harvest. Summer and winter, cold and heat, and that he would rain upon the just and unjust. I say because all these things are promised us in things of nature. Shall we not also believe the gracious promises? Be thou faithful unto death, and I will give thee a crown of life. The question only will arise whether we are faithful. We may forget many things, but a christian does not forget that he has had his soul filled with the love of Jesus, if he is pressed with infirmities and misfortunes; yet it may be profitable and not pleasurable.

He knows our frame, that it is but dust; he that made us is acquainted with the inmost recesses of the heart. Therefore let dissolution come and he is happy that trusts in God. Let joy spring up anew in our hearts, as we advance in life, for now is our salvation nearer than when we believed. The believer is safe, for his life is hid with Christ in God. Do you feel this assurance my aged friend? If so, then take courage. A few more setting Suns, will land you beyond the reach of sin and temptations; bear your pain a little longer; say to Satan his time is almost over with you, as you soon expect to be out of his reach, like certain insects: let him take the younger trees and spoil them if he can; yet he can do nothing but by permission.

How I pity the aged that are without hope and God, in the world. When they reflect, how many prayers they have rejected, and the wooings of the Holy Spirit and how long the dresser of the vineyard has come and sought fruit, and found none, and that he will say assuredly: "Cut it down." They may have a hope but it is flimsey as the spider web. Their hope will fail and where are they? And when we say to the aged sinner,— "Repent ye" what then?--does he? No! he turns away, and says it is time enough yet. Blessed Jesus help me to love thee more and serve thee better! as I advance in life! let my prospects for heaven be clearer, and brighter unto the perfect day! We have for many years professed faith in Jesus, to be children and heirs of the promised inheritance; and are we such in truth, my dear friend? Are we like autumn bearing fruit, and coming to the grave like a shock of corn fully ripe? When we honor God, he blesses us; and then when our gray hairs are thus formed in the ways of righteousness, we shall receive a crown of glory. How is it my dear friend, are you waiting for the coming of our dear Saviour? Many that are young, wish to remain on account of their children, or other friends; and we are permitted, and sometimes we promise to live better. I do not wonder we fear death for it is the penalty of our transgression, and after all, it is the gate to endless joy. I sincerely hope when we die, we shall die like Christians: have our reason and the presence of our king, to conduct us safely over the cold stream of Jordon. I pray God that he will keep us by his Almighty power, for it is through grace that we are saved, not of ourselves but by the gift of God.

I leave you with these reflections and may you grow in grace, and in knowledge of our Lord and Saviour, Jesus Christ, and write, that my soul may be refreshed. Remember those in connection with your prayers, and that the God of peace may rest down upon you, is the desire of your unworthy friend.

ABIGAIL HOUSE.

Y DEAR FRIEND:

Had I a thousand tongues I could not describe to you the low and disconsolate feeling with which I am oppressed. Not a friend who careth for my condition, I have out-lived all their affections; and what remains? Why, a trembling fear, that I shall not make God my only trust, my reason and my experience teach that there is no trust nor abiding confidence in anything; but the promise of him who has said:— "I will never leave nor forsake those that put their trust in me!" Even down to old age we shall find our promises sure: and I, even I, cannot help being cheered, while I write, notwithstanding I feel the chilling blasts of despair, while my nature is so closely allied to the cold region. Storm and Sunshine is our common lot; and what are all our ups and downs when compared to one that has no hope? His way is always dark and drear—always in opposition to the just requirements of God. Not subject to his law, neither indeed can be, while his heart is drawn away by his own legitimate desires, and less sunny days appear in view. We would fondly hope such ones will escape the gloomy prospects which threaten them, and may some kind and gentle hand wipe from their eyes the tears of repentance and sorrow. Then would their hearts flow with gratitude and love, and peace, like a river, glide with radiant hues, and hope be like an anchor that will hold the vessel fast; then onward and upward, will our pathway of duty lie, seeking the happinesss of others; and every days work will strengthen and animate us on the journey of life, and at its close we shall receive a rich reward, and hear the sentence of "Come ye blessed of my father inherit the joys of thy Lord." Yours in haste,

ABIGAIL HOUSE.

A BEAUTIFUL DESCRIPTION OE CHRIST.

———

Given by Publius Governor of Judea—Taken from the Life of Colby.

There appeared in these our days, a man of great virtue, named Jesus Christ, who is yet living amongst us, and of the Gentiles is accepted as a Prophet of truth, but by his own Disciples called the Son of God. He raised the dead, and cureth all manner of diseases. A man of stature, somewhat tall and comely: with a very reverend countenance; such as the beholder may both love and fear. His hair is of the color of a fillbert, full ripe, and plain almost down to his ears: but from his ears downwards, somewhat curled, more orient of color, and waving about his shoulders, In the midst of his head, goeth a seam or partition of his hair, after the manner of the Nazarites. His forehead is very plain and smooth; his face without spot or wrinkle, beautiful with comely red. His nose and mouth so formed as nothing can be reprehended, His beard somewhat thick, agreeing in color to the hair of his head not of any great length, but forked in the midst, and of an innocent, mature look. His eyes gray, clear and quick. In reproving; he is terrible, and in admonishing courteous and fair spoken, pleasant in speech mixed with gravity. It cannot be remembered that any have seen him laugh: but many have seen him weep. In proportion of body,— well shaped and straight; his hands, and arms right delectable to behold. In speaking, very temperate, modest, and wise. A man of singular beauty surpassing the children of men.

Lenox, Ashtabula County, Ohio, May 24th, 1857.

MUCH ESTEEMED BROTHER:

Yours of April 29th is received, with forty questions on immortality, and be assured it was a source of comfort and consolation: I often experience a drouth or famine, not for the want of bread nor of water, but for a word of consolation. I am thankful I have the word of truth whereby a peaceful spirit can be obtained and cultivated to profit—the promises therein contained will never fail us, and I truly believe our Heavenly Father will not withhold any good thing from those that walk uprightly. We need not live to three score years to know this truth: that everything on earth will fail us, which shows most conclusively, where our trust should be. I do not hesitate to say, his grace is sufficient for all who put their trust in him. Even down to old age he is still our strength and supporter, thanks be to his precious name that he hath given us hope in his mercy. My heart's affections are stirred up within me while I write, and think on this great subject, the Gospel, that makes us wise unto Salvation. While we anticipate being like him, who suffered death for us when we shall see him as he is, what manner of persons ought we to be, in all holy conversation and godliness?

How much need of strength when we have done all to stand; girt with truth in this, our evil day, when was the time we did not need the whole armor on? Surely our enemy has always been seeking whom he might devour. How often are Saints led to say in times of temptation, that their feet had well-nigh slipped, and then the promise is applied: that he will not suffer them to be tempted above what they are able to bear, but will make a way for their escape; there is a balm for every wound. Our life is hid with Christ in God—can we realize our safety? How many there are, it is to be feared are crying for peace and safety when sudden destruction will come upon them and there will be none to deliver. Yet will they say, is not the Lord among us—the world is now what it ever was, hostile to the followers of Christ, and still how much pains there is taken to blend them together. There is no neutral position for any man: they will be for, or against; and if we sow to the flesh we must reap corruption. May we be increasingly prepared to sow to the Spirit, and obtain eternal life.

How my heart is grieved from time to time when I see the dear Saints groping in darkness and blinded with the gods of this world, and can hardly understand how easily the Holy Spirit is grieved, even if they do not consider it a crime, and pass on until they do not think it necessary to be guided by its sweet influences. O may it be our constant desire to say with the Psalmist: "Take not thy Holy Spirit from us, that we may teach transgressors thy ways; that sinners may be converted unto thee." The greatest desire I have is to see the children of God, growing in grace and knowledge of God, and see them joined together *fitly*, to be of one heart, and one judgment, but how can I expect it until the scriptures are fulfilled, for in the latter days there shall be great falling away. I think we can discover many who have already apostatized.

THE PILGRIM'S SONG.

My rest is in Heaven, my rest is not here;
Then why should I tremble, when trials are near?
Be hushed my sad spirit, the worst that can come,
But shortens my journey, and hastens thee home.

It is not for me to be seeking my bliss,
And building my hopes in region like this:
I look for a City which hands have not piled,
I pant for a country by sin undefiled.

R

The thorn and the thistle around me may grow—
I would not lie down e'en on roses below:
I ask not my portion, I seek not a rest,
Till I find them forever on Jesus' lov'd breast.

Afflictions may press me, they cannot destroy,
One glimpse of his love turns them all into joy:
And the bitterest tears, if he smiles but on them—
Like dew in the sunshine, grow diamond and gem.

Let trials and danger my progress oppose,
They only make Heaven more sweet at the close:
Come joy, or come sorrow, whate'er may befall,
A home with my God, will make up for it all.

With a scrip on my back, and a staff in my hand,
I march on in haste, through an enemy's land;
The road may be rough, but it cannot be long,
And I'll smooth it with hope, and cheer it with song.

——

A COLONIZATION SONG.

——

Will you be colonized on the African shores?
And your fears will sleep, and you will rouse them no more.
    Will you, will you, will you, will you be colonized?
    Will you, will you, will you, will you be colonized?

'Tis a land that with honey and milk doth abound,
Where the lash is not heard, and the scourge is not found.

If you stay in this land where the white man hath rule,
You will starve by his hand in both body and soul.

For a nuisance you are, in this land of your birth,
Held down by his hand, and crushed to the earth.

My religion is pure, and it came from a'ove,
But I cannot consent the black negro to love.

It is true, there are judgments that hang o'er the land,
But they all turn aside when you follow the plan.

'Tis a land where Sun-beams will addle your brains,
And savage banditti rove over the plains.

You're ignorant I know, in this land of your birth,
And religion though pure, cannot remove the curse.

But only consent, though extorted by force,
What a blessing you'll prove, on the African coast.

Tis a land where sand-banks made hot from the skies,
Like clouds arise round you to dazzle your eyes.
   Will you, will you, will you, will you be colonized?
   Will you, will you, will you, will you be colonized?

THE FREE SLAVE.

Go, go! thou that enslavest me; now, now thy power is o'er,
Long, long have I obeyed thee: I'm not a slave any more!
   No, no,—oh! no, I'm a free man ever more!

Thou, thou, broughtest me over deep, deep sorrow and pain,
But I have left thee forever, nor will I serve thee again.
   No, no,—oh! no, no I'll not serve thee again.

Tyrant! thou hast bereft me, home, friends, pleasures so sweet
Now, now forever I've left thee, thou and I never shall meet.
    No, no,—oh! no thou and I never shall meet!

Joys, joys, bright as the morning; now, now on me will pour,
Hope, hope sweetly is dawning, I'm not a slave any more!
    No, no,—oh! no, I'm not a slave any more.

Hark, ten thousand harps and voics, sound the note of praise
    above,
Jesus reigns, and heaven rejoices, Jesus reigns the God of love
See he sits on yonder throne, Jesus rules the world above.
    Hallelujah! Hallelujah! Hallelujah!—Amen.

Jesus hail! whose glory brightens all above and gives it worth;
Lord of life, thy smile enlightens, cheers and charms thy Saints
    on earth;
When we think of love like thine, Lord we own it, love divine
    Hallelujah! etc.

King of glory reign forever, thine an everlasting crown,
Nothing from thy love can sever, those whom thou hast made
    thine own;
Happy objects of thy grace, destined to behold thy face;
    Hallelujah! etc.

Saviour hasten thine appearing, bring, oh! bring the glorious
    day,
When the awful summons hearing, heaven and earth shall pass
    away,
Then with golden harps we'll sing, glory, glory, to our king!
    Hallelujah! etc.

A CRADLE HYMN

Hush my dear lie still and slumber,
  Holy Angels guard thy bed,
Heavenly blessings without number,
  Gently falling on thy head.

Sleep my babe thy food and raiment,
  House and home thy friends provide,
And without thy care or payment,
  All thy wants shall be supplied.

How much better thou 'rt attended,
  Than the Son of God could be,
When from Heaven he descended,
  And became a child like thee.

Soft and easy is thy cradle,
  Coarse and hard thy Saviour lay,
When his birth-place was a stable,
  And his softest bed was hay.

Blessed babe what glorious features,
  Spotless, fair, divinely bright;
Must he dwell with brutal creatures,
  How could Angels bear the sight?

Was there nothing but a manger,
  Cursed sinners could afford?
To receive the heavenly stranger,
  Could they thus affront their Lord?

Soft, my child, I did not chide thee,
  Though my song might sound too hard,
Tis thy mother sits beside thee,
  And her arms shall be thy guard.

While I read the shameful story,
  How the Jews abused their king,
How they served the Lord of glory,
  Makes me angry while I sing.

See the kinder Shepherds round him,
  Telling wonders from the sky,
There they sought him, there they found him,
  With his Virgin mother by.

See the lovely babe a dressing,
  Lovely infant how he smiled,
When he wept, the mother's blessing,
  Soothed and hushed the holy child.

Lo! he slumbers in a manger,
  Where the horned oxen fed,
Peace my darling there's no danger,
  Here's no oxen near thy bed.

'Twas to save thee, child from dying,
  Save my dear from burning pains,
Bitter groans and endless cryings,
  That thy blessed Redeemer came.

Mayest thou live to know and fear him,
  Trust and love him all thy days,
Then go dwell forever near him,
  See his face and sing his praise.

I could give thee a thousand kisses,
  Hoping what I most desire:
Not a mother's fondest wishes,
  Can to greater joys aspire.

                           DR. WATTS.

THE BRIDEGROOM'S DOVE.

My dove! the Bridegroom speaks to whom?
  Whom thinkest thou, meaneth He?
Say, O my soul, canst thou presume,
  He thus addresseth thee?
Yes, 'tis the Bridegroom's voice of love,
Calling thee, O my soul! His dove.

The dove is gentle, mild, and meek;
  Deserve I then the name?
I look within in vain to seek,
  Aught which can give a claim,
Yet made so by redeeming love,
My soul thou art the Bridegroom's dove!

Methinks my soul, that thou may'st see,
  In this endearing word,
Reasons why Jesus likens thee,
  To this defenceless bird;
Reasons which shew the Bridegroom's love,
To his poor helpless timid dove.

The dove of all the feathered tribe,
  Doth least of power possess;
My soul what better can describe,
  Thine utter helplessness?
Yet courage take, the Bridegroom's love,
Will keep, defend, protect his dove.

The dove hath neither claw nor sting,
  Nor weapon for the fight;
She owes her safety to her wing,
  Her victory to flight;
A shelter hath the Bridegroom's love,
Provided for his helpless dove.

The hawk comes on with eager chase,
  The dove will not resist,
In flying to her hiding place,
  Her safety doth consist;
The Bridegroom opes his arms of love,
And in them folds his panting dove.

The dove can nothing now molest,
  Safe from the fowler's snare;
The bridegroom's bosom is her nest,
  Nothing can harm her there;
Encircled by the arms of love,
Almighty power protects the dove.

As the poor dove, before the hawk,
  Quick to her refuge flies,
So need I, in my daily walk,
  The wing which faith supplies,
To bear me where the Bridegroom's love,
Places beyond all harm his dove.

My soul of native power bereft,
  To Calvary repairs;
Immanuel is the rocky cleft,
  The secret of the stairs;
Since placed there by the Bridegroom's love,
What evil can befall his dove?

Though Sinai's thunder round her roar,
  Though Ebal's lightnings flash,
Though heav'n a firey torrent pour,
  And riven mountains crash;
Through all, the still small voice of love,
Whispers: Be not afraid, my dove.

What though the heavens away may pass,
 With fervent heat dissolve,
And round the Sun this earthly mass,
 No longer shall revolve;
Behold a miracle of love:
The Lion quakes, but not the dove.

My soul, now hid within a rock,
 (The rock of ages call'd,)
Amid the universal shock,
 Is fearless, unappall'd;
A cleft therein prepared by love,
In safety hides the Bridegroom's dove.

O happy dove, thus weak, thus safe;
 Do I resemble her?
Then to my soul, O Lord vouchsafe,
 A dove-like character;
Pure, harmless, gentle, full of love,
Make me in spirit, Lord a dove.

O! thou who on the Bridegroom's head,
 Did as a dove come down:
Within my soul thy graces shed,
 Establish there thy throne;
There shed abroad a Saviour's love,
Thou holy, pure and heavenly dove.

ON READING THE SPEECH OF MR. GIDDINGS DELIVERED
APRIL 10TH, 1848.

———

Be bold and courageous, and fear not the South,
Their speech cannot harm you though poured from their mouth:
It will fall to the ground, as powerless as ever,
Nor fear their proud threats—never—no! never!

Be bold and courageous, and fear not to die,
May your spirit ascend up to God in the sky,
And hear the blest sentence from the lips of the king:
Well done faithful servant—come enter within.

Be bold and courageous, as you're wont to be,
You will soon come off conqueror as we shall see;
Though the conflict is sharp, and the struggle severe,
Still trust in God's grace, be calm and sincere.

Be bold and courageous, and never give o'er,
And should you lack wisdom, then ask God for more;
He ne'er will upbraid you, though often request,
Even if he should fail you " 'tis all for the best."

Be bold and courageous, what 'er may oppose,
I Am! will be with you, to conquer your foes;
Draw not back your hand; like your name-sake of old:
While his arm was outstretched his subjects were bold.

Be bold and courageous, contine to blow
The trumpet of Ram's-horns till the city 's laid low;
The judgments of heaven, will punish for sin,
Because of God's image, sometimes called a thing.

Be bold and courageous, where ever you be,
Nor care not for those who say 'tis for fee;
But pour forth the truth in volleys of smoke,
Let the Democrats writhe when you expose Mr. Polk.

I hope they 'll no longer be fighting at arms,
But lay aside party and sound the alarm,
Let the Wilmot proviso be our motto and guide,
And nought but pure principles we will abide.

Therefore be courageous and tug at the oar,
For if we gain that, what can we gain more?
May your hands be stayed up like Moses of old,
That in after ages your acts may be told.

While the bondman is waiting with expectations high,
To think his redemption is soon drawing nigh,
Then our hearts will rejoice, and be merry with glee,
At the thoughts of our Nation's grand jubilee.

May heaven protect you through all coming strife,
Though oft-times we feared you would fall by the knife;
We look to you therefore as our head and our leader,
And as oft as you speak may each be a reader.

Most Honorable Sir, let thy course still prevail,
Should all be united on our Senator Hale,
Then each lay aside his long valued notions,
(Yourself if you please) brought forth for promotion.

Now Sir, should you ask whose nonsense are these,
I answer directly its one that makes cheese;
Please pass over and pardon my many misgivings,
Adieu, live forever—Joshua R. Giddings.

ABIGAIL HOUSE.

ON HEARING THE RESULT OF THE BUFFALO CONVENTION.

———

Hurrah for Van Buren, hurrah for free soil!
Hurrah for right principles for which we will toil!
Let us yet save our Nation from Slavery's power;
No longer should freemen to Southerners cower.

Hurrah for Van Buren, hurrah all that can!
Hurrah for Van Buren, hurrah to a man!
Come up to the help of the people we cry:
To rescue from danger, methinks you will try.

Hurrah for Van Buren, come stand at your post!
Though Taylor and Cass men may think they 're a host!
Yet still we believe you may carry your point;
For true we discover them all out of joint.

Hurrah for Van Buren, and bless the glad day,
Also the Convention, and the Nominee!
We did shout when the news of it fell on our ear,
That the crisis to us, had come even this year.

Hurrah for Van Buren, again let us shout!
On the seventh of November, pray prove yourselves stout!
For a Nation divided we read cannot stand,
Therefore draw together and save our blest land.

Hurrah for Van Buren once more we do say!
For all have an interest, and enlist now we pray,
Arise to the battle that 's coming ere long,
Come up to the polls, be valiant and strong.

Hurrah for Van Buren, and for many more!
Which have stood at their posts, and yet they endure;
We cannot pass by them, without giving cheers,
So hurrah to all such as are not in the rear!

Now ladies we 'll give a hearty response,
For long have we sought to relieve from their bonds,
Those that are made of such material as we,
To give them their freedom how happy they 'd be.

It is true we are helpless like the Slaves of the South,
Yet we feel to hurrah with the breath of our mouth,
Though anciently some staid, by the stuff it is said,
So let us submit to our husband and head.

Kind heaven forgive—though first in transgression,
We feel thy rebuke, and would fain make confession:
But we must be still if we cant count as much,
As that portion of South, that cannot be touched.

My dear Christian friends, a word and I'll stop:
Our religion 's in danger, without civil prop,
Now take the alarm, though woman hath said,
Or else you may yet, have a nail drove in your head.

ABIGAIL HOUSE.

CHRIST IN THE GARDEN.

———

While nature was sinking in stillness and rest,
The last beams of daylight shone dim in the West;
O'er the fields by the moonlight to lonely retreat:
In deep meditation I wandered my feet.

While passing a garden, I paused there to hear,
A voice faint and faltering from one that was near,
A voice to the mourner affected my heart,
While pleading in anguish the poor sinner's part.

In offering to heaven the poor sinner's prayer,
He spoke of the torment that sinners must bear:
His life as a ransom he offered to give,
That sinners redeemed in glory might live.

I listened a moment then turned to see,
What man of compassion this stranger could be,
When, lo! I discovered knelt on the cold ground,
The loveliest being that ever was known.

His mantle was wet with the dews of the night,
His locks by pale moon-beams were glistening and bright
His eyes bright like diamonds to heaven were raised,
Whilst angels in wonder stood round him amazed. '

So deep was his sorrow, so fervent his prayers,
That down on his bosom rolled sweat blood and tears;
I went to behold and ask him his name,
He answered 'tis Jesus, from Heaven I came.

I am thy redeemer, for thee I must die,
The cup is most painful, but cannot pass by,
Thy sins like a mountain, are laid upon me;
And all this deep anguish I suffer for thee.

I heard with attention the tale of his woe,
While tears like a fountain of water did flow,
The cause of his sorrow to hear him repeat,
Afflicted my heart and I fell at his feet.

I trembled with horror and loudly did cry:
Lord save a poor sinner, oh! save or I die!
He smiled when he saw me, and said to me—live!
Thy sins which are many, I freely forgive.

How sweet was that moment he bade me rejoice,
His smiles, oh! how pleasant, how cheering his voice!
I flew from the garden to spread it abroad,
I shouted Salvation, oh! glory to God!

I'm now on my journey to mansions above,
My soul's full of glory, of peace, light, and love;
I think of the garden, the prayers and the tears,
Of that loving stranger that banished my fears,

The day of bright glory is rolling around,
When Gabriel descending the trumpet will sound:
My eyes then with raptures of glory will rise,
To gaze on the stranger with unclouded eyes.

THE WHITE PILGRIM.

———

I came to the spot where the white Pilgrim lay,
   And pensively stood by the tomb,
When in a low whisper I heard something say:
   How sweetly I sleep here alone.

The tempest may howl, and loud thunder may roar,
   And gathering storms may arise;
Yet calm are my feelings, at rest is my soul,
   The tears are all wiped from my eyes.

The cause of my Master propelled me from home,
   I bid my companion farewell;
I left my sweet children who now for me mourn,
   In far distant regions to dwell.

I wandered an exile, a stranger below,
   To publish Salvation abroad,
The trump of the Gospel endeavored to blow,
   Inviting poor sinners to God.

But when among strangers and far from my home,
   No kindred nor relative nigh,
I met the contagion and sunk in the tomb,
   My spirit to mansions on high.

Go tell my companion and children most dear,
   To weep not for Joseph tho' gone,
The same hand that led me thro' scenes dark and drear,
   Has kindly assisted me home,
                   Yours in haste,
                         AMANDA.

www.ingramcontent.com/pod-product-compliance
Lightning Source LLC
Chambersburg PA
CBHW020354030726
47496CB00007B/2133